I0793212

IMAGES
of America

CHATSWORTH

CAPITAL OF THE PINE BARRENS

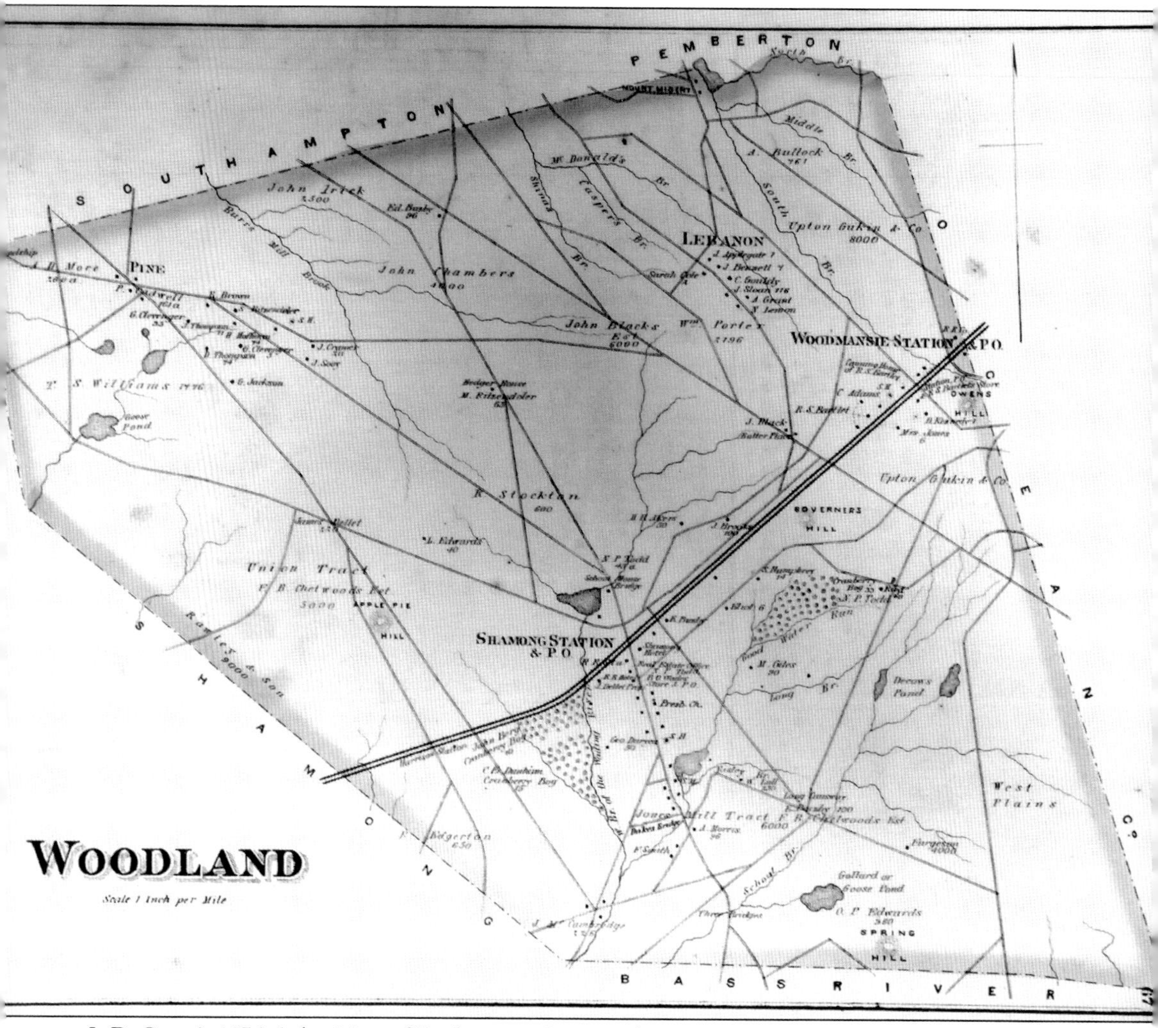

J. D. Scott's 1876 Atlas Map of Burlington County shows Woodland Township as it existed at that time. The names of landowners are shown on the map. (Courtesy of the Burlington County Historical Society.)

On the Cover: This photograph of workers harvesting cranberries with wooden scoops typifies the harvest in the early 1900s. The scoops were heavy and made of wood with wooden or metal teeth that combed through the vines pulling off the berries. The berries were then loaded into boxes before being taken to the packinghouse for sorting. (Courtesy of William S. Haines Sr. family.)

IMAGES
of America

CHATSWORTH

CAPITAL OF THE PINE BARRENS

Ellen V. Fayer, Stan Fayer,
and Walter A. Brower

ARCADIA
PUBLISHING

ISBN 978-0-7385-7288-8

Published by Arcadia Publishing
Charleston, South Carolina

Printed in the United States of America

Library of Congress Control Number: 2009939867

For all general information contact Arcadia Publishing at:
Telephone 843-853-2070
Fax 843-853-0044
E-mail sales@arcadiapublishing.com
For customer service and orders:
Toll-Free 1-888-313-2665

Visit us on the Internet at www.arcadiapublishing.com

To members of the Woodland Township Historical Society who are no longer with us. They are Ida Mae Carr, Lillian Bozarth, and William S. Haines Sr.

Contents

ACKNOWLEDGMENTS

We are profoundly grateful to all who, in many and diverse ways, contributed significantly to the preparation of this history pictorial. We are especially mindful of those who responded to our calls for photographs and who so willingly recalled the importance of each. We owe all of them our heartfelt thanks.

How fortunate we were to have the assistance of Diane Sooy and Donna Horner, members of the book committee, who labored many hours with us. Their suggestions related to genealogical questions and numerous other aspects of this book's preparation were always welcomed and were of much value to us.

It is the words of encouragement that we received from so many, both far and near, that enabled us to pursue the important goal of putting together a pictorial publication that we believe will be of interest both within and beyond New Jersey's borders.

We would be remiss were we to fail to note those who were instrumental in the formation of the Woodland Township Historical Society: R. Marilyn Schmidt, Ida Mae Carr, Albert Morison, Lillian Bozarth, Deborah and Barry Grove, and Donna and Elton Horner. Each worked diligently to have their dreams become reality. To the society's current members, we convey our sincere appreciation for their interest and support.

To others who were keenly interested in this project and gave us support, we say, "Thank you."

—Ellen V. Fayer, Stan Fayer, and Walter A. Brower

INTRODUCTION

Where we love is home, Home that our feet may leave, But not our hearts.

—Oliver Wendel Holmes
From *An American Hometown*

Throughout the last four decades, Chatsworth has experienced a notable resurgence of interest in the town's location, history, and its people by persons throughout New Jersey and the East. Located in Woodland Township, Burlington County, in the pine barrens of Southern New Jersey, it is widely known as the "Capital of the Pines." It traces its roots to the 1700s, when settlers migrated to the area not only from other sections of the state but also from abroad. The early settlers came primarily to mine, forge bog iron, and to farm. There were four small settlements during the early years, Johnson Place, Jones Mill, Pasadena, and the largest, Shamong, which was renamed Chatsworth in 1901. Shamong was a popular overnight stagecoach stop for those traveling from Philadelphia to the Jersey Shore who would spend the night at the Peacock Inn on Main Street. The White Horse Inn, probably one of the oldest buildings in town, was available for lodging by those visiting or working in the area.

The continuous increase in the local population with many families with children necessitated that schools be built. Five one-room elementary schools were constructed. Meager by any standard, there was no electricity, no water, and no amenities one might expect to see in a school. They were schools with one teacher, usually a male, and accommodating more students than there were seats. Those schools were closed in 1915, when a larger school was built in Chatsworth to meet the needs of all the children in the township.

The village's first church building was constructed in 1873 to serve the Presbyterian parishioners. Destroyed by fire 20 years later, a new church facility was constructed and the congregation affiliated with the Methodist denomination. It has continued to be a vital part of the community.

A development that was to have a major impact on the growing community was the arrival of the railroad in 1850. There were no privately owned vehicles and no public transportation at that time. It was the railroad that opened many doors to the outside world for the citizens who would travel to and from Bridgeton, Philadelphia, and New York for shopping. The railroad also made it possible for local citizens to ship to market the sphagnum moss, pine cones, and cattails they gathered and to also receive items needed for daily living. The railroad, along with the area's natural beauty and its pure air, attracted persons from the populated cities of the Northeast and elsewhere to visit and in several instances, to relocate. A major development was the construction of a club at the lake in 1897 known as the Chatsworth Club by Prince Mario Ruspoli, an attaché of the Italian embassy in Washington, D.C. The prince also built a country villa, similar to an estate of the Duke of Devonshire in England, where he and his wife lavishly entertained notables from the United States and abroad. By the early 1900s, the club had over 500 members, among whom were the Astors, Morgans, Drexels, and Vanderbilts, and a sitting vice president of the United States, Levi P. Morton.

It was during the mid- to late 1800s that Chatsworth played a major role in the development of the cranberry industry in New Jersey. The cranberry growers provided employment for many local citizens. The growing of cranberries in the area continues to be a major industry. So major that for the last 27 years, thousands of people travel to Chatsworth each October to participate in the Annual Cranberry Festival, which is responsible for the complete rehabilitation of the White Horse Inn that had its beginning in the early 1860s. It was early in the 1900s that the location of Chatsworth became a year-round center for sportsmen and women to partake of the numerous recreational opportunities. These were namely hiking, fishing, and unlimited hunting, and in later years, canoeing and bicycling. Early in the 1900s, hunters built facilities, known as "deer clubs," that continue to be used during hunting season and throughout the year.

Chatsworth played a vital part in the 1920s in the development of the cultivated blueberry industry. Many local citizens owned blueberry farms (known as fields), and each day during the harvesting season, June and July, they would send their berries to markets not only in New Jersey and Philadelphia, but to distant locations. Many in the community looked forward each year to the harvesting of the blueberries as another way to earn money to support their families.

In 1913, a meeting took place in Pemberton to discuss plans for a colony house for the care and training of the mentally disabled in Burlington County. It was estimated that New Jersey had over 6,000 persons who needed care and training. That facility, the first of its kind in New Jersey, became a reality in 1914 and was called Four Mile Colony. It was situated on 500 acres of state forestlands, sections of which the residents were clearing and preparing for cultivation. In 1915, the colony had 32 residents, and plans were made to construct a dormitory that would house 40 residents. The residents were taught various crafts and skills commensurate with their abilities. The first superintendent was J. Frank Macomber, who was assisted by his wife. They were credited with handling the residents in an ideal manner and maintaining an institution that was a credit to the county. By 1930, there were 563 residents at the colony. The facility also contained a spotless concrete piggery housing 158 pigs from which they obtained meat, a herd of 20 Holstein cows, and a dairy, which provided milk. Fruits and vegetables were grown and preserved by acceptable canning methods. The residents were taught woodworking and weaving, and some participated in the glee club and the colony band. There was also a baseball team for those who wished to participate in sports. Many residents of Chatsworth and Woodland Township were employed by the colony.

Of special note is the 1939 wreck of the Blue Comet, 1 mile west of the Chatsworth Station. Operated by the Central Railroad of New Jersey, the train was advertised as being the "Seashore's Finest Train." It was a special train as the nation's first all-reserved deluxe coach train designed to give its passengers first-class service at low coach fares as they traveled to and from New York City and Atlantic City. Each car was named for a comet and painted a beautiful blue and cream color, both inside and out. It attracted the attention of people from long distances to travel to Chatsworth to await the passing of this very special train. Local citizens remember the evening of the wreck and continue to be proud that the Blue Comet's legacy of excellence was a part of Chatsworth's history.

The 1930s and 1940s, the years of the Great Depression, were difficult for the residents of Chatsworth. Whether gathering sphagnum moss, pine cones, cattails, or wild huckleberries, cutting wood to be shipped to far off places, or cranberry and blueberry harvesting, both men and women worked from before dawn until after sunset each day to earn money to provide for their families. Most families had a garden from which they harvested and preserved vegetables for the winter. The "Pineys," as local residents are often called, were industrious people whose example for hard work has been handed down from generation to generation.

The war years of the early 1940s found the citizens of Chatsworth responding with remarkable enthusiasm to manning the two local airplane lookout towers and participating as wardens during the weekly air raid drills that were held. Of special note is how proud everyone was that over 50 of the city's young men were serving in the military. The local citizens took the numerous rationing restrictions in stride and went about their daily routines.

Today Chatsworth, with a population of approximately 2,000, remains the largest settlement in Woodland Township, along with Lebanon Lakes, Jones Mill, and Johnson Place, all within the area covered by the Pinelands Protection Act of 1979. Chatsworth is more than just another village in the New Jersey Pines. It is a small village with an intriguing history, a village that captures the imagination of people in distant places who come to discover, explore, and enjoy the peace and tranquility of the area. The uniqueness of Chatsworth, its location and its bucolic environment, caught the endorsement of the 2007 issue of *National Geographic Adventure* as being "one of the 50 top towns in the country that exemplifies those characteristics that enables its citizens to be proud of their history and their culture."

One

Our Town

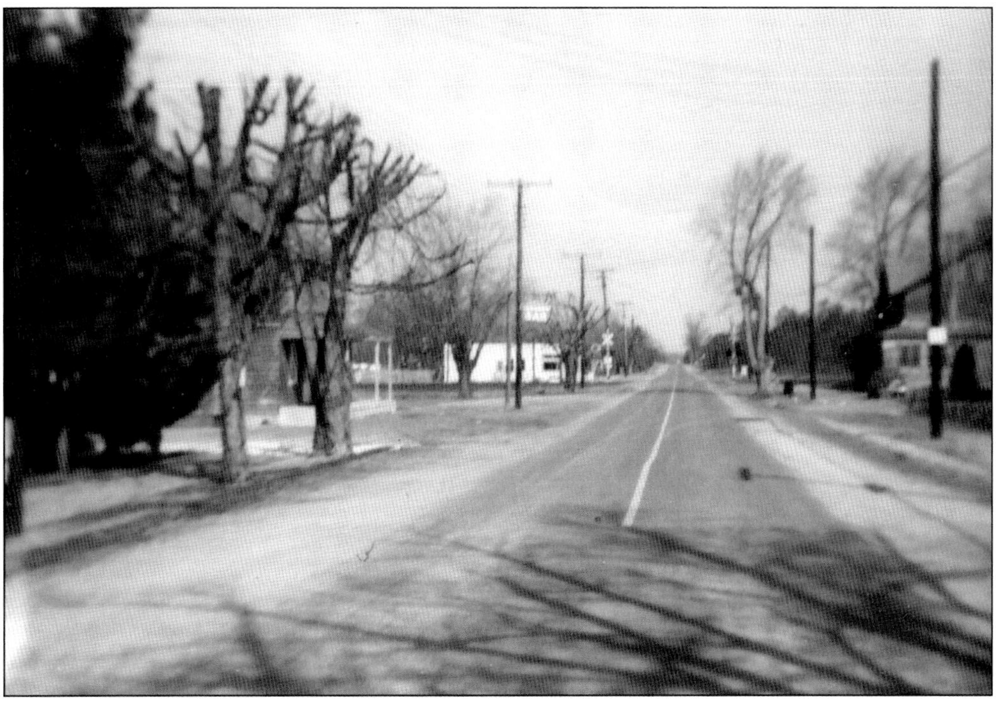

This 1960s Main Street scene shows the Peacock Inn on the left and the White Horse Inn on the right. Across the railroad tracks is Applegate's pool hall and ice cream parlor. The Peacock Inn was torn down in the 1970s, and the pool hall and ice cream parlor no longer exists. (Courtesy of Vera Topham.)

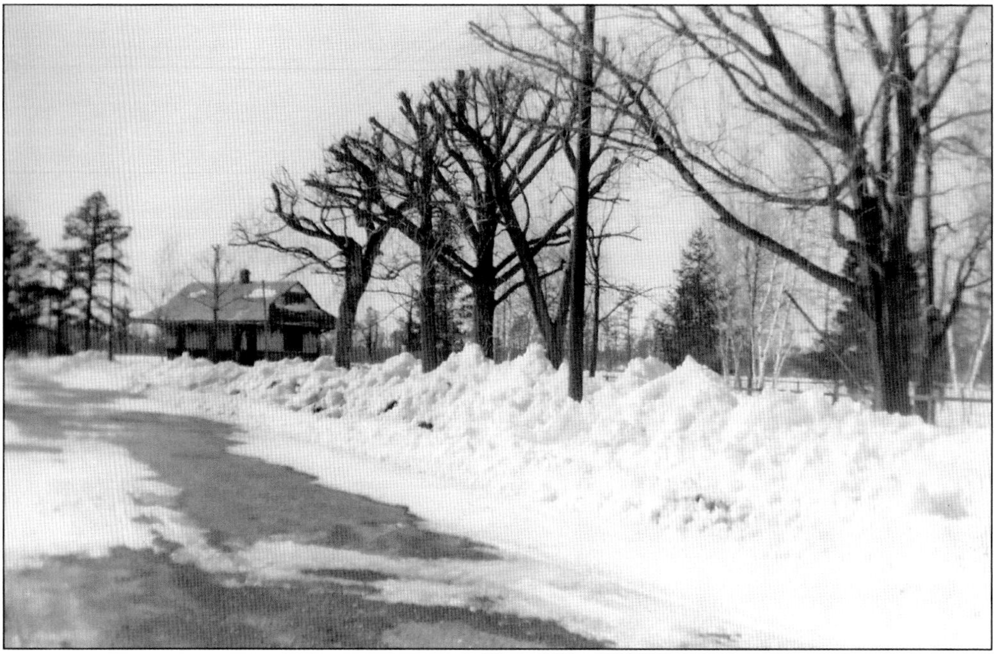

Heavy snowstorms were common in Chatsworth as shown in this 1937 photograph depicting the railroad station in the background. It was not uncommon for harsh snowstorms to almost completely immobilize the town until the roadways and streets could become usable. Some plowing has taken place, but there are still snowbanks along the roadside. (Courtesy of Buzby collection.)

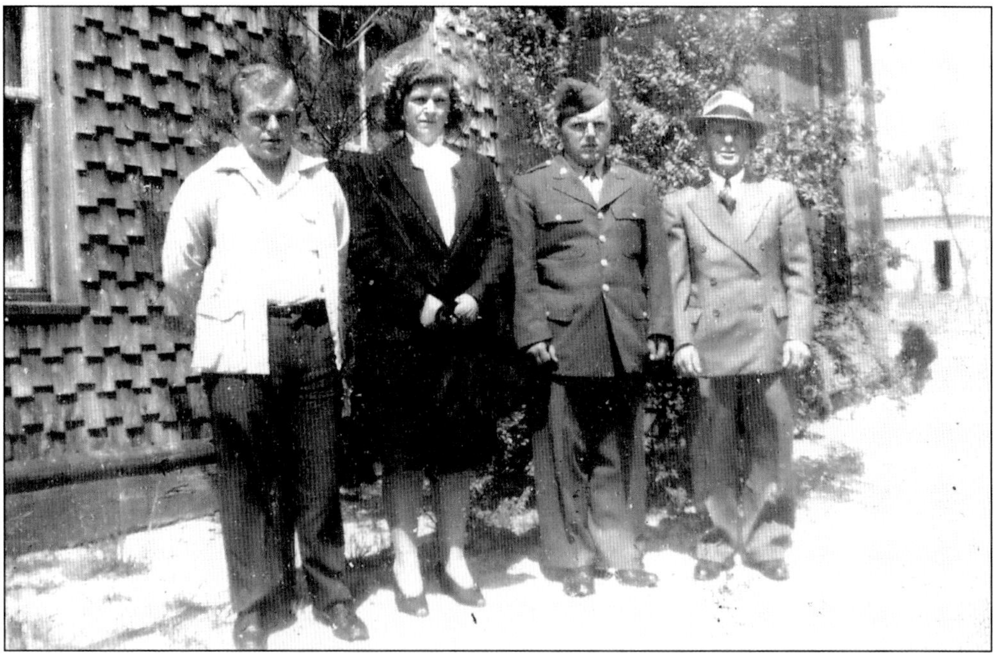

Charles and Daisy Leek Beach with sons Harry and Charles Jr. are shown in this photograph, taken next to their home on Main Street in the area adjacent to today's location of the township municipal building. Their home was called the "Slab House." It had been brought into town in four sections and then joined together on the site. (Courtesy of Sooy family.)

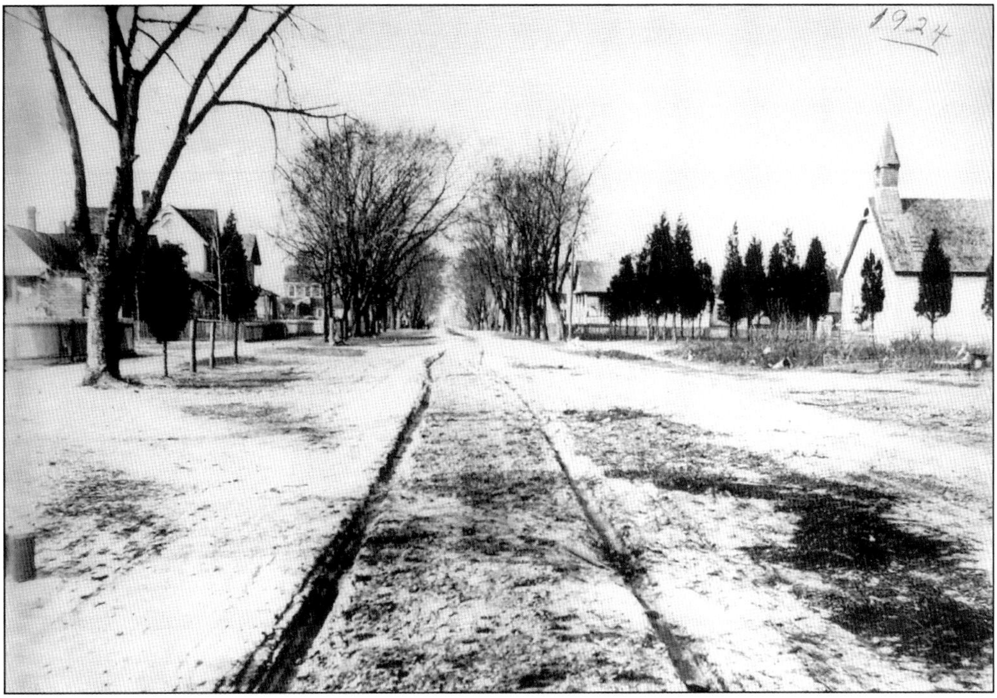

This is a view looking north on Main Street in 1924. On the left are the homes of the Messlers, Bozarths, and Greens, and in the distance is Buzby's store. On the right are the Methodist church and the parsonage. The unpaved street saw the horse and buggy as the major source of transportation. Note that there are no telephone or electric lines in town. Limited telephone service became available in 1910, while electricity did not arrive until 1932. (Courtesy of Frank Applegate family.)

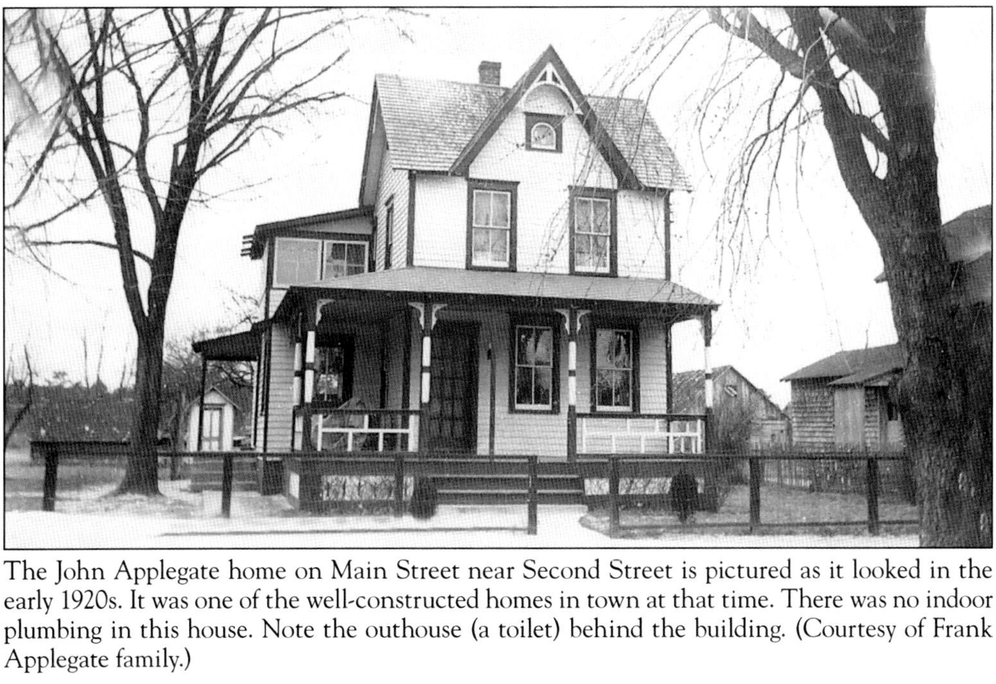

The John Applegate home on Main Street near Second Street is pictured as it looked in the early 1920s. It was one of the well-constructed homes in town at that time. There was no indoor plumbing in this house. Note the outhouse (a toilet) behind the building. (Courtesy of Frank Applegate family.)

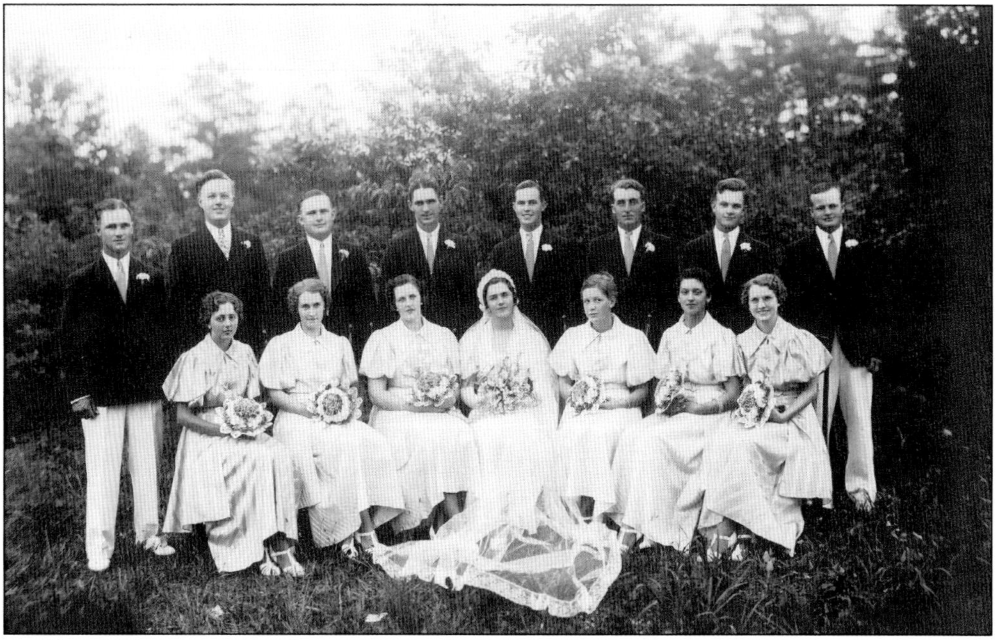

Wedding bells rang at the Chatsworth Methodist Church for the June 20, 1936, wedding of Julia Sloan and Stanley Worrell. Those in the wedding party were, from left to right, (first row) Louise Brower, Verna Pepper, Ella Kathryn Sloan, Julia Sloan, Amelia Stevenson, Rose Ranalli, and Mary Ella Pepper; (second row) Benjamin "Benn" Worrell, unidentified, Henry "Hank" Worrell, Bill Sloan, Stanley Worrell, Albertus Pepper, Ellis Worrell, and Milton "Mutt" Worrell. (Courtesy of Stan and Maureen Worrell.)

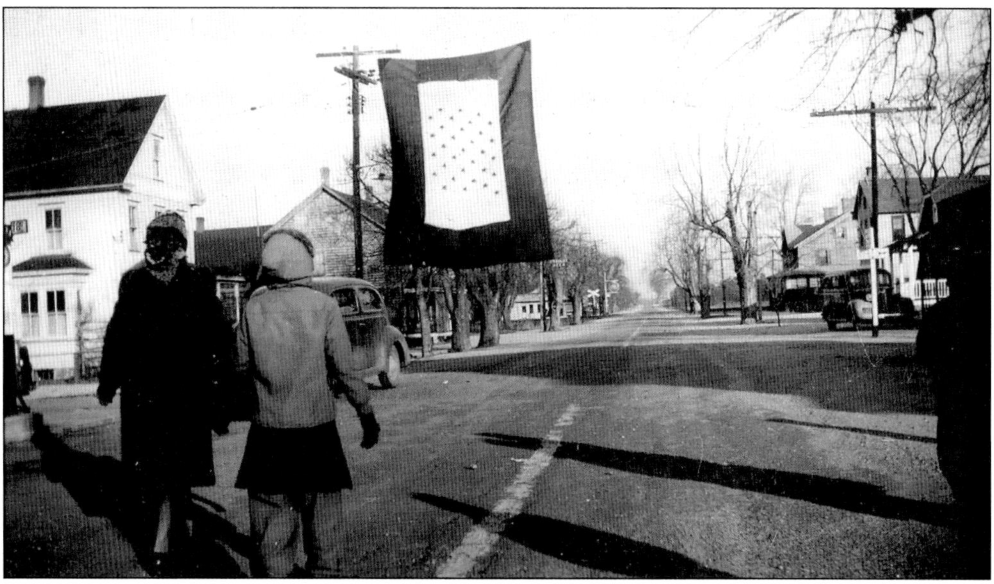

The Junior Red Cross Service Flag is prominently displayed at the intersection of Main Street and Route 532 in Chatsworth in 1943. The white building on the right is the town hall/fire house with the White Horse Inn closer to the railroad crossing. The roof of the Peacock Inn is visible near the flag. The two pedestrians on the street are unidentified. (Courtesy of Stan and Maureen Worrell.)

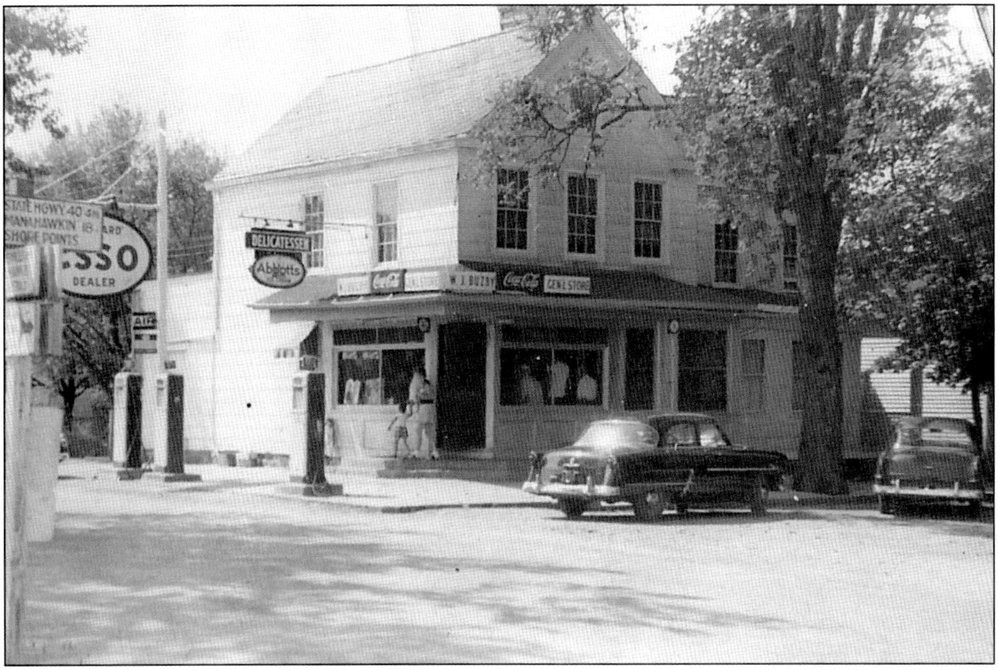

Buzby's store at Main and First Streets was more than a general store. It was also the gathering place for residents of Chatsworth. It was not unusual for the men of the community to gather in the evening to talk about the day's events. A look through the store window shows a group of persons taking time out of their busy day to chat. (Courtesy of Amelia Green collection.)

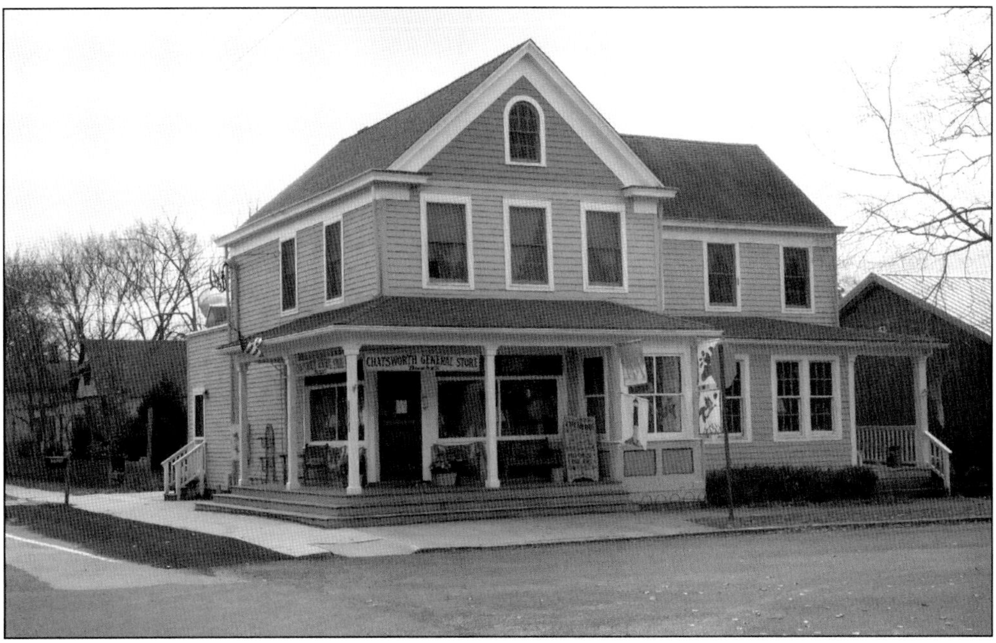

Buzby's store was constructed in 1865. This photograph shows the building as it is today. The structure was purchased and extensively rehabilitated by R. Marilyn Schmidt in 2000 and houses a gift shop called the Cheshire Cat. The structure is on the National Register of Historic Places. (Courtesy of Stan Fayer.)

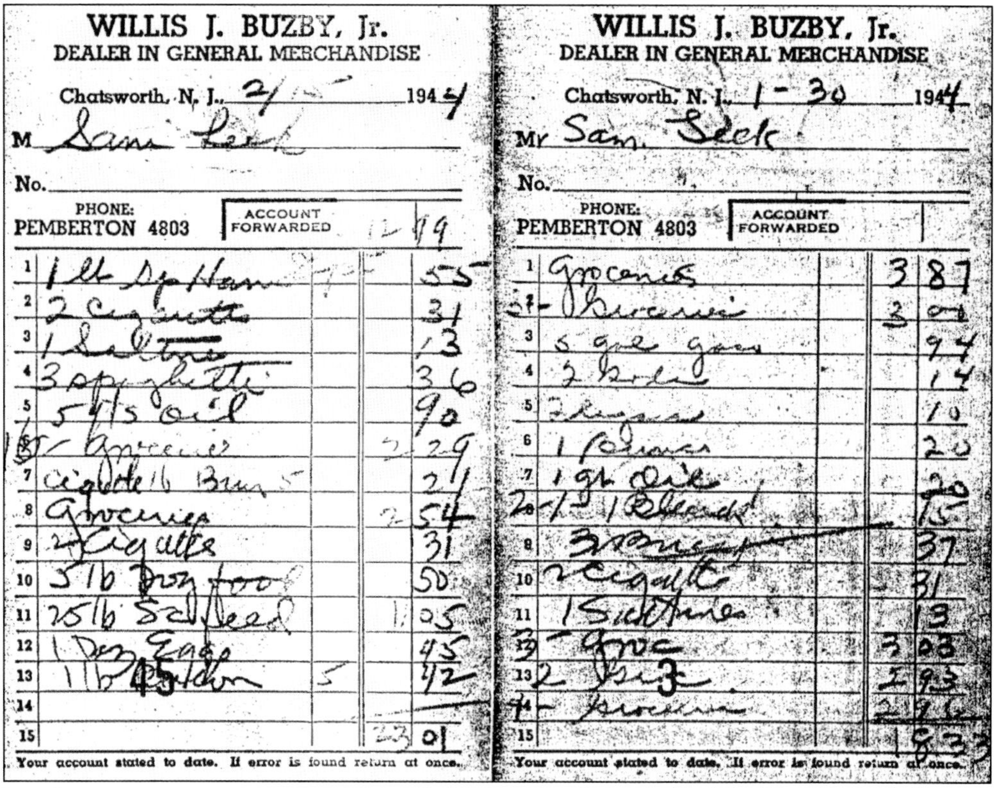

WILLIS J. BUZBY, Jr.
DEALER IN GENERAL MERCHANDISE
Chatsworth, N. J., 2/ 194
M Sam Leek
No.
PHONE: PEMBERTON 4803
ACCOUNT FORWARDED
Your account stated to date. If error is found return at once.

WILLIS J. BUZBY, Jr.
DEALER IN GENERAL MERCHANDISE
Chatsworth, N. J., 1-30 1944
Mr Sam. Leek
No.
PHONE: PEMBERTON 4803
ACCOUNT FORWARDED
Your account stated to date. If error is found return at once.

Local citizens were permitted to run a tab for their purchases at Buzby's. This 1944 tab for Sam Leek is indeed revealing about the cost of items when compared with today. Imagine paying 94¢ for 5 gallons of gasoline and 45¢ for a dozen eggs. (Courtesy of Sooy family.)

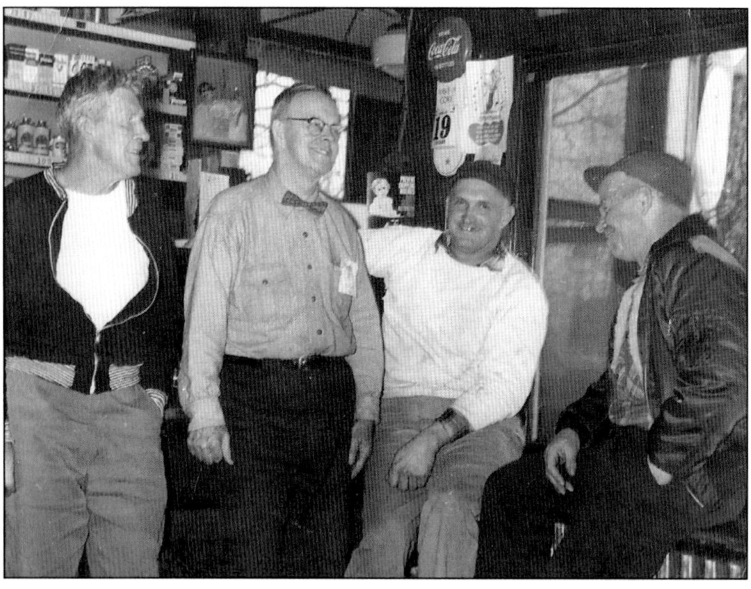

Known as a gathering place, Buzby's store was frequently the location for local citizens to get together for a discussion of local news. From left to right, Walter Inman, Jack Buzby, Irving "Diz" Mantel, and George Wills take time from work to have a chat. (Courtesy of Amelia Green collection.)

Willis J. "Jack" Buzby Jr. and his cat Billy stand in front of the well-stocked shelves of Buzby's store. Jack learned the operation of the store from his father, Willis Jefferson Buzby, and when his father died in 1939, he was well equipped to take over total management of the operation. He and Katie, his wife, operated the store until the late 1960s. (Courtesy of Buzby collection.)

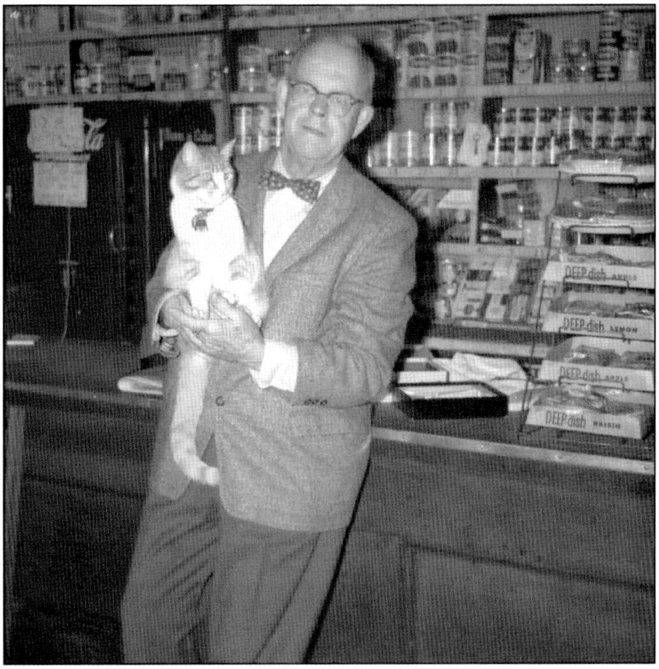

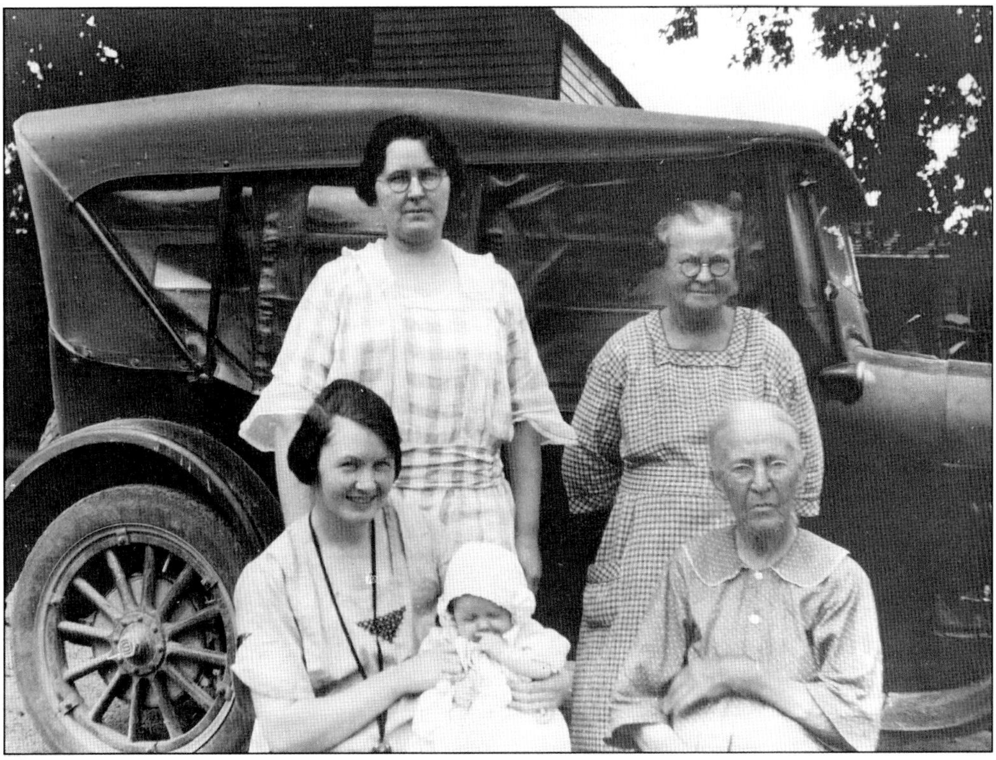

Five generations pose for this photograph taken in 1924. From left to right are (first row) Kate Buzby (the granddaughter of Victor Ritzendollar) holding Theresa (infant) and her great-grandmother Jane Adams Lee; (second row) Kate's mother, Wilhemina Inman Ritzendollar, and her mother, Amanda Lee Inman. (Courtesy of Buzby collection.)

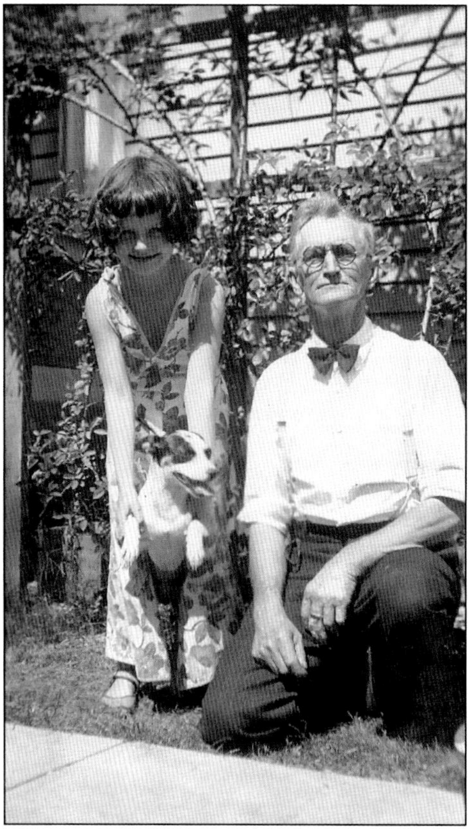

Theresa Buzby, daughter of Jack and Katie Buzby, are with her dog Buddy and grandfather John Henry Ritzendollar in 1929. The Ritzendollar family came to this country in 1853 and settled in Chatsworth by 1860. John Henry was the son of Victor Ritzendollar and the father of Kate Ritzendollar Buzby. (Courtesy of Buzby collection.)

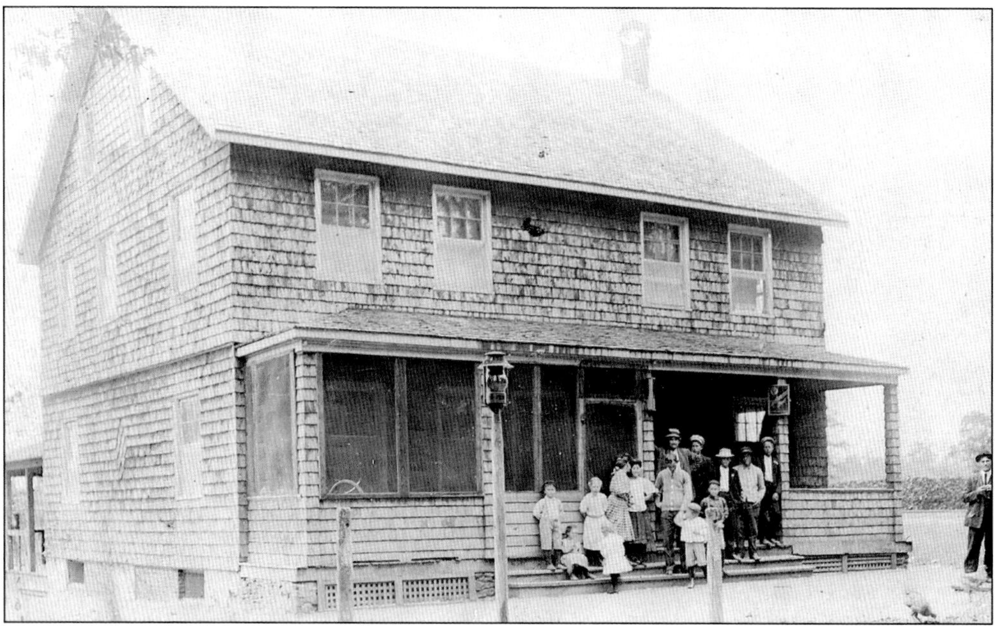

The Bozarth family and townspeople gather at the Peacock Inn on Main Street for this 1915 photograph. The building continued to stand and was in operation until the early 1970s. (Courtesy of Stan and Maureen Worrell.)

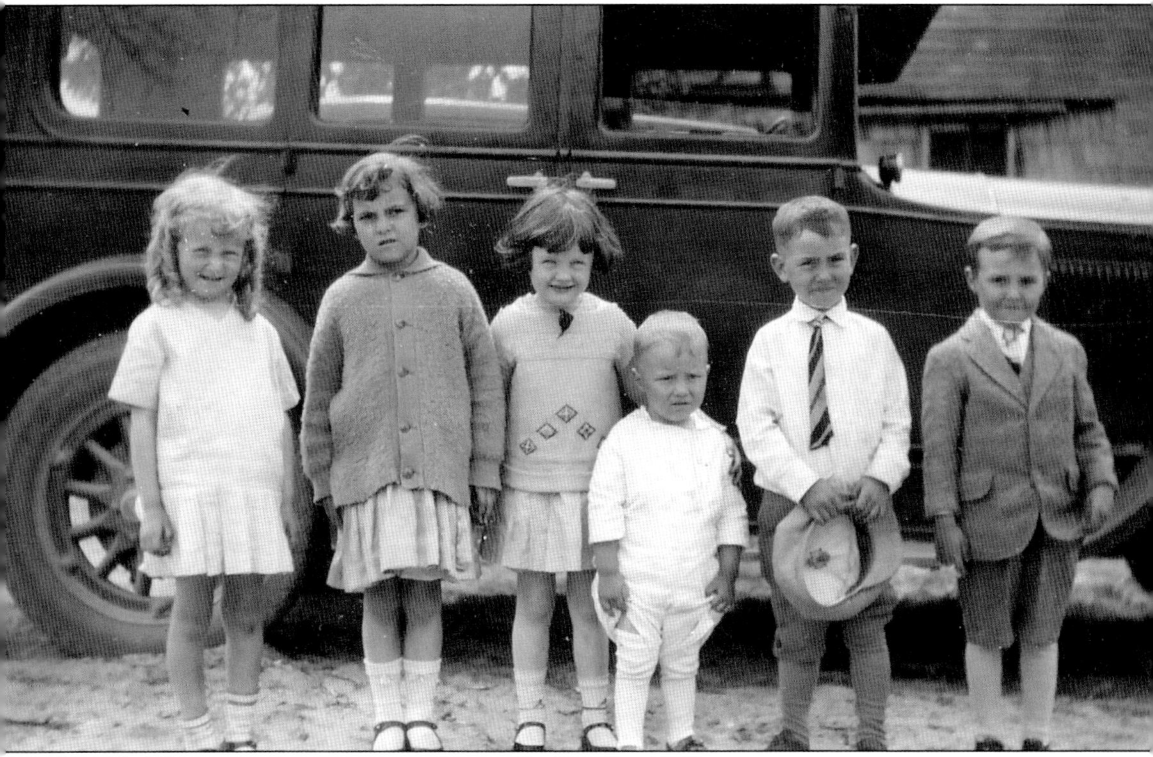

Perhaps these young people are waiting for the driver. In this 1928 photograph, they are all dressed up and appear ready to get into the awaiting vehicle. From left to right are Doris Jones, Kathryn Wills, Theresa Buzby, Norman Wills, John Wills, and Alfred Wills. (Courtesy of Buzby collection.)

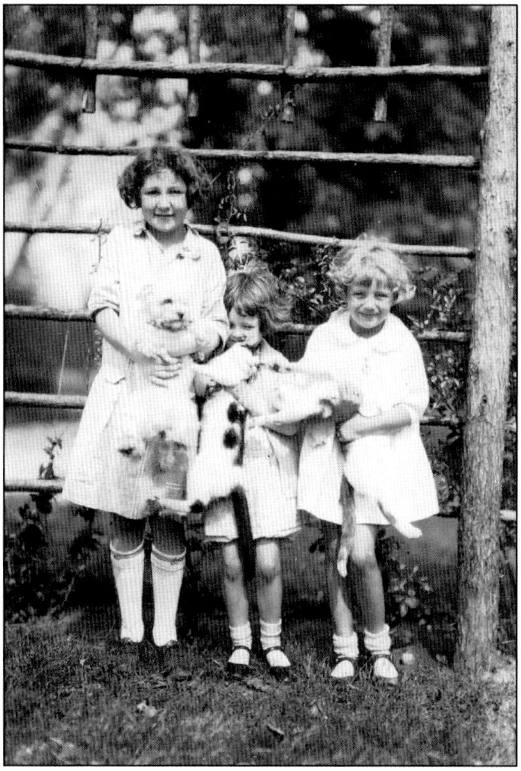

From left to right, Irma Dunfee, Theresa Buzby, and Almeda Brower, with their pets, get together for this 1928 photograph taken in the yard of the Dunfee home. Theresa and Almeda were cousins, Theresa being the daughter of Katie Ritzendollar Buzby and Almeda the daughter of Anna Ritzendollar Brower. (Courtesy of Buzby collection.)

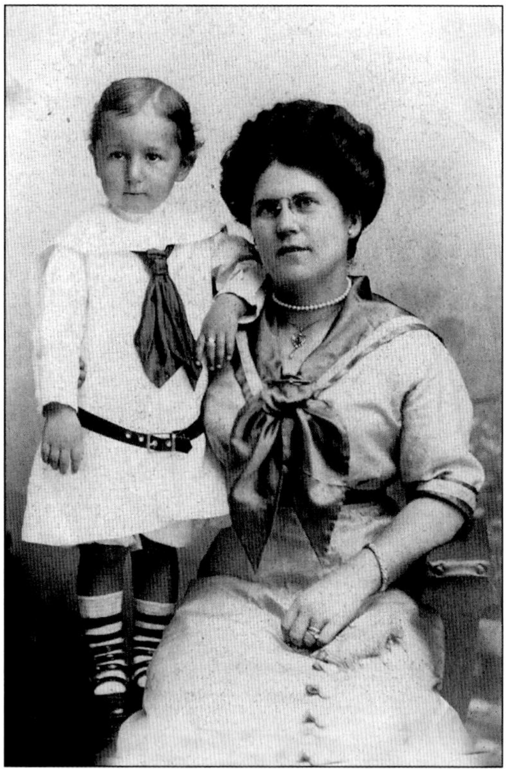

Bertha Dunfee, wife of the station agent in Chatsworth, and son Fred Jr. pose for this photograph taken in the early 1900s on the boardwalk while on a day trip to Atlantic City. It was not uncommon for residents of Chatsworth to travel to Bridgeton, Atlantic City, Philadelphia, or New York to shop. (Courtesy of Buzby collection.)

This is the home of Harry and Sadie Sloan on Lake Road, which Harry built in the 1920s and exists today. It is probably the only residence in Chatsworth with an unusually long, slanted roof. Harry Sloan was a builder who constructed many houses in Chatsworth. (Courtesy of Stan and Maureen Worrell.)

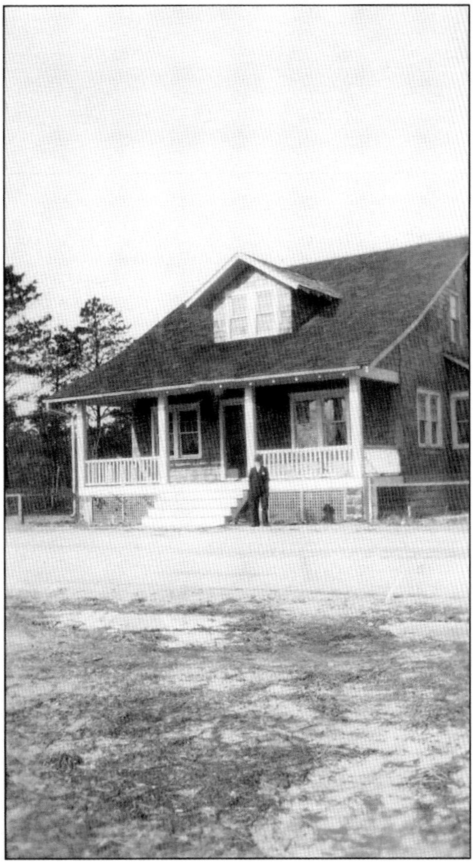

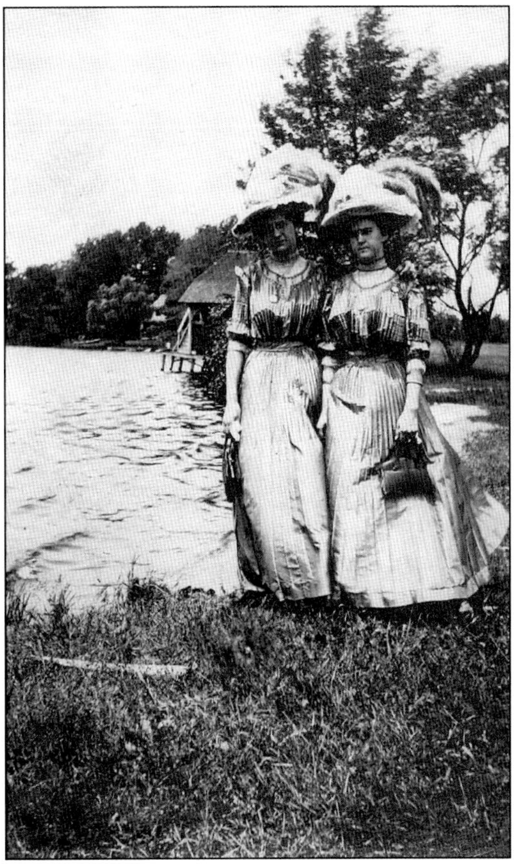

Florence Sloan and Sadie Taylor pose for this photograph taken in the early 1900s as they stood on the banks of the Chatsworth Lake. A sailboat can be seen on the shore of the lake in the distance. Note the similarity of dress, hat, and pocketbook. (Courtesy of Stan and Maureen Worrell.)

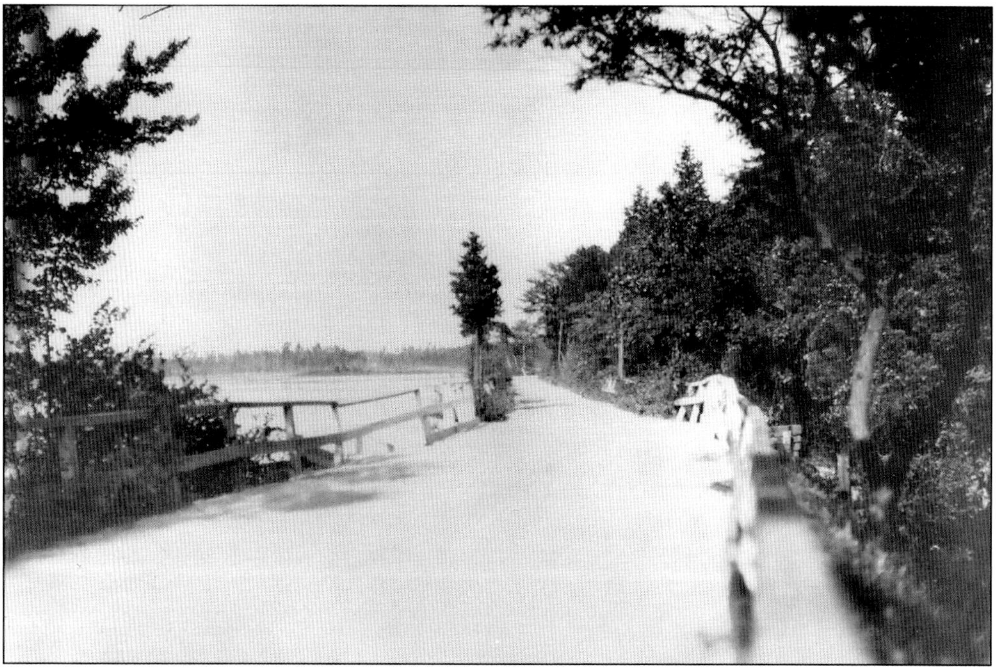

A scene taken in 1924 at the Chatsworth Lake shows what was then known as the Tabernacle Road. The lake was a popular swimming and diving spot for the local citizens. In later years, the road became Route 532 from Tabernacle leading to Chatsworth, Route 72, and Long Beach Island. (Courtesy of Charles Applegate collection.)

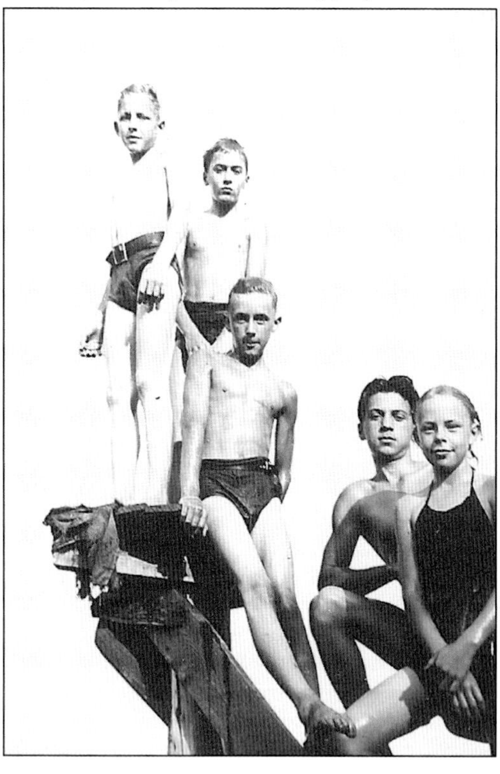

The Chatsworth Lake on Lake Avenue was always a popular swimming and picnic spot, especially with the young people. In this August 1942 photograph taken at the diving board are, from top to bottom, Jim Anderson, Bobby Bozarth, Jimmie Sloan, Billy Ranalli, and Dorothy Rita Green. (Courtesy of Amelia Green collection.)

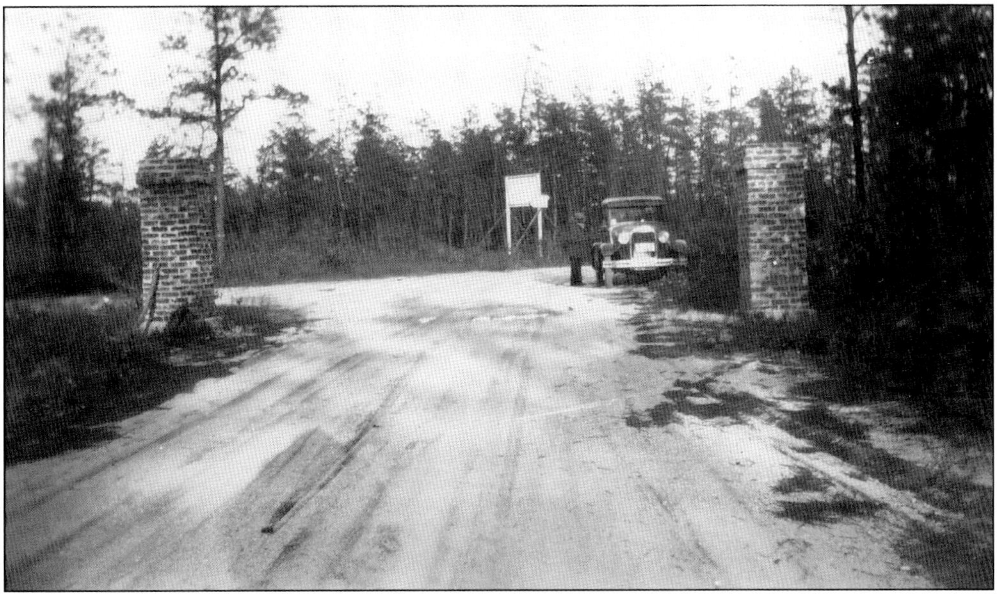

Two brick columns mark the entrance to the proposed Chatsworth Woods Country Club. The corporation was formed in 1927 by Charles Muntrick, Justin Ringler, Hans Katenhauser, G. Osberg, and Thomas J. Curran. The club did not materialize. Osberg lived in one of the few homes built there. The area is referred to as "The Streets" because of the streets planned for the development. (Courtesy of Stan and Maureen Worrell.)

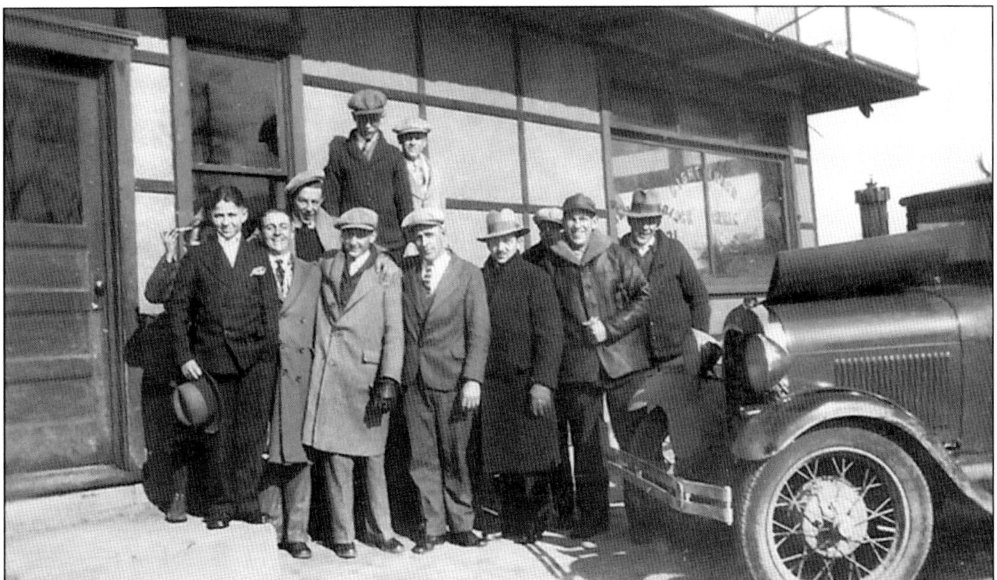

A gathering at Sloan's ice cream parlor near the railroad crossing in Chatsworth consisted of, from left to right, (first row) two unidentified, Albertus Pepper, Clifford Haines, three unidentified, Harold Stevenson, and Jack Buzby; (second row) Richard Green, Caleb Adams, and George Applegate. A 1930s automobile is pictured in the foreground. (Courtesy of Stan and Maureen Worrell.)

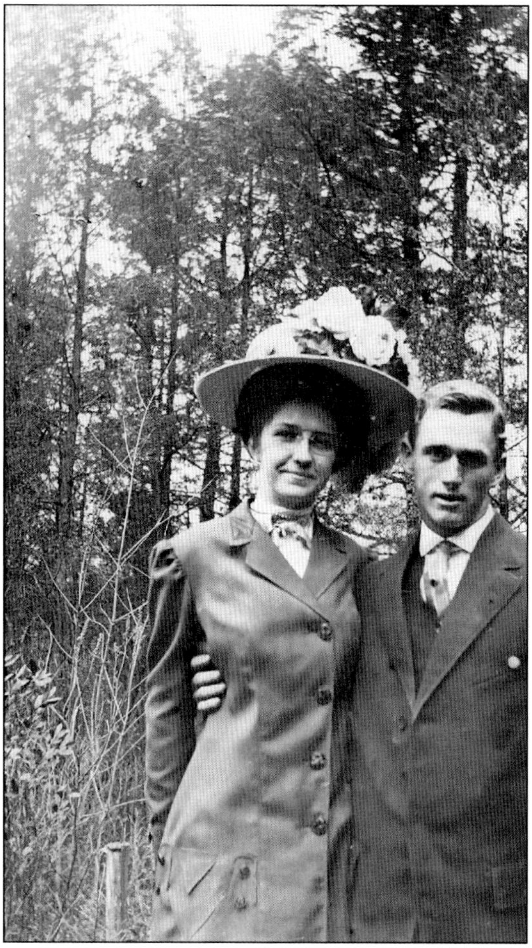

This 1913 photograph shows Sadie Taylor and Harry Sloan, who were married on January 2, 1913. For many years, they operated an ice cream parlor on Main Street adjacent to the railroad. Sadie was a long-standing member of the board of education in Chatsworth. (Courtesy of Stan and Maureen Worrell.)

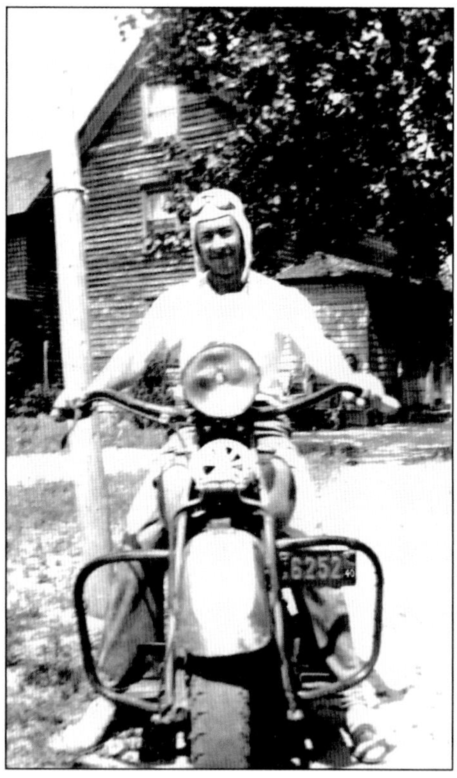

Charlie "Wings" Applegate is ready for a ride on his Indian motorcycle. The *c.* 1940 photograph was taken at his home on Main Street in Chatsworth. Charlie was the ultimate prankster and would ride through town standing on the seat of the cycle or hiding next to the gas tank, so that it appeared that the cycle was operated by a ghost. (Courtesy of Charles Applegate collection.)

Albertus V. Pepper Sr. was a lifelong resident of Chatsworth. He was a member of the team of men who recovered Emilio Carranza's remains after his fatal airplane crash in the Pine Barrens in 1928. He was the owner of Jones Mill Farm in Chatsworth where he grew blueberries. He served as mayor of Woodland Township in the 1950s and served on the board of education. At the time of his death in 2007, he was the oldest living member of the Chatsworth Methodist Church. (Courtesy of Amelia Green collection.)

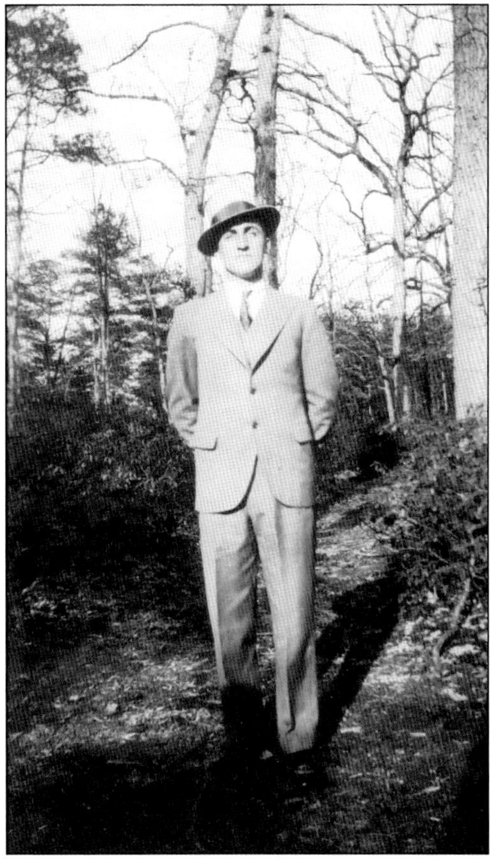

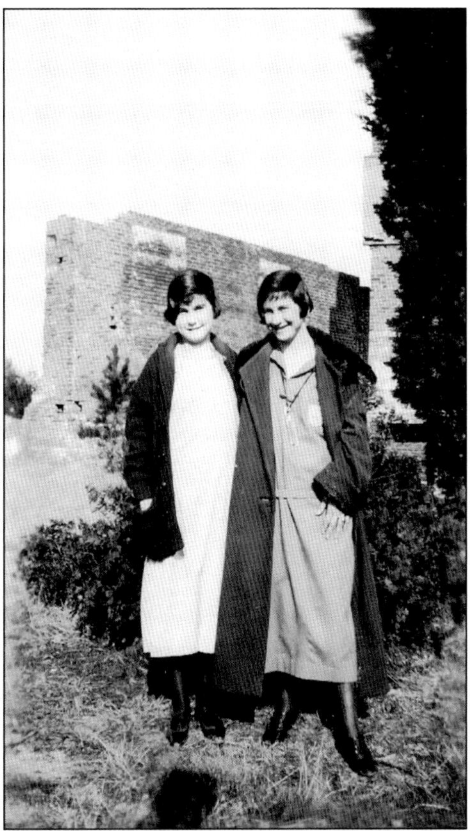

Ruth Estlow and Florence Wills Applegate pose for this photograph with the ruins of the Harrisville Paper Mill in the background. The mill, located at the Oswego Branch of the Wading River, is believed to have been the largest paper mill in New Jersey in the early 1800s. (Courtesy of Charles Applegate collection.)

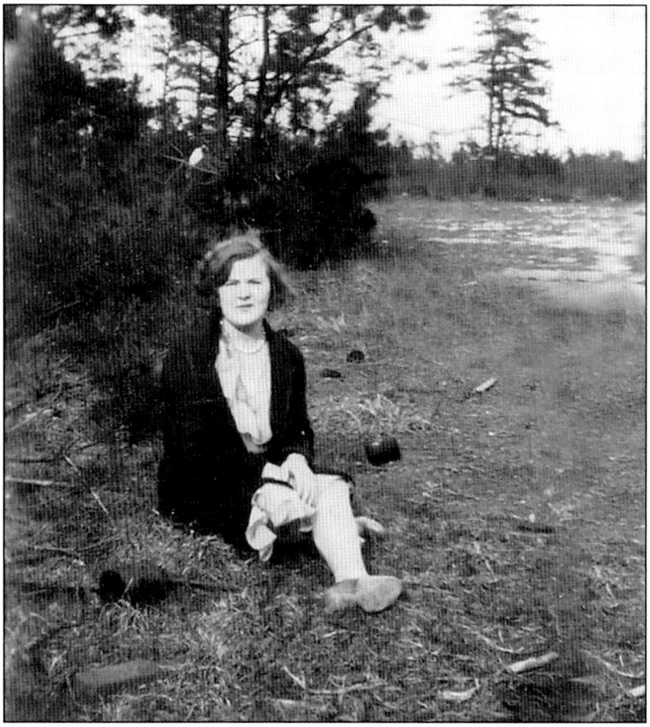

Eva Corlis spends a quiet moment at Chatsworth Lake in the mid-1920s. She later married Ernest Messler, a local fellow who worked in the cranberry bogs, and they lived on Main Street in Chatsworth in the 1930s. Eva was a seamstress at Four Mile Colony for many years. (Courtesy of Donna Horner.)

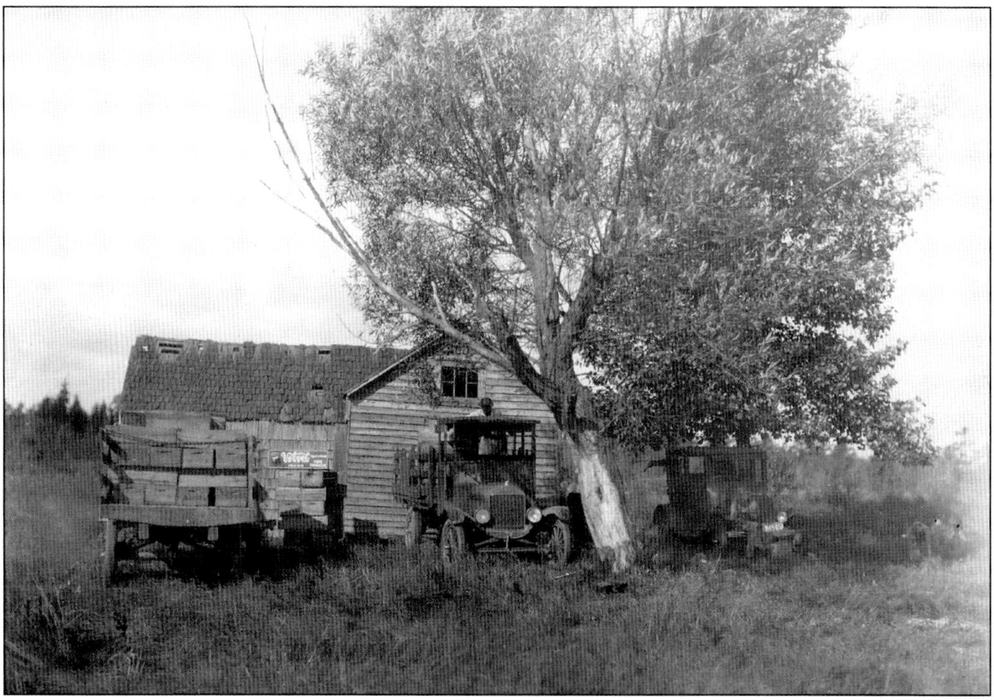

This mid-1930s photograph shows a packinghouse at the cranberry bogs owned by John Ritzendollar on the east side of Route 563 adjacent to the Schoolhouse Bridge. Note the old truck that was used to carry the harvested cranberries from the bogs to the packinghouse. (Courtesy of the Buzby collection.)

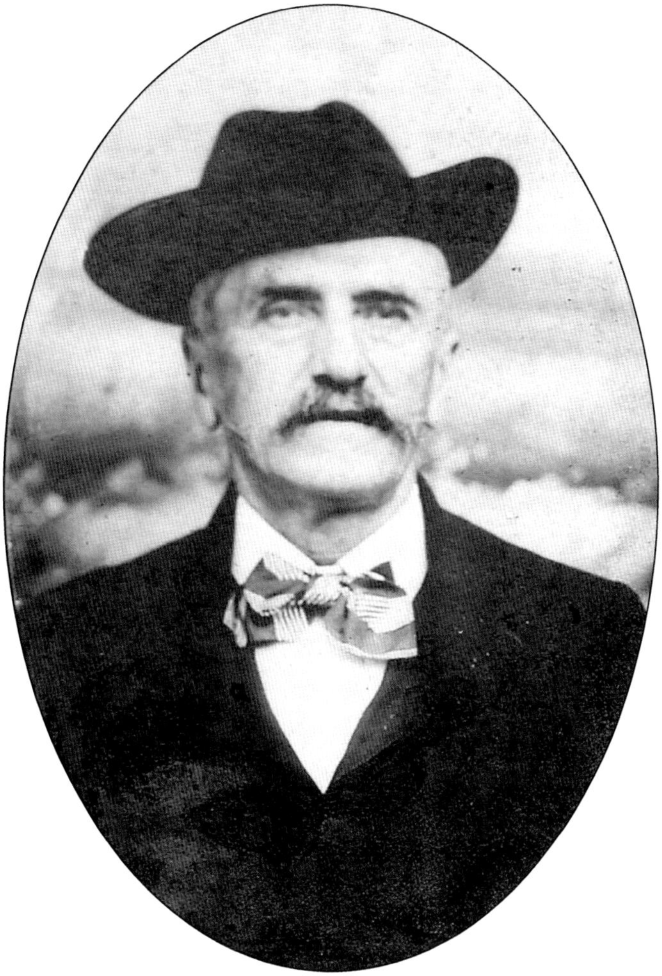

Victor Ritzendollar was a prominent leader in the community in its early years. Born in the Alsace Lorraine region of France in 1845, his family came to the United States five years later and settled in Chatsworth at the homestead, the Hedger House, to engage in farming. He was a cranberry grower with bogs on both sides of Main Street near the Schoolhouse Bridge. During the early years, he built and owned many homes in the area near the bogs. That area of Chatsworth was known as "Vicksburg." Victor Street in Chatsworth was named in his honor. He was a member of the school board, served as a justice of the peace, was a constable, a Burlington County Freeholder, a member of the Woodland Township Committee, and served as mayor. He was also a fire warden and a director of the New Jersey Cranberry Company. (Courtesy of Natalie Oakes Sturr.)

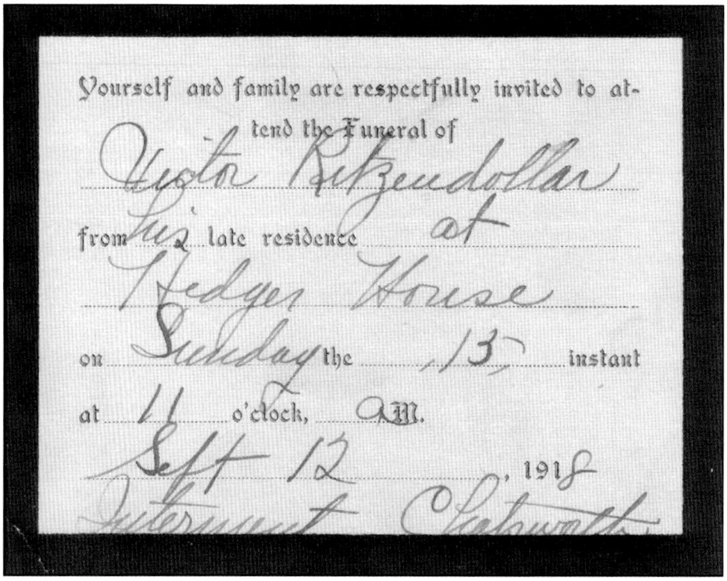

Yourself and family are respectfully invited to attend the Funeral of

Victor Ritzendollar

from his late residence at

Hedger House

on Sunday the 15 instant

at 11 o'clock, A.M.

Sept 12, 1918

Interment at Chatsworth

As was the custom in those early years, funeral invitations were sent or delivered. The *Mount Holly Herald* reported, "People came from all parts of Burlington County on Sunday to attend the funeral of Victor Ritzendollar at his home at the Hedger House. There were perhaps forty automobiles lined up at the house." (Courtesy of Natalie Oakes Sturr.)

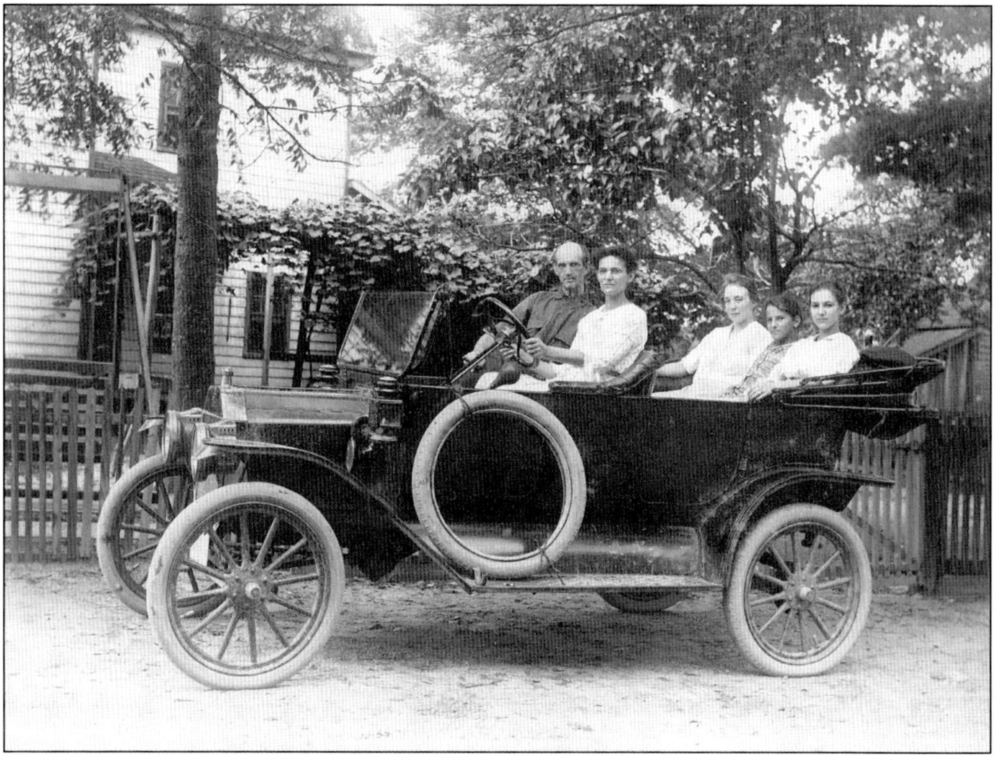

Eliza Ritzendollar, wife of Victor Ritzendollar, is the driver of the touring car, one of the first in the township. This photograph was taken at the Hedger House, the Ritzendollar homestead. Seated behind Eliza is her daughter Anna who, in 1924, became postmistress in Chatsworth. Driving in those days was restricted to open fields, clear spaces, and on sand roads that required drivers to always remain in the ruts made by horse-drawn buggies. It was many years later that paved roadways came to the Chatsworth area. Others in the car are not identified. (Courtesy of Walter A. Brower Jr.)

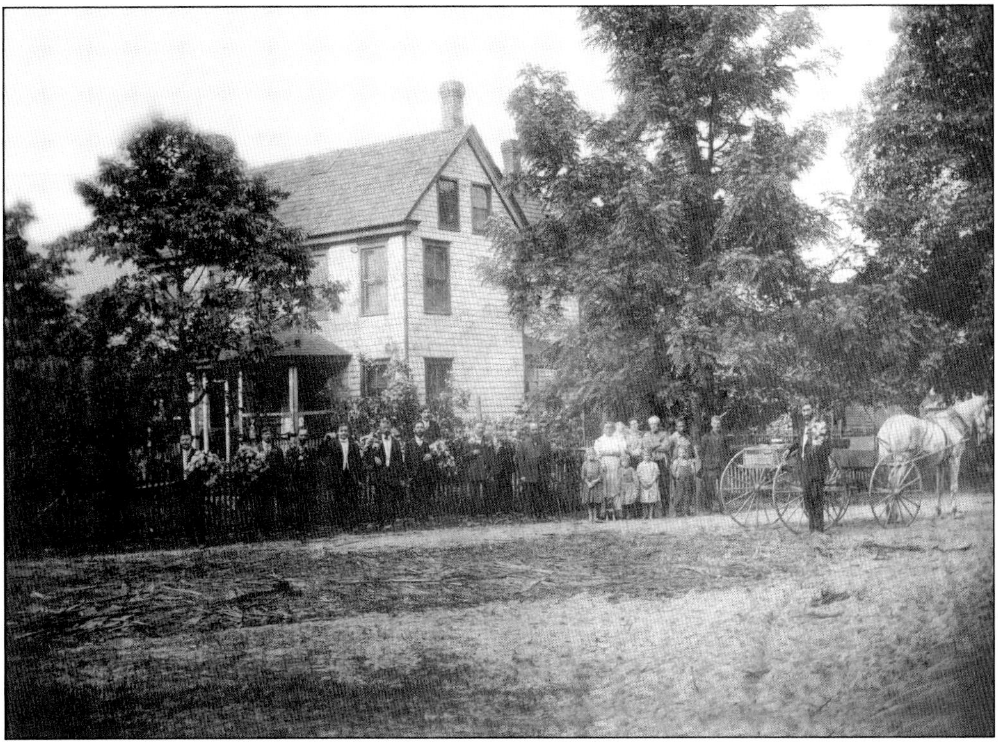

This photograph of the Hedger House, homestead of Victor and Eliza Ritzendollar, taken in the 1920s, shows a gathering of family and friends for what appears to be a funeral, probably of one of the farm employees. Victor operated a large farm at this location that included fruit trees and grape vines, and he also owned cranberry bogs in the Chatsworth area. (Courtesy of Walter A. Brower Jr.)

The David and Sarah Applegate homestead was located on Prince Street. The buildings of the Applegate Land Improvement Company are situated behind the home. Other homes on Prince Street belonged to William Steward, J. R. Dunfee, and George Wills. From 1943 until 1975, the post office was located on Prince Street. (Courtesy of Frank Applegate family.)

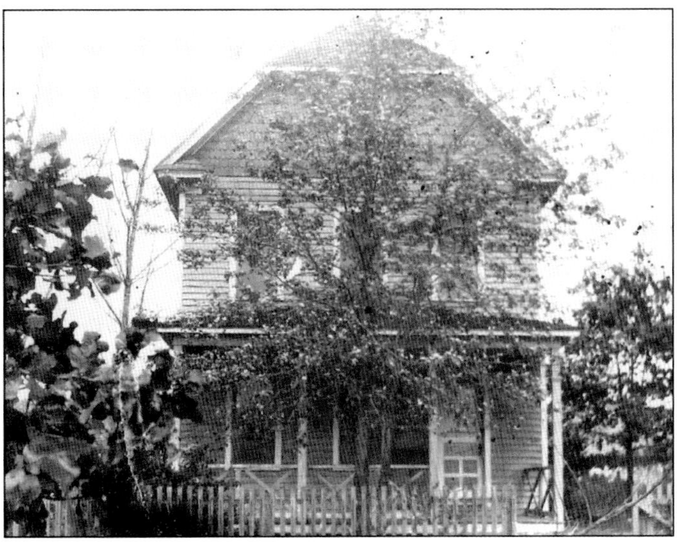

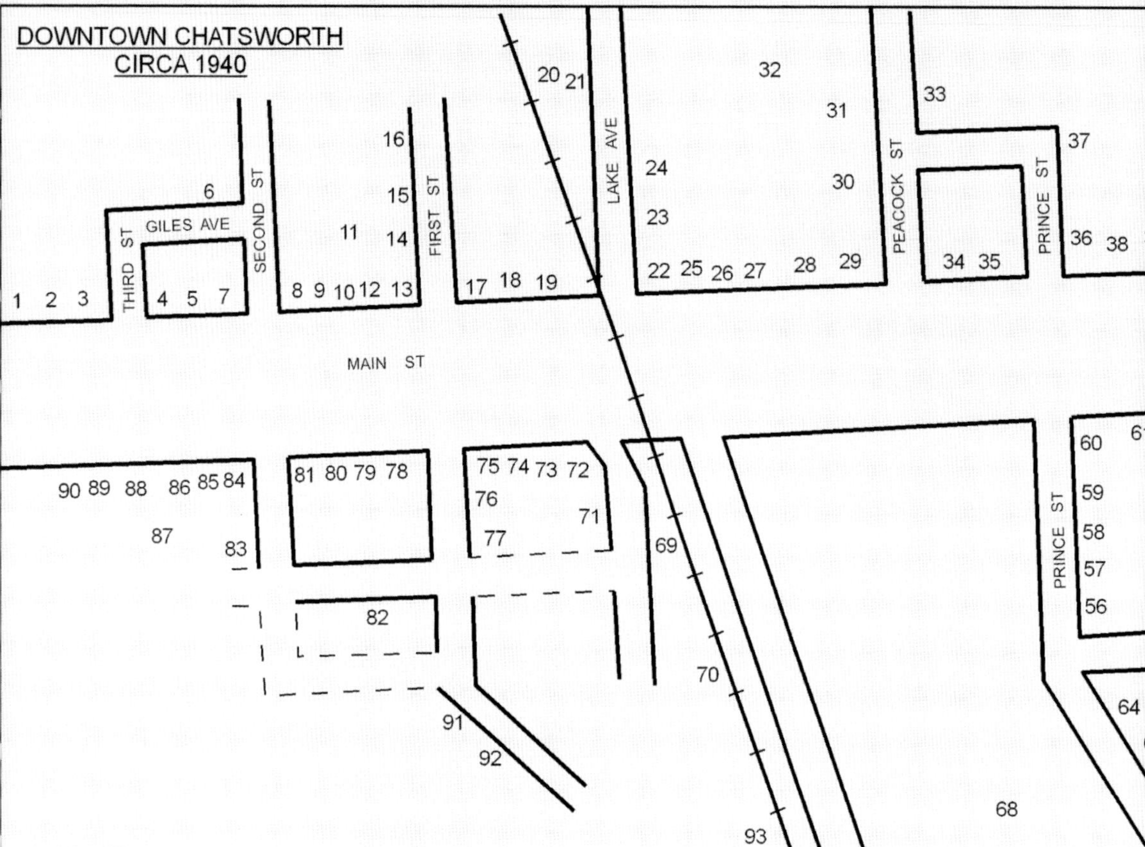

MAP KEY

1 WOODLAWN CEMETERY
2 HARMONY GUN CLUB
3 HEWITT A.
4 BROWER E.
5 BEACH C.
6 SCHOOL
7 BOZARTH A.
8 HAINES H.
9 McCARTHY H.
10 GREEN R.
11 HEWITT E.
12 WORRELL S.
13 BUZBY W. STORE
14 RITZENDOLLAR J.
15 DUNFEE F.
16 STEVENSON J.
17 BUZBY W.
18 STEVENSON P.
19 PEACOCK INN
20 EGENLAUF C.
21 STEVENSON J.
22 APPLEGATE E.
23 SLOAN H.
24 HAINES E.
25 PRICKETT A.
26 TAYLOR W.
27 APPLEGATE A.
28 SLOAN W.
29 SLOAN W. STORE
30 SAWMILL SLOAN
31 CLAIR L.
32 LEMMON R.
33 STEVENSON J.
34 RANALLI B.
35 KING C.
36 KATT O.
37 SOOY H.
38 JANNONE L.
39 WILLS S.
40 KENNEDY F.
41 KENNEDY SAWMILL
42 CORLIS L.
43 APPLEGATE M.
44 BROOMES J.
45 CRANBERRY BOG
46 SCHOOLHOUSE BRIDGE
47 HEADLEY M.
48 WILLS J.
49 KENNEDY H.
50 APPLEGATE SAWMILL
51 MT. ROYAL GUN CLUB
52 GLENDORA GUN CLUB
53 WICHWARD H.
54 MESSLER E.
55 APPLEGATE CRANBERRY HOUSE
56 DUNFEE J. R.
57 APPLEGATE D.
58 STEWART W.
59 WILLS G.
60 POST OFFICE
61 BROOMES J.
62 BATES R.
63 PORTER G.
64 WOODBURY GUN CLUB
65 CLAIR C.
66 BUCK FEVER GUN CLUB
67 SIMPKINS M.
68 CURRA
& 3 C
69 HOLLO
70 CARR
71 KING T.
72 WHITE
STEVE
73 TOWN
74 BROWE
75 BROWE
76 ANDER
77 CRANB
78 ESTLO
79 ESTLO
80 PARSO
81 CHURC
82 KING E
83 PEPPE
84 PEPPE

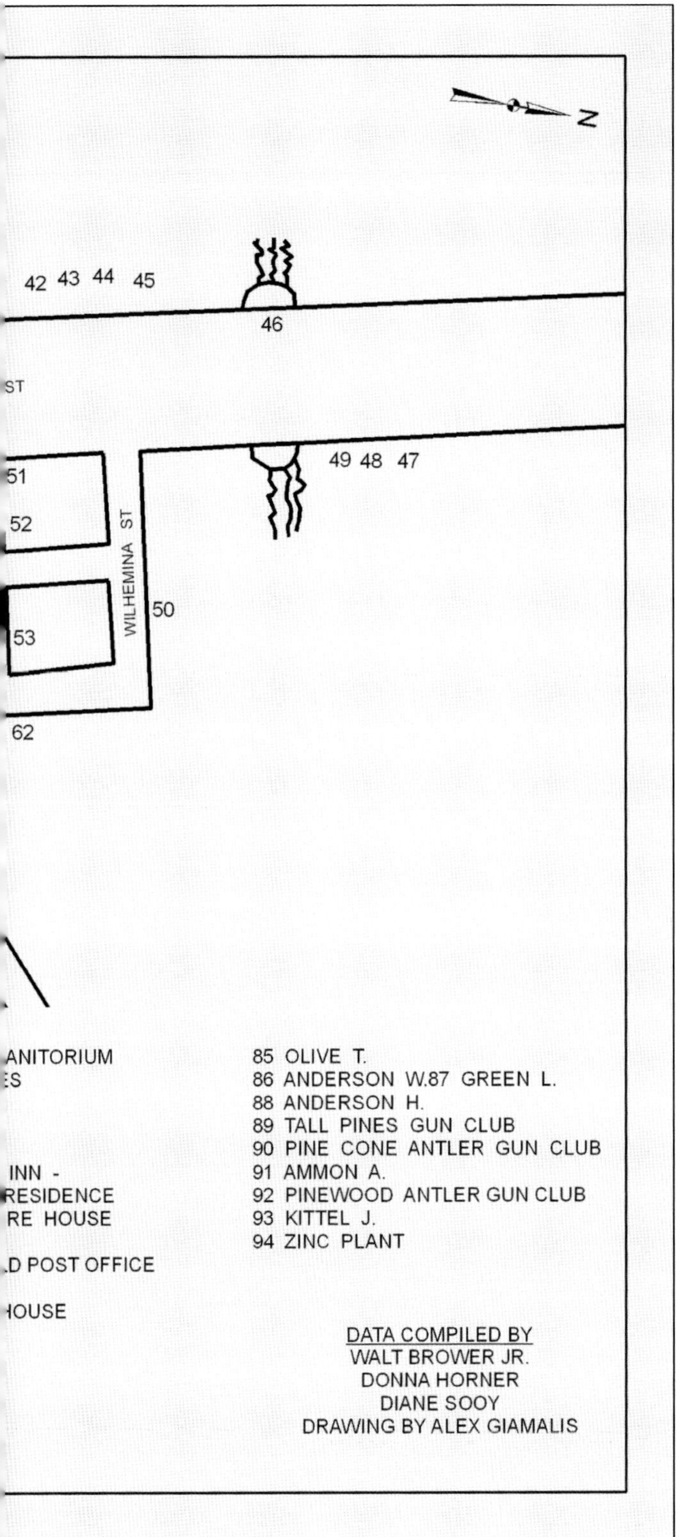

Pictured here is a map of Chatsworth c. 1940. The drawing is by Alex Giamalis, and the changes were made by David Richert. (Data compiled by Walter Brower Jr., Donna Horner, and Diane Sooy, November 2009.)

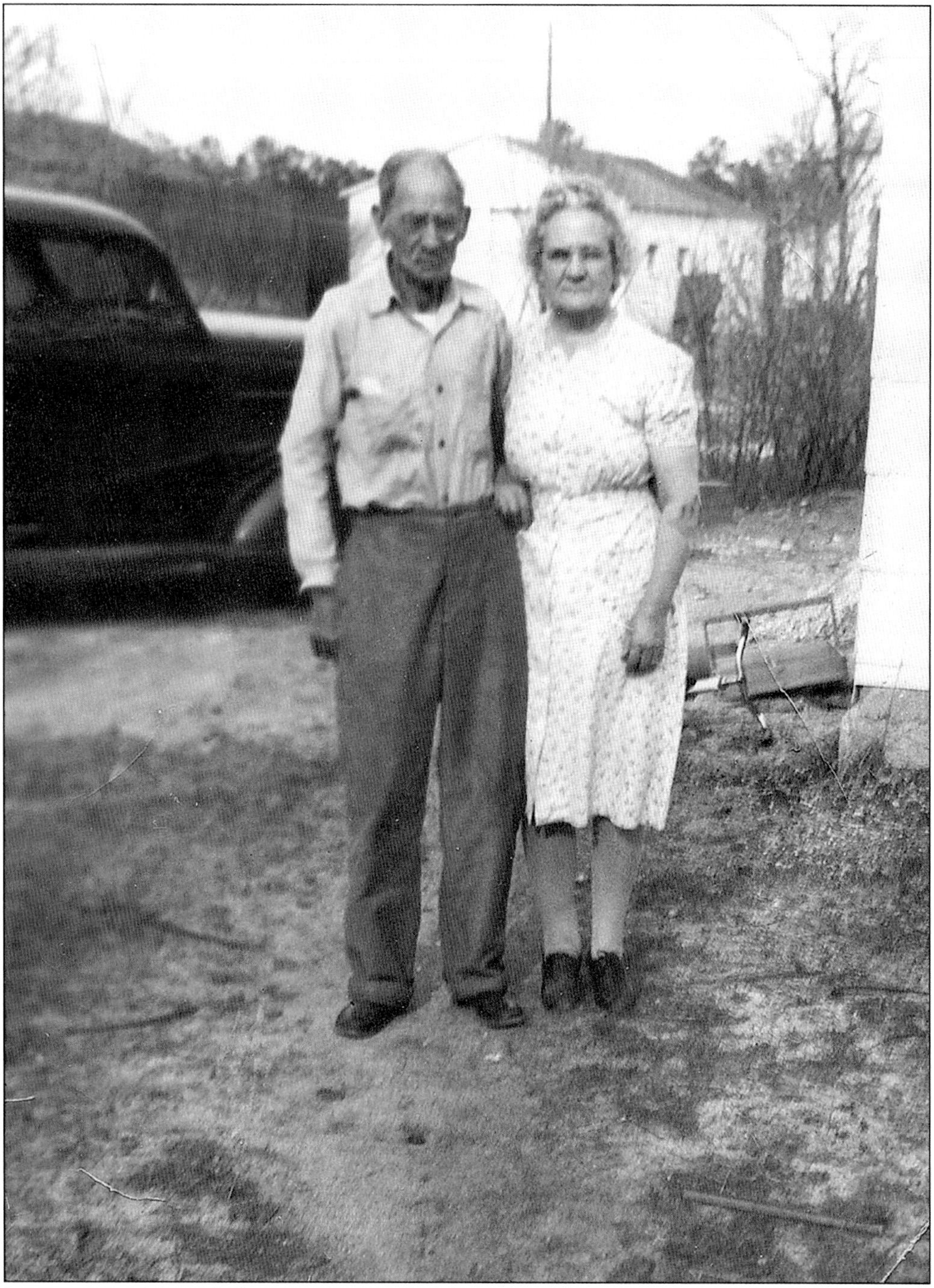

Longtime residents of Chatsworth, David and Sarah Applegate pose for this photograph near their home on Prince Street. They were married when David was 33 years old. David Applegate was employed as a superintendent in the cranberry bogs. The Applegate Land and Improvement Company was formed by the Applegates. (Courtesy of Frank Applegate family.)

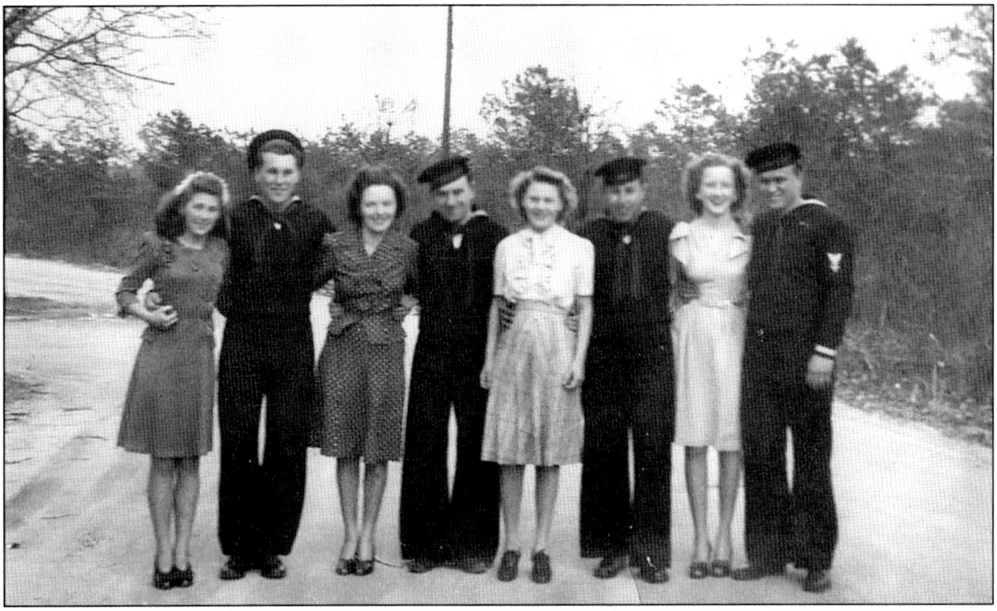

Four servicemen home on leave during World War II pause for this photograph with their wives, taken on Prince Street in the 1940s. They are, from left to right, Betty and Robert Dunfee, Gertie and Frank Applegate, Leila and Melvin Cranmer, and Selena and Russell Dunfee. (Courtesy of Frank Applegate family.)

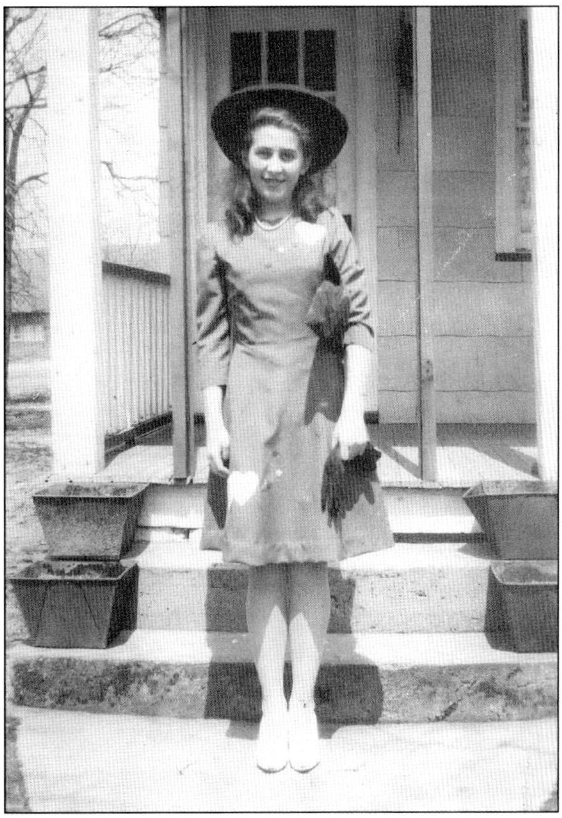

Betty Wills poses for this photograph in the 1940s. She married Robert Dunfee, and the couple had three daughters. After the death of Robert Dunfee, she married Raymond Carter. She became postmistress in 1966 and served until 1983 when she retired, and her daughter Cathy L. Dunfee Pepper became the postmistress. At that time the post office was moved to a modular facility on Second Street. (Courtesy of Amelia Green collection.)

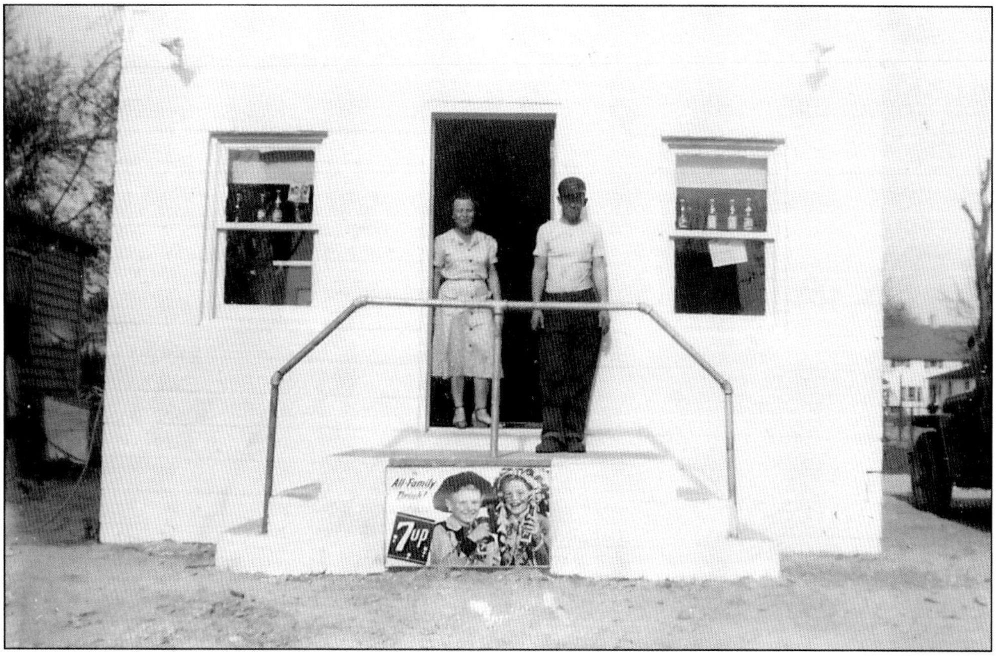

John Broomes's store on Main Street near Prince Street was the only provider of gasoline after Buzby's store was closed. In addition to selling gasoline, the local citizens took their automobiles to Broomes for repair. John Broomes operated a luncheonette in the building, which also contained pinball machines. (Courtesy of Donna Horner.)

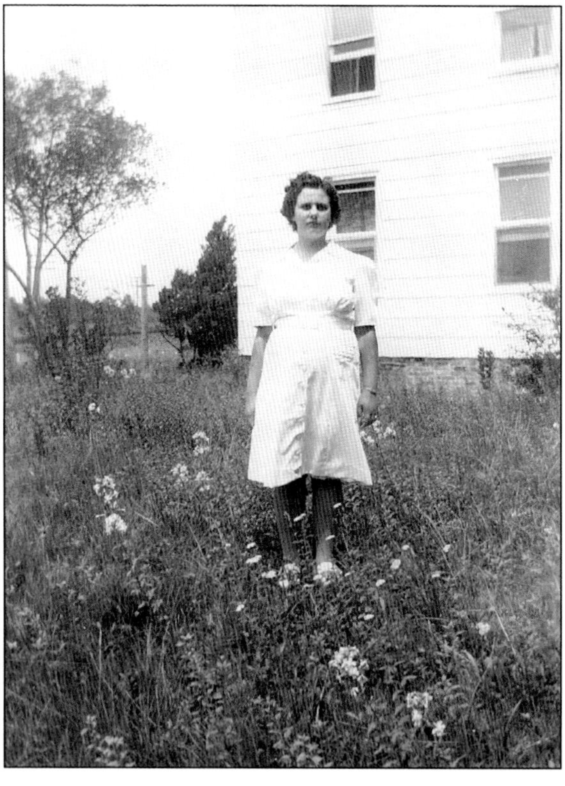

Jean Holloway is shown at her home adjacent to the railroad in Chatsworth. Jean worked in the blueberry packinghouse and helped propagate blueberry bushes by making cuttings (whips), which were placed in hotbeds to root. Many Chatsworth residents worked long hours during the blueberry season. (Courtesy of Sooy family.)

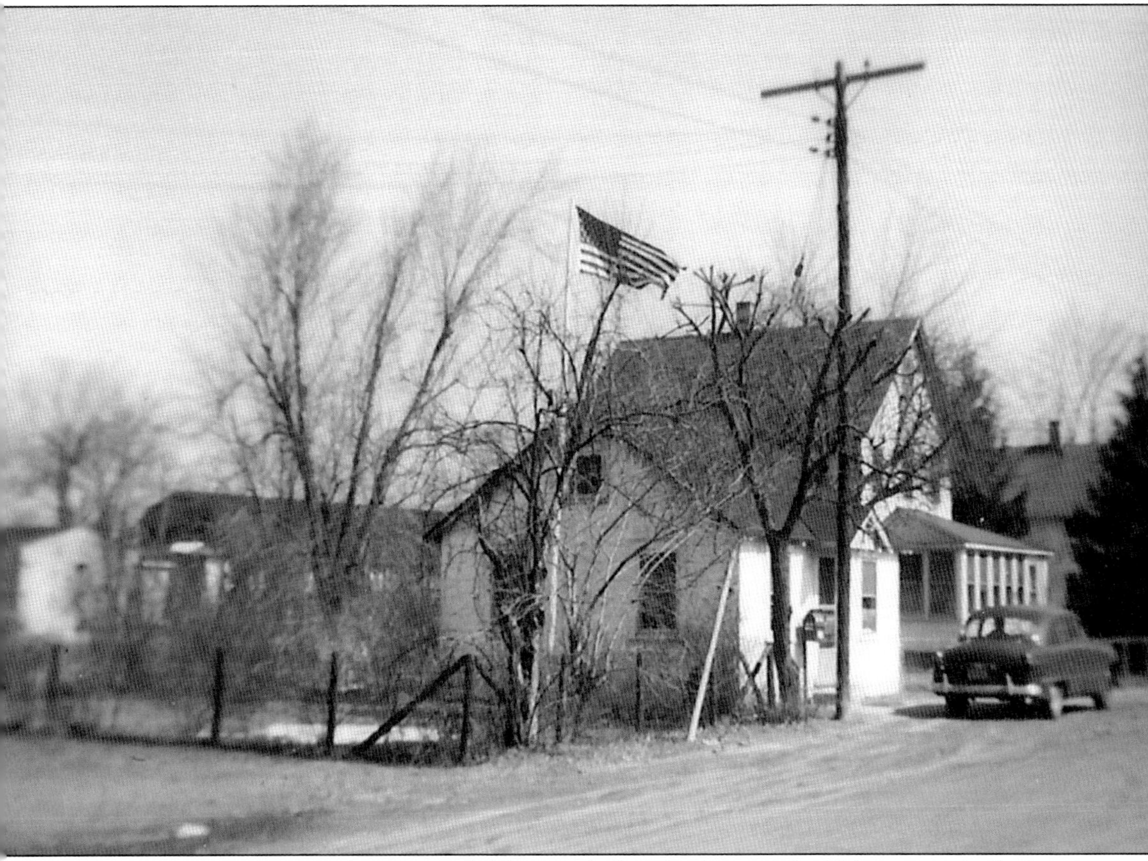

Mail service in Chatsworth was provided by train before the dawn of the 20th century. In the later 1800s, the post office was located in the general store on Main Street owned by John Applegate. It was moved to Buzby's store in 1914 with Willis J. Buzby and his sister Myrtle O. Buzby as postmasters, until Myrtle died in November 1915 from pneumonia and diphtheria. Upon her death, Willis Buzby Sr. became the postmaster until Anna Brower became the postmistress, and the post office was moved diagonally across the street to a building owned by the Browers. Anna served as postmistress until her death, and in 1943, Elizabeth Wills became postmistress, and the post office was moved to the building above, located on Prince Street and owned by the Wills. Elizabeth Wills served until her death in 1966. Her daughter Betty Wills Dunfee Carter, who had been a clerk since 1951, became acting postmistress. (Courtesy of Charles Applegate collection.)

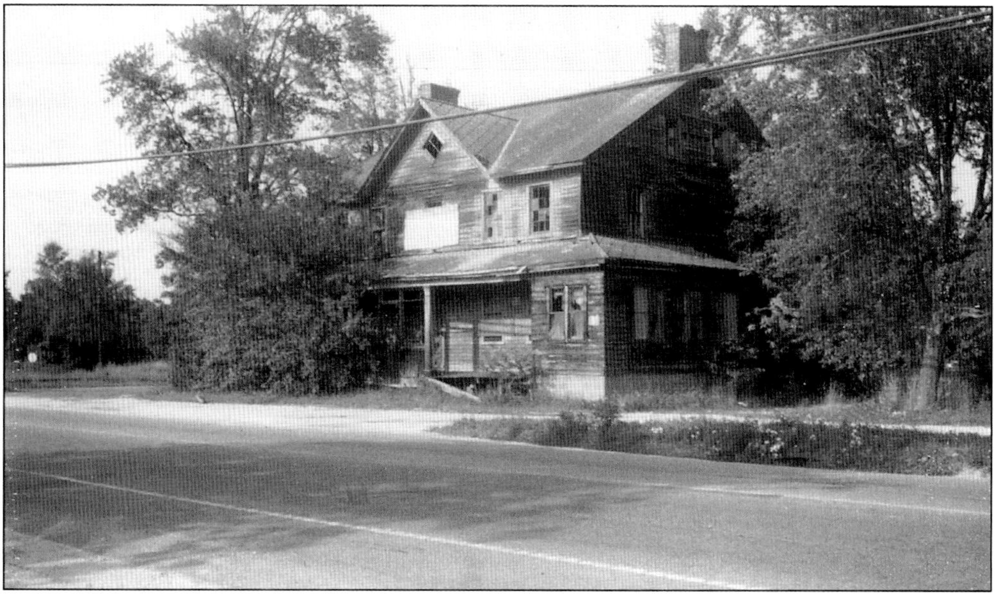

The White Horse Inn, constructed in the 1850s, is one of Chatsworth's historic buildings. Although constructed as an inn, through the years it was also the location for church services, a library, and the place for the making of roping (wreaths) during the holiday season. Early in its history, it was owned by Prince Mario Ruspoli and Jonathan Godfrey. For many years it was the residence of the Alfred Stevenson family. As the years passed, the building sustained considerable deterioration. Twenty-seven years ago, the need to save the building became a matter of interest, and today the inn has been restored and is used as a community center. It is also the home of the Woodland Township Historical Society. (Above, courtesy of Margie Wills Hall; below, courtesy of Stan Fayer.)

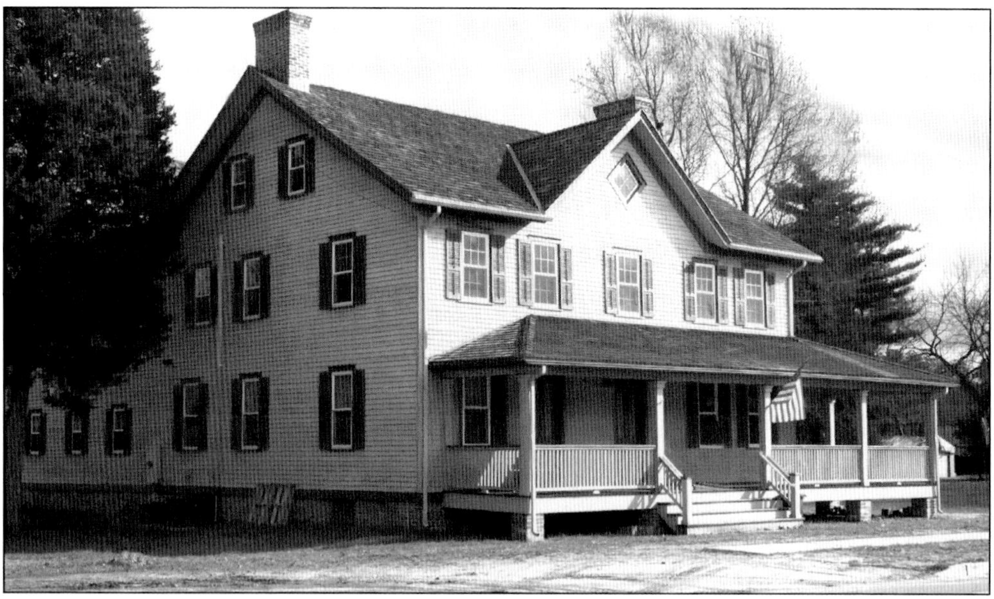

Diane Sooy and Doug Hallick pause for a photograph that was taken in 1962 after the eighth grade dance at Tommy Sinkowski's (now the Evergreen Dairy Bar) on Route 70 in Southampton. Diane lived on Main Street in Chatsworth, and Doug lived on Sooy Place Road at Johnson Place. (Courtesy of Sooy family.)

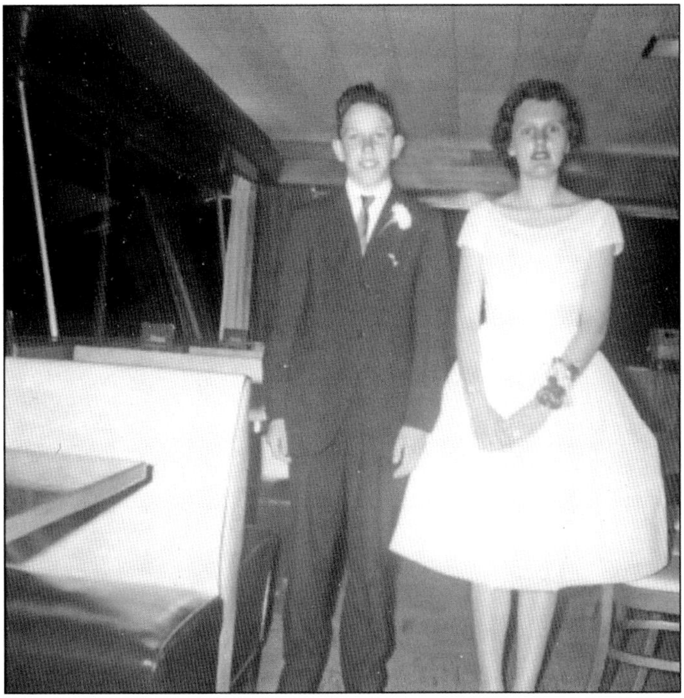

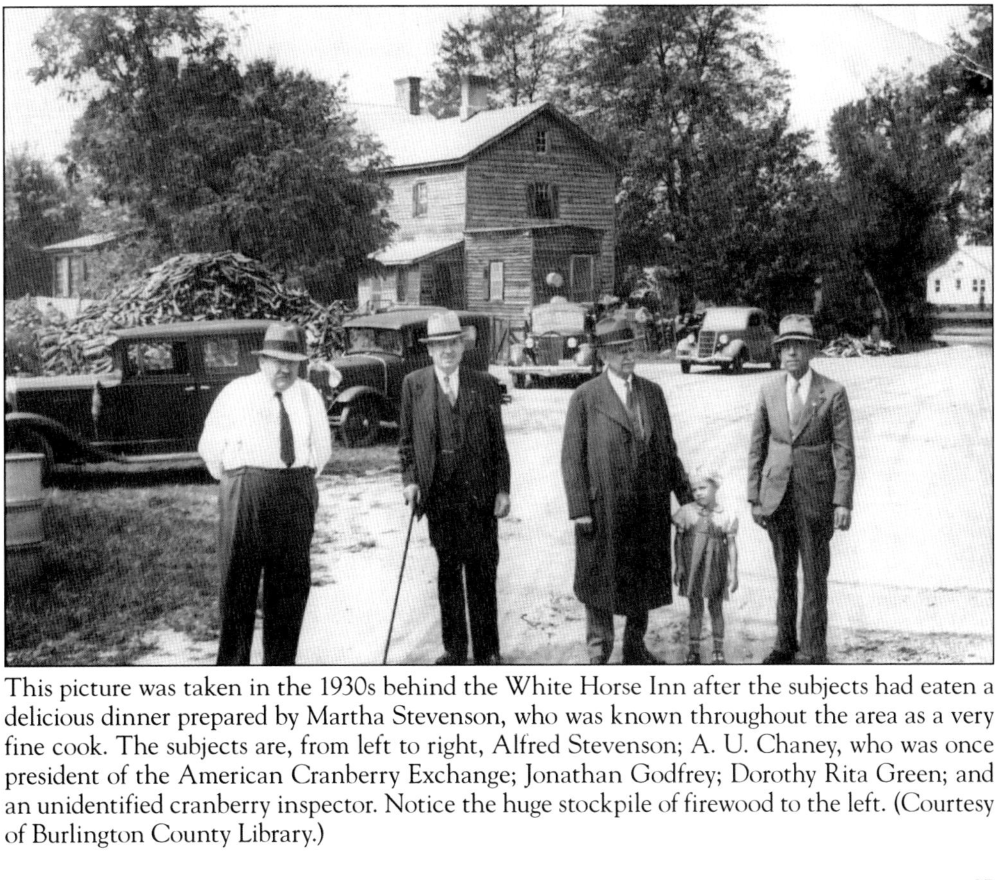

This picture was taken in the 1930s behind the White Horse Inn after the subjects had eaten a delicious dinner prepared by Martha Stevenson, who was known throughout the area as a very fine cook. The subjects are, from left to right, Alfred Stevenson; A. U. Chaney, who was once president of the American Cranberry Exchange; Jonathan Godfrey; Dorothy Rita Green; and an unidentified cranberry inspector. Notice the huge stockpile of firewood to the left. (Courtesy of Burlington County Library.)

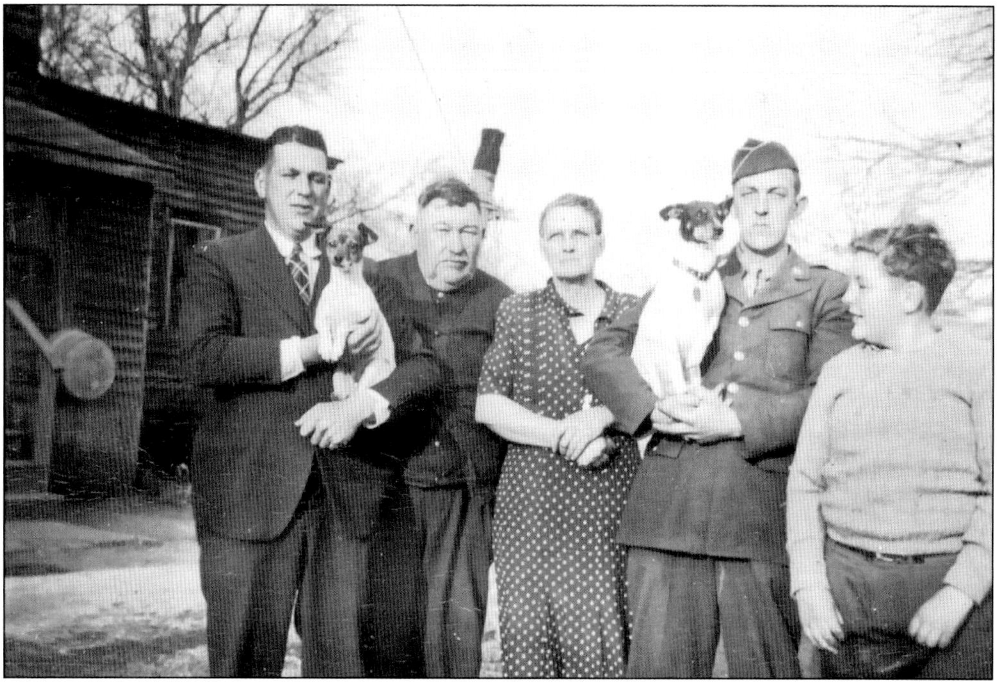

Members of the Stevenson family gather for a photograph outside their home on Main Street taken in 1942. They are, from left to right, Harold, Alfred Sr., Martha, Alfred Jr., and Jonathon Stevenson. The dogs are Butch and Jake. (Courtesy of Amelia Green collection.)

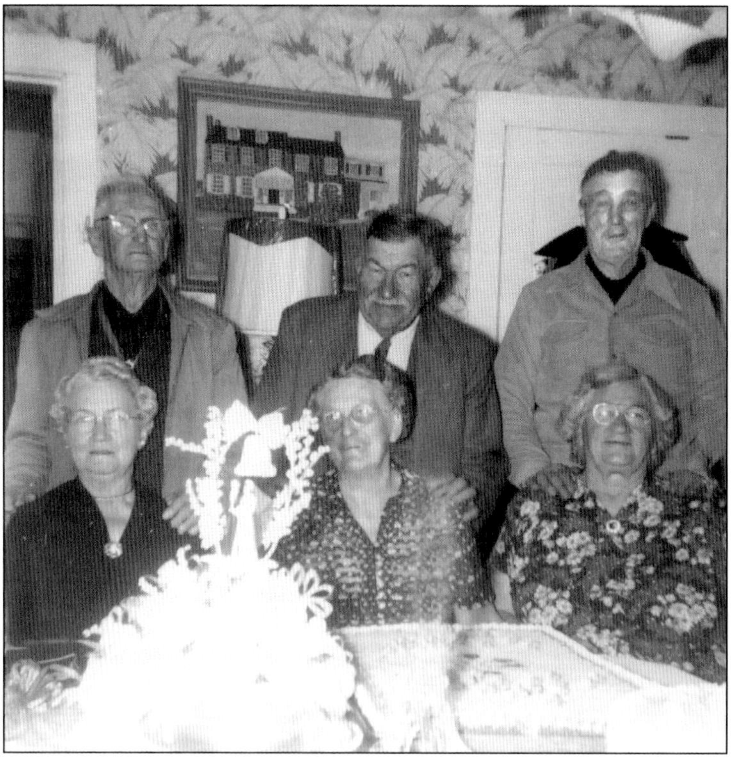

Gathered for the 50th wedding anniversary held at the White Horse Inn in 1954 in honor of Martha and Alfred Stevenson (center) are, from left to right, (first row) Mina Ritzendollar, Martha Stevenson, and Addie Holloway; (second row) John H. Ritzendollar, Alfred Stevenson, and Joseph Holloway. The Stevensons settled in Chatsworth in 1911, and the White Horse Inn was their home. (Courtesy of Sooy family.)

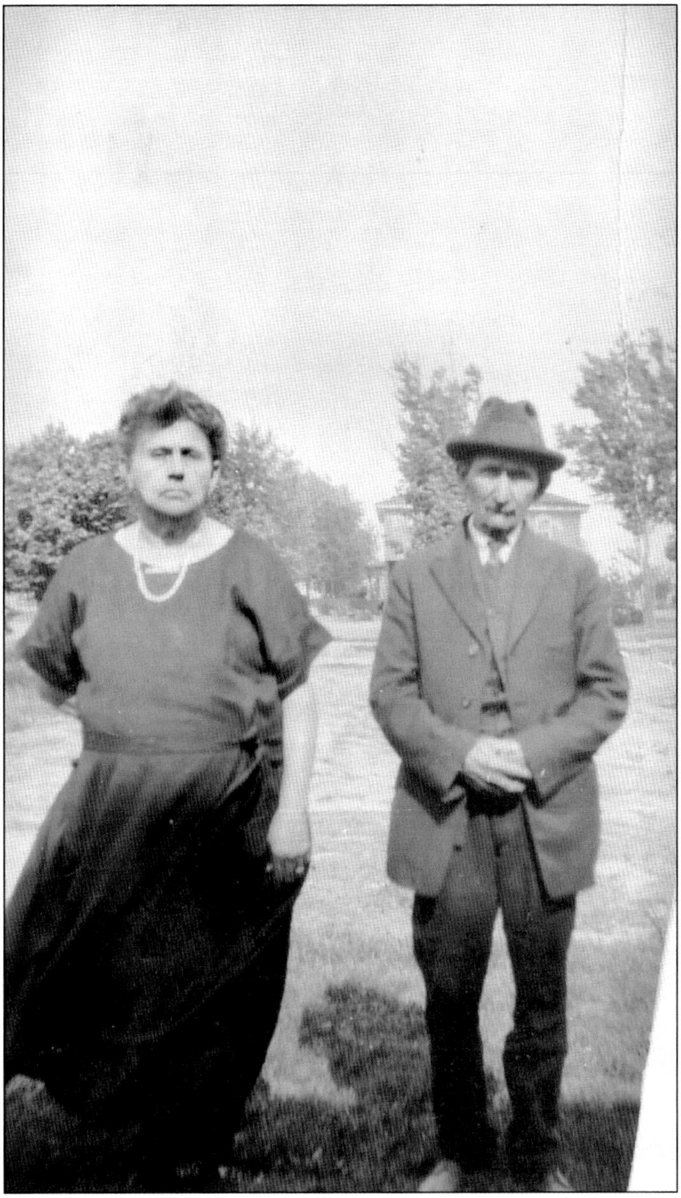

Louisa G. and Peter T. Brower, residents of Chatsworth and the parents of 11 children, one of whom was Walter A. Brower Sr., are shown here. Peter served in the Civil War in Company E, 18th Regiment, VRC, from 1862 until 1865. He died in 1928. John Mason, private, Company F, 1st New Volunteer Cavalry, served from 1861 until 1865. Towards the end of his life, he lived on a cranberry bog at Speedwell and died in 1890. Both of these Civil War veterans are buried in Woodlawn Cemetery, Chatsworth. Two brothers from Johnson Place, Archie and John Thompson, enlisted in 1861 in the "Olden Legion" of the New Jersey Volunteers. The unit was reorganized into the 10th Regiment, and both served in Company C of the 10th Regiment. John Thompson lost his life during the Battle of the Wilderness, fought on May 5–6, 1864, near Fredericksburg, Virginia. Archie Thompson was present at Lee's surrender at Appomattox, Virginia, on April 9, 1865, and returned to Johnson Place. He died in 1869 at the age of 31. (Courtesy of Walter A. Brower Jr.)

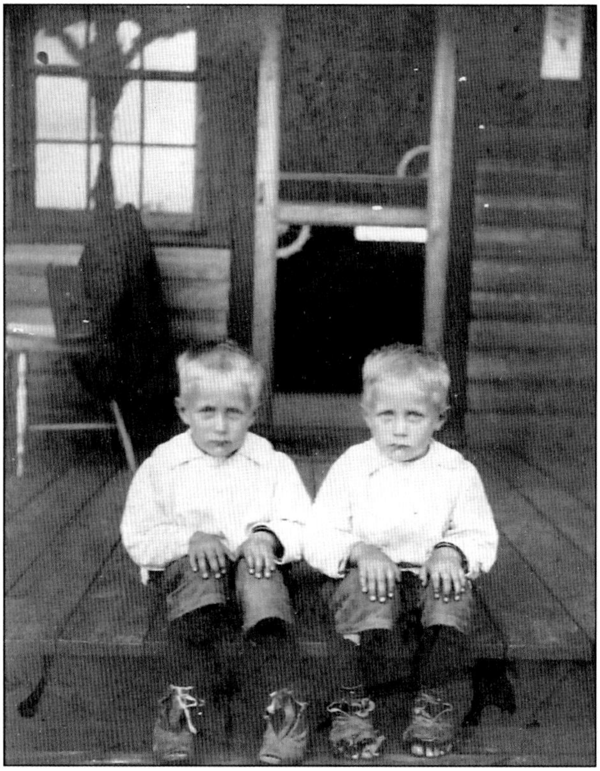

The twin sons, Howard and Walter, two of 11 children born to Louisa and Peter Brower, sit on the steps of their home in this 1902 photograph. Not only are they dressed alike, their facial expressions are quite similar. Howard was killed in an automobile accident in 1931; Walter served in a leadership role in the community until his death in 1971. (Courtesy of Grace Brower Donnelly.)

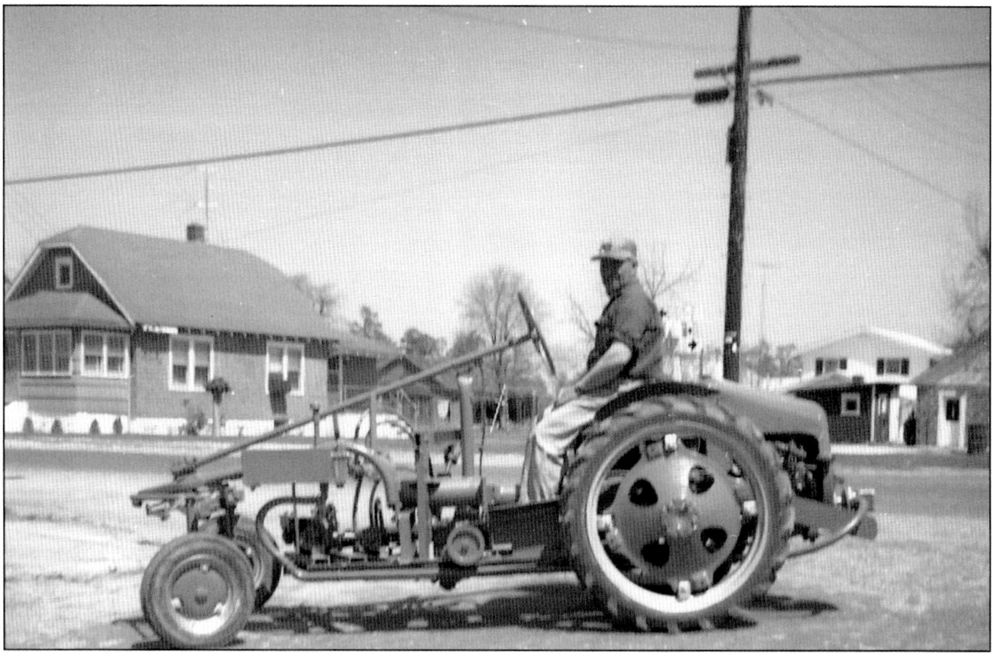

Russell Anderson, an employee of the township, paused for this photograph taken in the mid-1950s while at work on projects in Chatsworth. The photograph was taken on Main Street and shows a local residence that was constructed in the early 1900s by Harry Sloan, a local builder. Russell later served as the mayor in Woodland Township. (Courtesy of Buzby collection.)

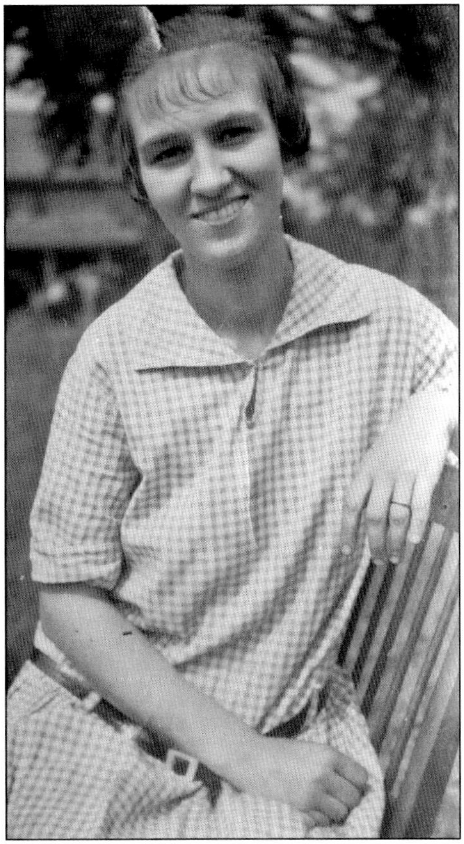

These photographs of Walter A. Brower Sr. and Anna Ritzendollar Brower were taken in 1934. Walter was a member of the Township Committee from 1935 to 1950, during which time he also served several terms as mayor, and Anna was Chatsworth postmistress for 20 years. She was also one of the organizers of the Parent Teacher Association and continued to assist that organization in its activities at the Chatsworth Elementary School. She was also a homemaker. Anna was one of the few persons in Chatsworth baptized in the White Horse Inn by the church when services were being held in the inn. Walter was a supervisor for the Burlington County Highway Department for more than 40 years; was a charter member of the Chatsworth Fire Company No. 1, which was formed in 1939; and was affiliated with the Chatsworth Methodist Church. The couple had three children, Grace, Almeda, and Walter Jr. (Both, courtesy of Walter A. Brower Jr.)

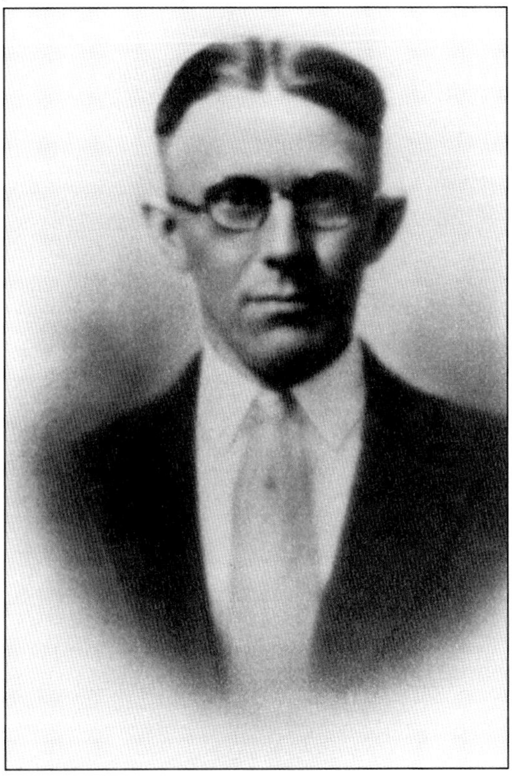

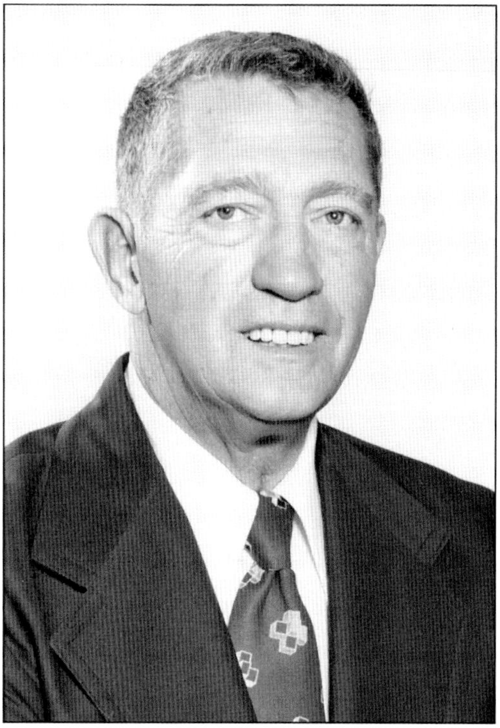

John "Jack" Shaner served as mayor of Woodland Township in 1971, 1972, and 1973. Prior to service as mayor, he provided the leadership that saw the rebirth of the Chatsworth Fire Company, acquisition of a new fire truck, and construction of the new firehouse. Local citizens were pleased to have a local fire company and less dependence on fire companies from other towns in the county. (Courtesy of Robin Shaner Hollingshead.)

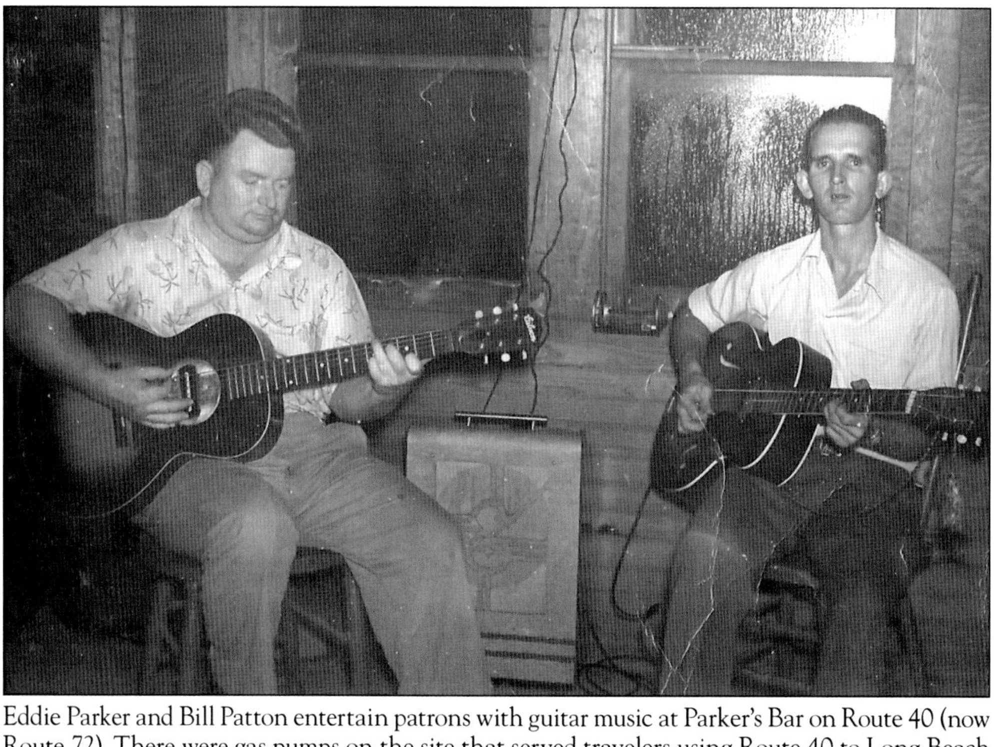

Eddie Parker and Bill Patton entertain patrons with guitar music at Parker's Bar on Route 40 (now Route 72). There were gas pumps on the site that served travelers using Route 40 to Long Beach Island. In the 1930s, the Parkers operated the second gas station in the township. (Courtesy of Clarice Higgenbothem.)

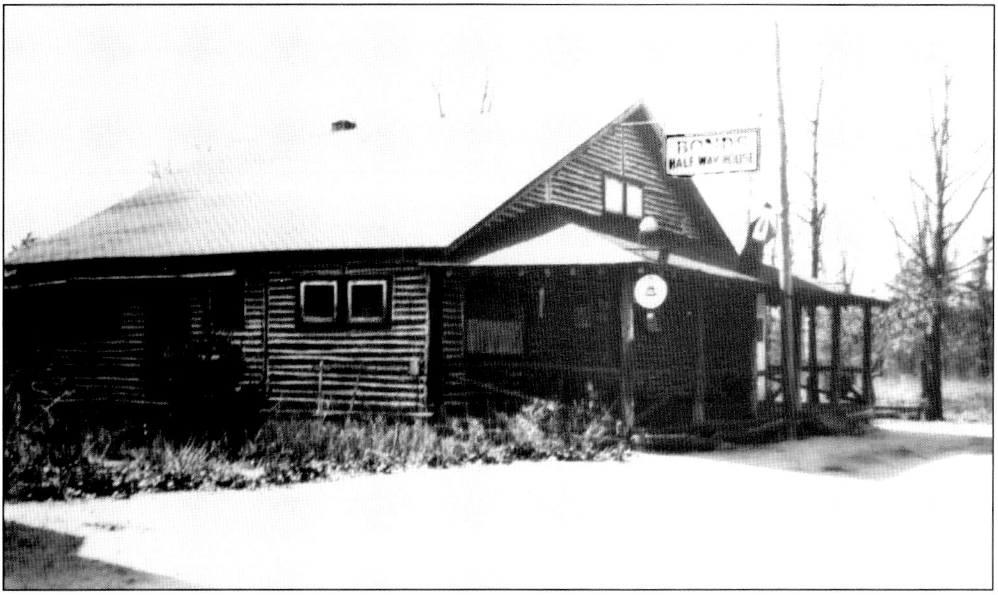

Bond's Bar on Route 72, a few miles out of town, was owned by Jack and Betty Bond in the 1930s. The facility remains a popular bar today, not only for local residents but for those traveling to the Jersey Shore from the Camden-Philadelphia areas. It is now known as Mayo's Halfway House—halfway meaning that it is halfway from Philadelphia to the shore. (Courtesy of the William S. Haines Sr. collection.)

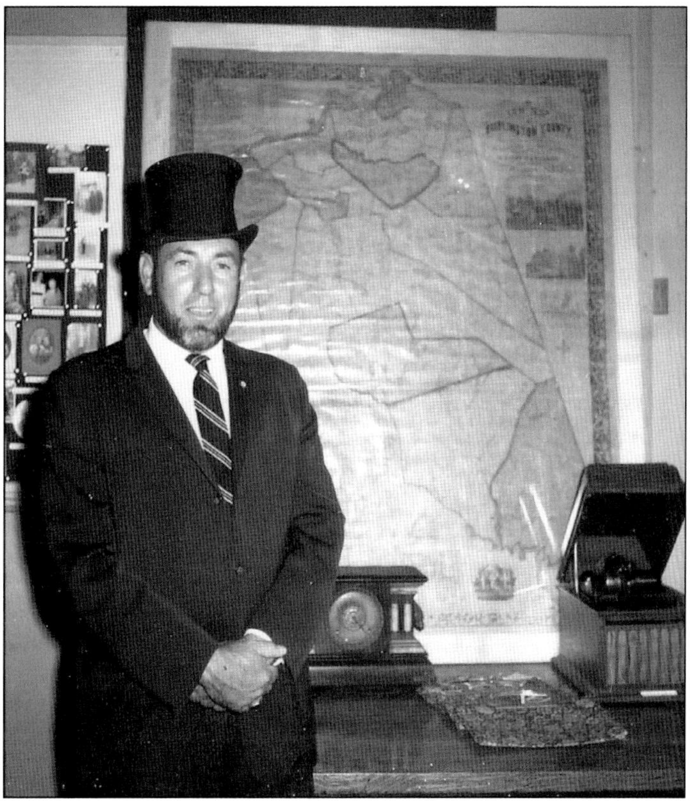

Peter T. Brower poses for this photograph during the centennial celebration in 1966. He served in the army, where he did construction work in the Caribbean. He served as tax assessor, was a township commissioner, and was the mayor of Chatsworth (Woodland Township) from 1959 until 1966. He was a successful blueberry farmer in the Chatsworth area. (Courtesy of Vera Topham.)

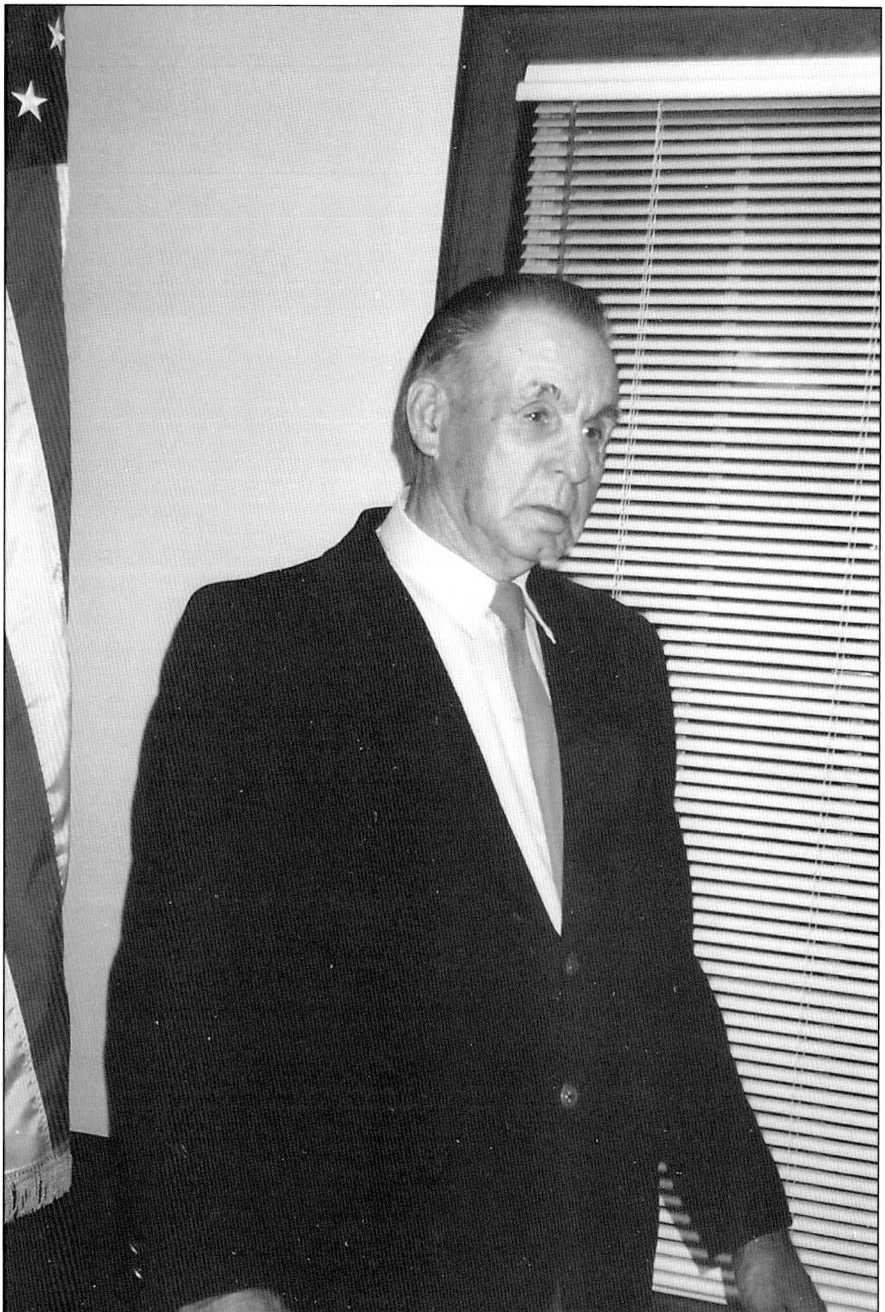

John Bowker was the mayor of Woodland Township from 1975 to May 1996. During his administration, the Pinelands Commission was formed and served to govern development in the Pinelands. His family has lived in the Chatsworth area for several generations. Other residents who served as mayor are Walter Sloan (1925–1934), Walter Brower (1935–1939 and 1942–1949), Harold Stevenson (1940–1941), Albertus Pepper (1950–1952), Russell Anderson (1953–1957), Otto Katt (1958), Peter T. Brower (1959–1966), Eugene V. Minks (1967), Jack Shaner (1971–1973), and Russell Anderson (1974). (Courtesy of Ken and Deborah Bowker.)

Two

EDUCATION AND RELIGION

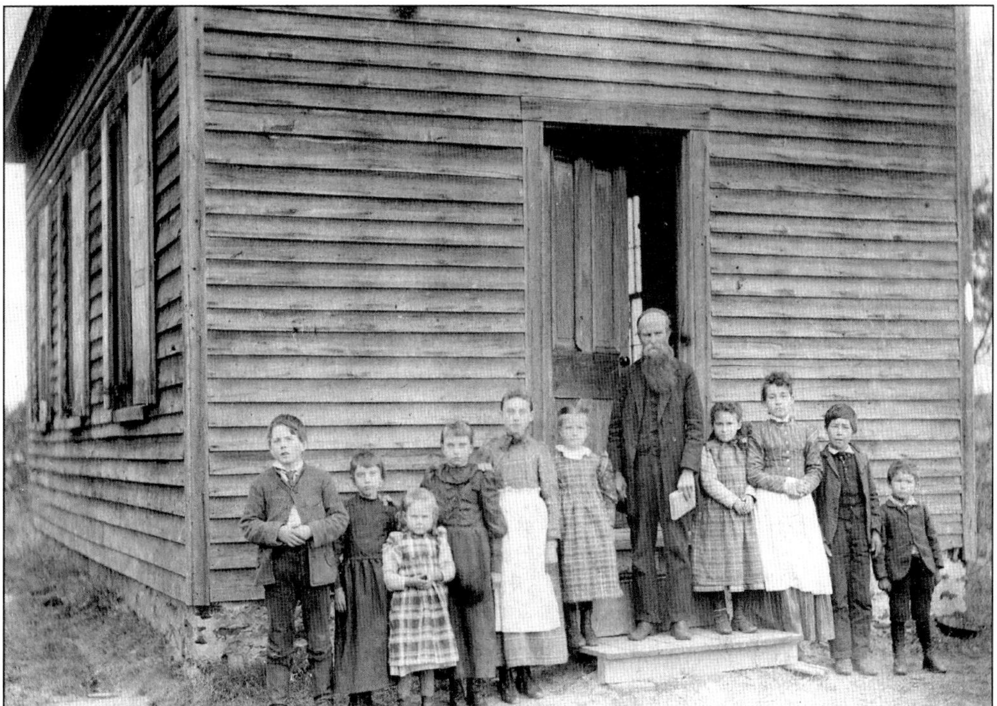

Although the early settlers of Chatsworth lacked financial resources, they wanted to educate their children. The Johnson Place School was built in 1876–1877 by Alfred A. Adams for $640. The students in this c. 1893 photograph are, from left to right, Charles Taylor, Rebecca Bozarth, Eliza Thompson, Sally Bozarth, Lizzie Bozarth, Hester Taylor, Mr. Mallit (the teacher), Mande Clevenger, Jane Clevenger, Bill Clevenger, and Charles Clevenger. (Courtesy of Penny Tice Lucas.)

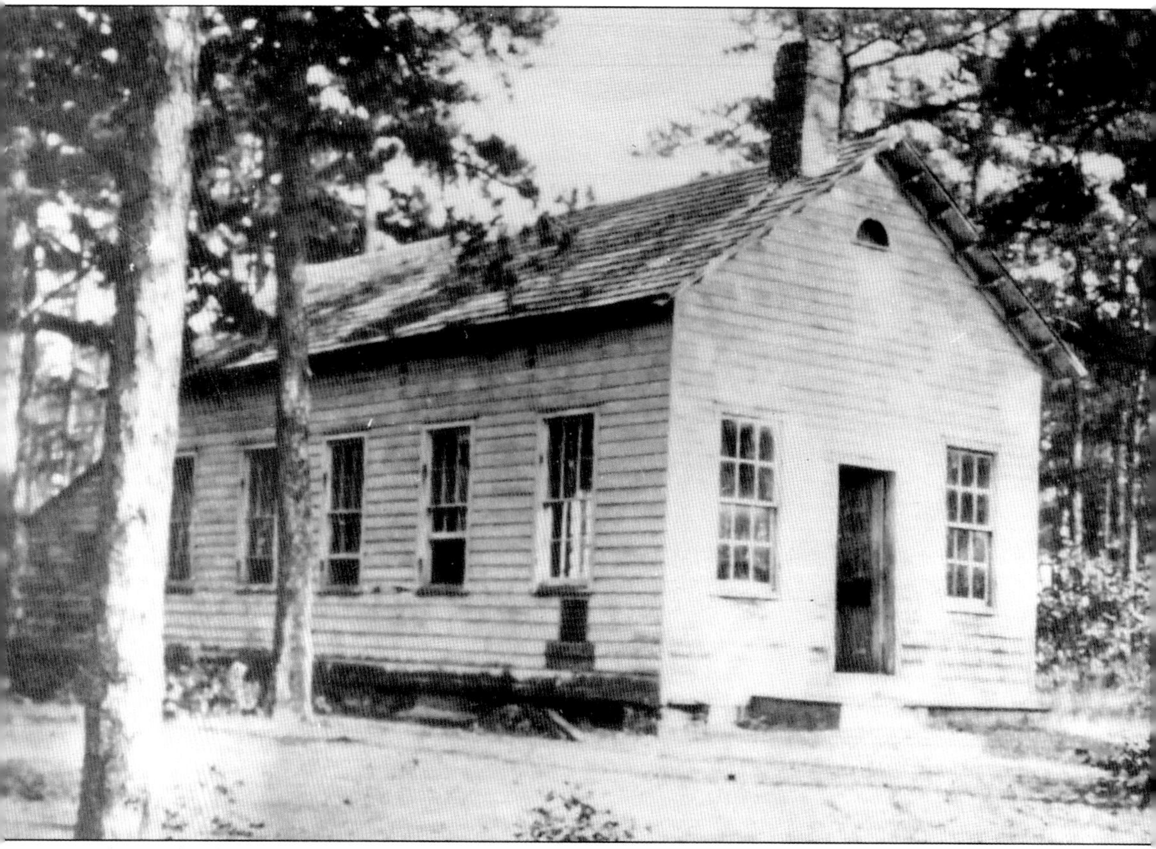

This is the first Chatsworth School in 1900. It was a one-room school for all grades with one teacher, an elderly man who boarded with various families. He was quite strict and was known for giving whippings. There were 60 to 65 pupils ranging in age from five to 15 or 16. School hours were 9:00 a.m. to 4:00 p.m., with an hour for lunch. School was in session for approximately seven and one-tenth months each year. The school was equipped with a big coal stove in the middle of the room. The teacher's desk was in front. There was no indoor plumbing. Books were provided to the pupils, but they were required to bring slates or pencils and paper. Reading, spelling, arithmetic, geography, history, and civics were the lessons taught. The children walked to school, or their parents brought them in a horse and wagon. (Courtesy of Alberta Applegate collection.)

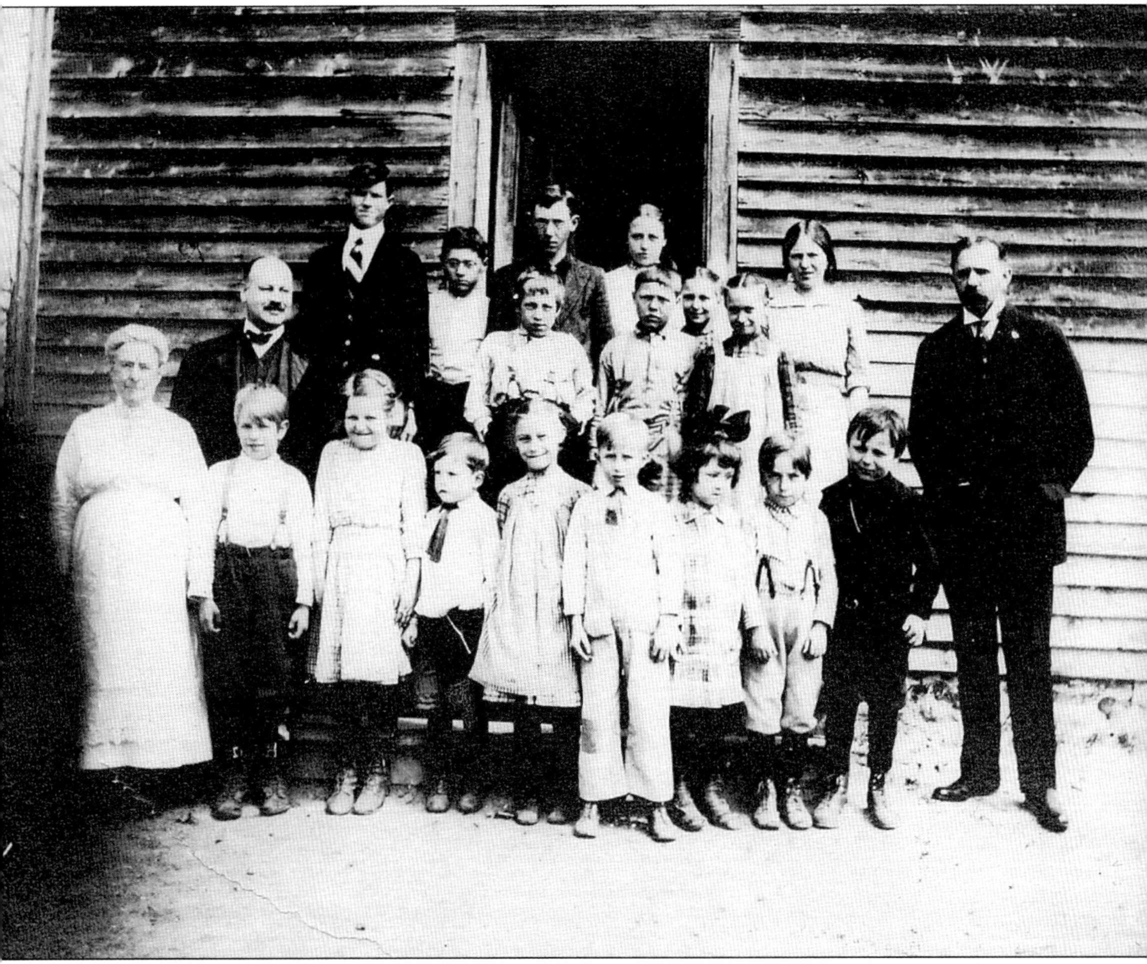

This photograph of the students of the Johnson Place School represented the entire student body and was taken prior to the school's closing in 1918. Mary Davis, the teacher (extreme left), was also instrumental in establishing the chapel in Johnson Place, which served the local residents for many years. Upon her death, her niece Maude LeDuc continued her aunt's work with the chapel. The students are, from left to right, (first row) unidentified, Mary Lippincott, Charles Tice, unidentified, Eugene Tice, Juanita Lambert, unidentified, Mark Lippincott, and unidentified; (second row) county superintendent (name unknown), unidentified, Orville Haines, Alice Tice, Hattie Tice, and Elva Thompson; (third row) Robert Ware, unidentified, Fred Lambert, and unidentified. Seating was at a premium in the one-room schoolhouse, with two students often occupying one seat. Students had to provide their pencils and writing pads. The school had one stove to heat the building. Students walked to school regardless of weather conditions. Water from which all students drank using the same dipper was carried in a bucket from a nearby home. There was no electricity. (Courtesy of Stan and Maureen Worrell.)

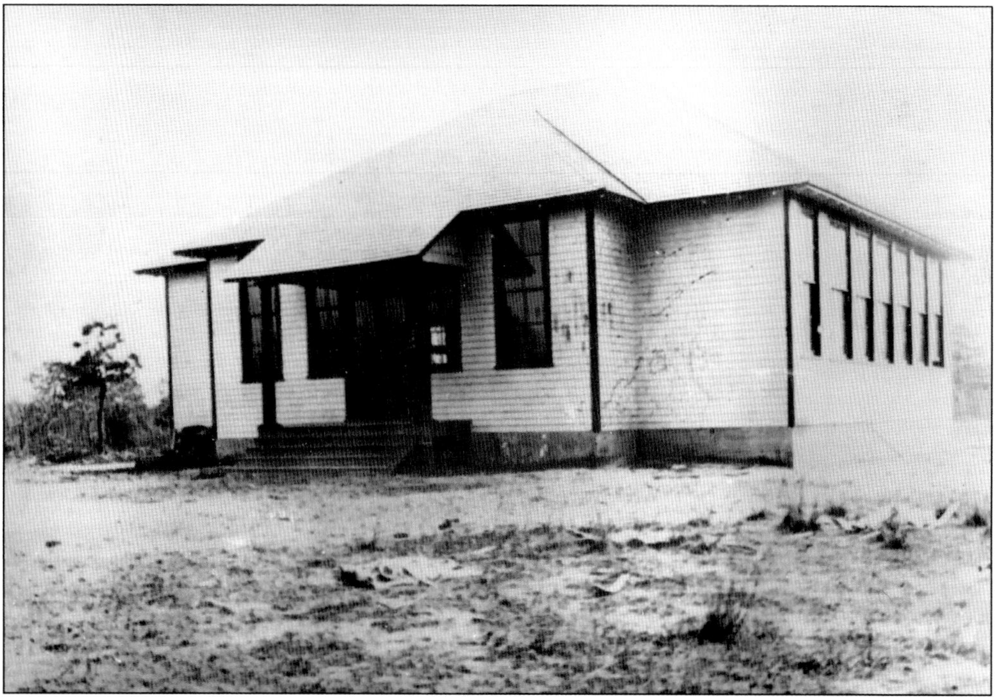

Other one-room schools were in Woodmansie, Four Mile, Mount Relief, and Woodland. Coal stoves heated these buildings. During 1906–1907, one male teacher was employed for $315 annually. Five women were employed at an aggregate salary of $960. In 1915, a new two-room school was constructed in Chatsworth, and it was the only school in use by 1918. (Courtesy of Margie Wills Hall.)

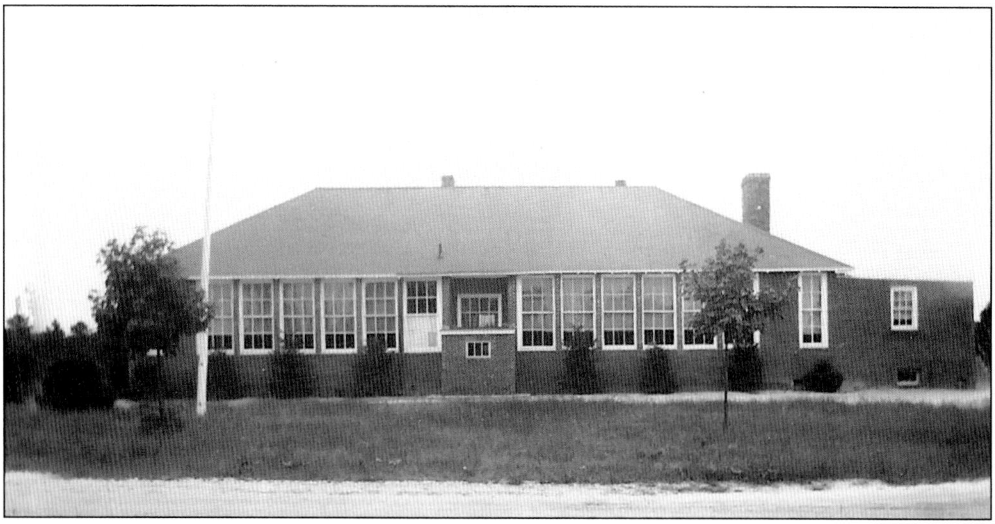

In 1938, the PTA room became a lunchroom. The enlarged four-room, modern school is shown here as it looked in 1940. The entire building was brick veneered that year. The coal stoves had been replaced by modern heating, and this was the first year that a matron had been hired to prepare school lunches. (Courtesy of Alberta Applegate collection.)

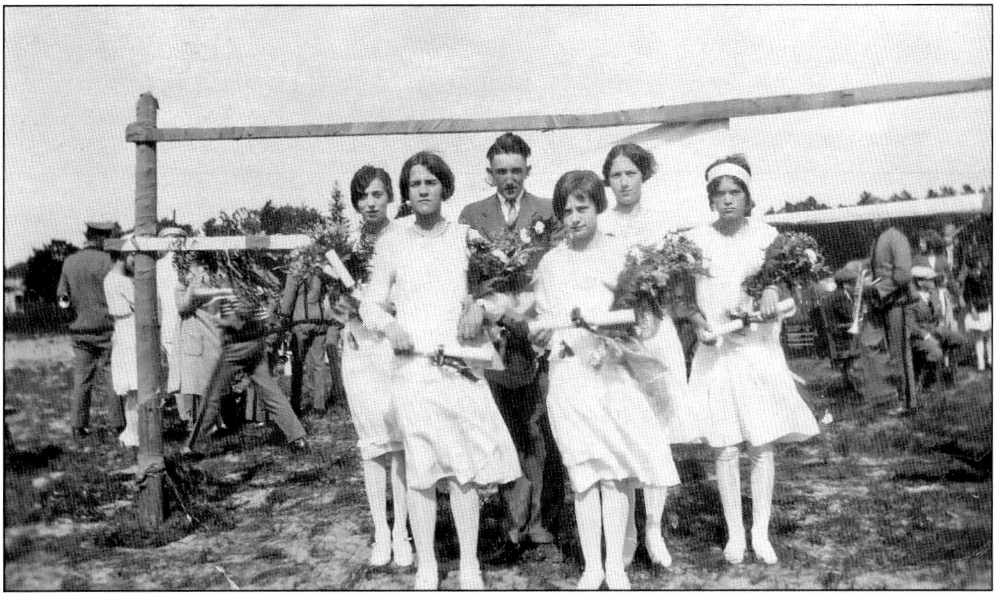

The eighth grade graduation class of the Chatsworth School gathers in the schoolyard for a photograph on a breezy day in 1928. They are, from left to right, Marguerite Brower, Mary Evelyn Applegate, Kenneth Dunfee, Virginia Green, Dorothy Ritzendollar, and Dorothy Lemmon. (Courtesy of Stan and Maureen Worrell.)

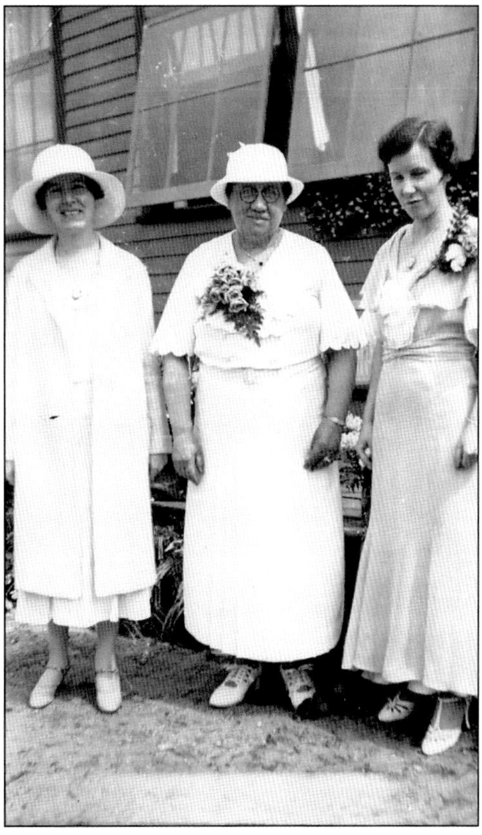

The three teachers at the Chatsworth School in 1932 were, from left to right, Anna Kane (grades three through five), Lillian Wilbert (principal and grades six through eight), and Della Holloway (grades kindergarten through second). Lillian Wilbert was the founder of the Parent Teacher Association. (Courtesy of Alberta Applegate collection.)

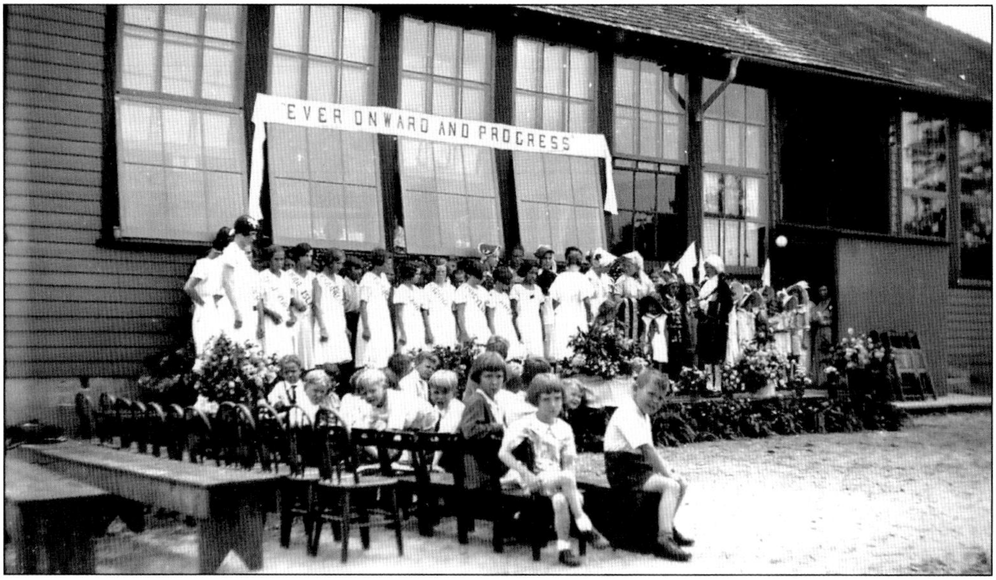

The students of the Chatsworth School practice for a patriotic presentation in 1932. The students from the lower grades sit idly by, while the upper-class students rehearse for the presentation. The student population was under 100. Students residing in town walked to school, while those living at Johnson Place, Jones Mill, and Pasadena were transported. (Courtesy of Buzby collection.)

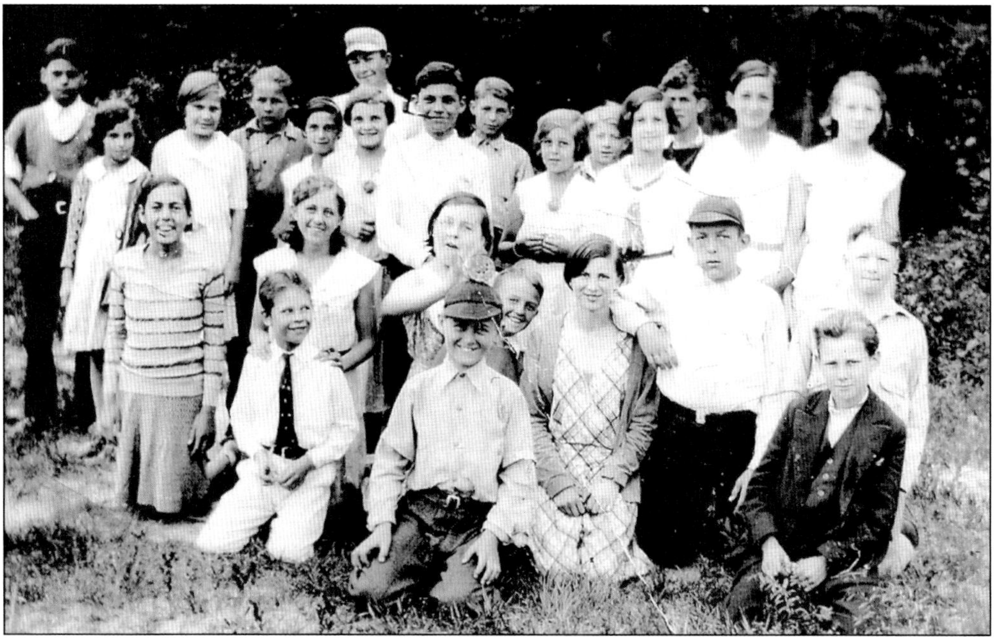

Students of the sixth, seventh, and eighth grade classes of the Chatsworth School gather for this group photograph. They are, from left to right, (first row) Charles Bates, Donald Bozarth, unidentified, Dorothy Lambert, Harold Stevenson Jr., Jonas Giberson, and Lewis Corlis; (second row) Elizabeth Brower, Louise Brower, and Jean Lee; (third row) Kathryn Wills, Rena Applegate, Alice Erles, Edith Tice, Fred Ranalli, Thelma Bowker, ? Giberson, Grace Brower, and Mildred Messler; (fourth row) Joe Ranalli, Wilbert "Webb" Anderson, Charles Applegate, John Bowker, Elton Carr, and Charles Leek. (Courtesy of Margie Wills Hall.)

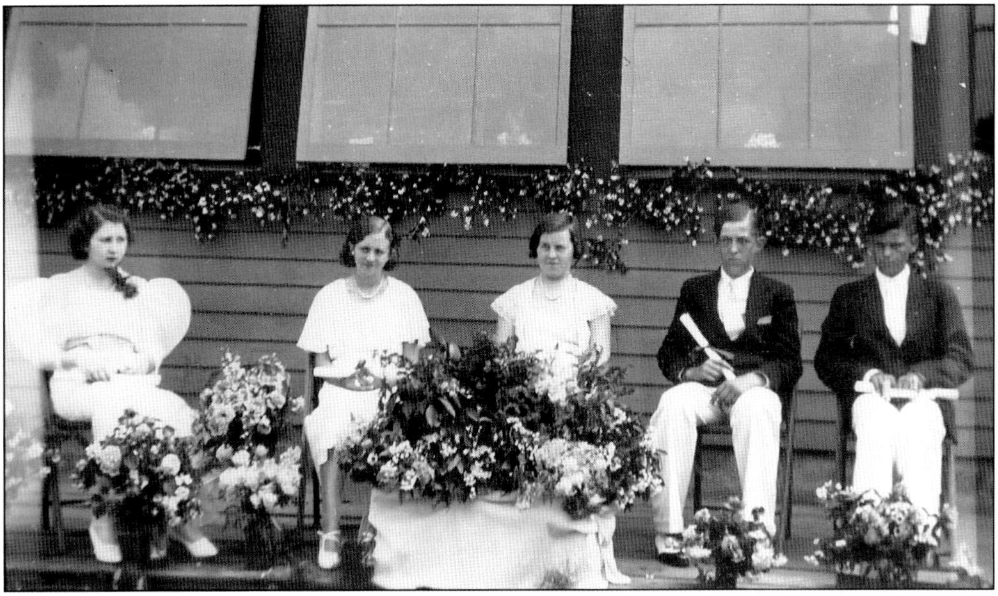

It is graduation day in 1936 for five members of the eighth grade at the Chatsworth Elementary School. The graduates are, from left to right, Irma Dunfee, Louise Brower, Jean Lee, Alfred Stevenson Jr., and Joseph Ranalli. During their enrollment at the school, clubs were formed to aid in the students' learning experiences. (Courtesy of the Buzby collection.)

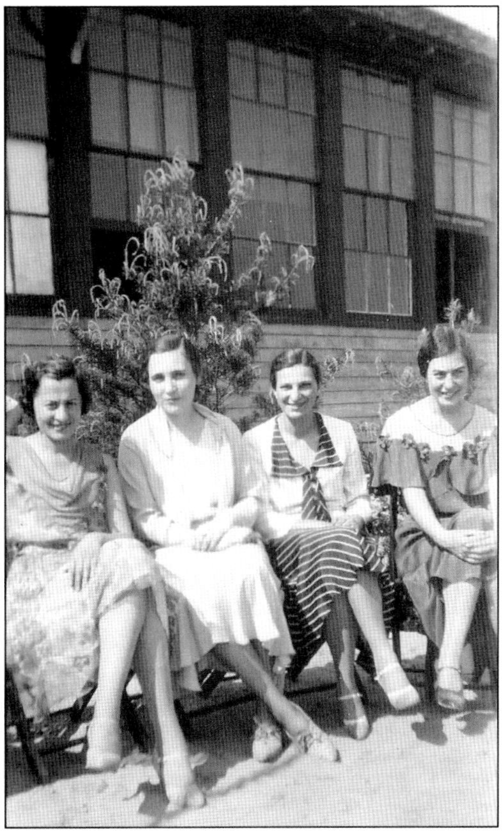

The four teachers of the Chatsworth School in the late 1930s were, from left to right, Miss Peterson, Miss Zalinsky, Miss Moskovich, and Miss Warrick. They received a salary of $1,000 for the year. There was no public transportation during that time, and consequently the teachers lived in town where they boarded with local residents. (Courtesy of the Buzby collection.)

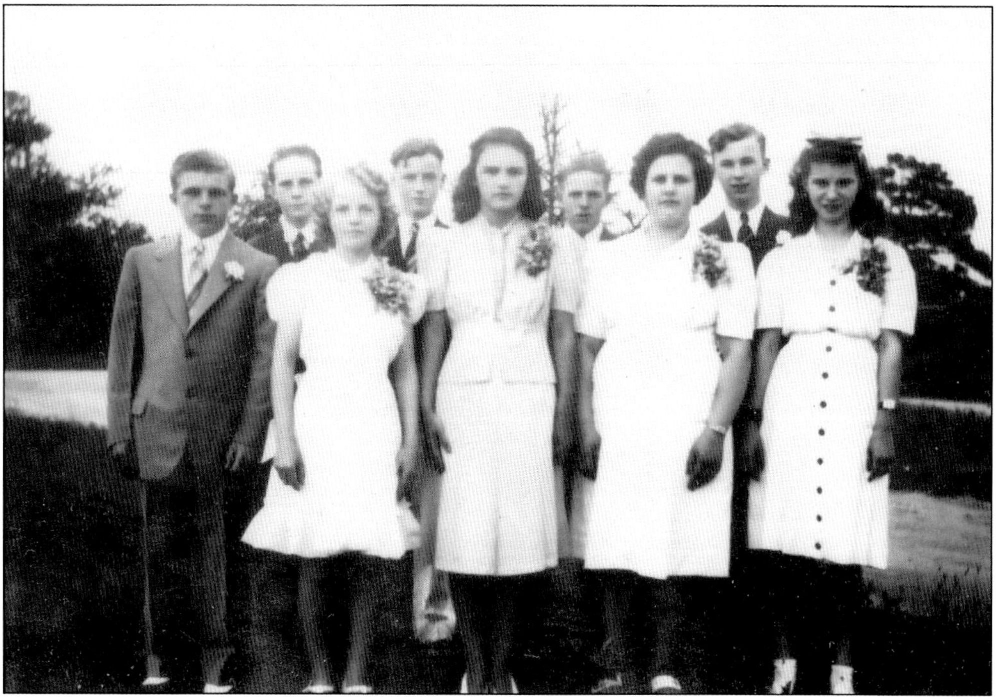

This June 1942 photograph captures the graduating class of the Chatsworth School. They are, from left to right, (first row) Shirley Ammon, Helen Leek, Jean Hollway, and Elizabeth King; (second row) Harry Beach, Floyd Tice, Albert Ammon, Fred Kennedy Jr., and James Bates. (Courtesy of Alberta Applegate collection.)

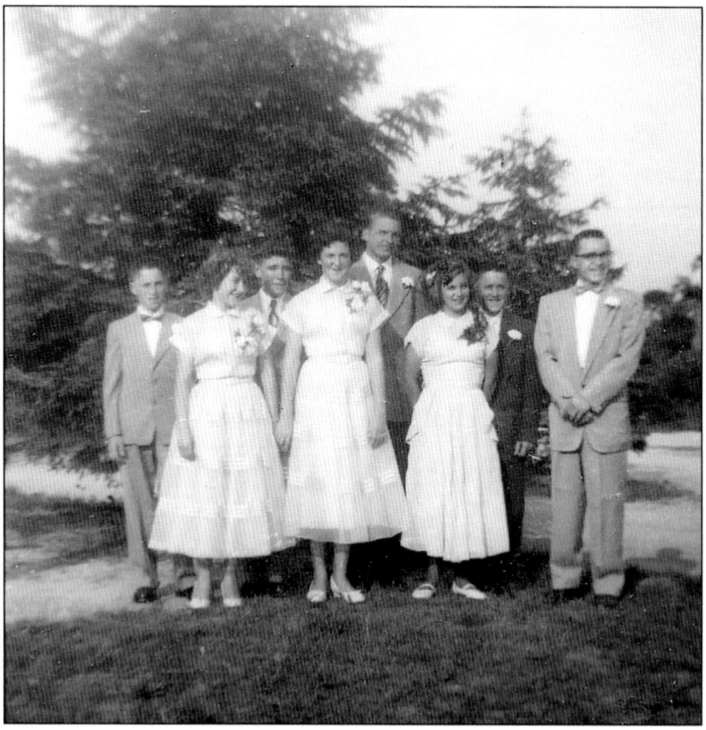

The students of the Chatsworth School class of 1952 were Daniel Clair, Ruth Bowker, Alfred Leek, Phyllis Haines, Fred Lemmon, Ruth Anderson, Robert Leek, Morris Chambers, Charles Clair, Fred King, Robert Hartpence, and their teacher Charles Treutel. (Courtesy of Alberta Applegate collection.)

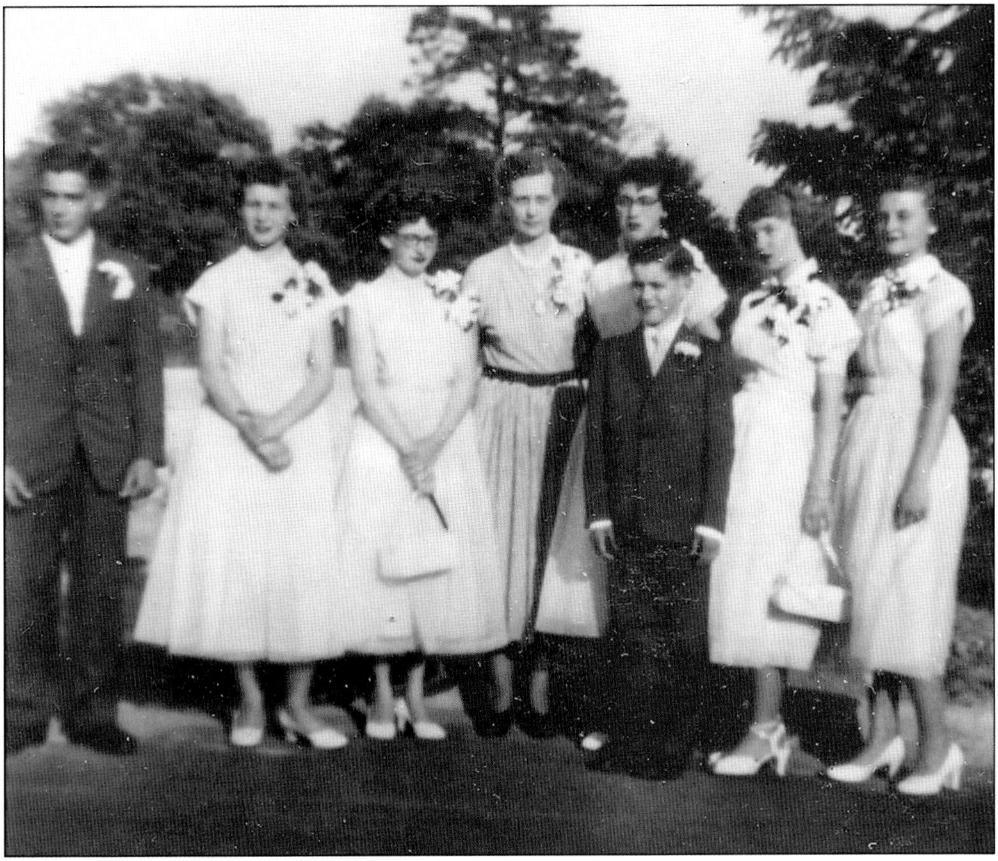

The Chatsworth School class of 1953 gathers for a photograph near the school. They are, from left to right, Sydney Lockwood, Shirley Bowker, Mary Jane Brophy, teacher Marion Phillips, Mary Adams, Robert Lockwood, Clara Chambers, and Deanna Pepper. Enrollment had begun to climb, and an additional teacher was hired. A youth canteen had been organized and was sponsored by the board of education and the Parent Teacher Association. (Courtesy of Alberta Applegate collection.)

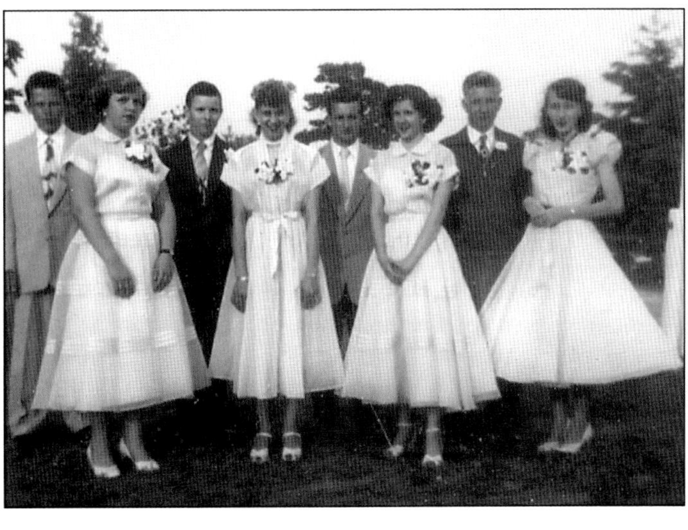

In 1954, the Chatsworth School graduation class of eight students consisted of, from left to right, Barry Holloway, Janet Lemmon, Buddy Simpkins, Roxie King, Joe Mastalski, Margie Wills, Rodney Emmons, and Veronica Kiernan. (Courtesy of Alberta Applegate collection.)

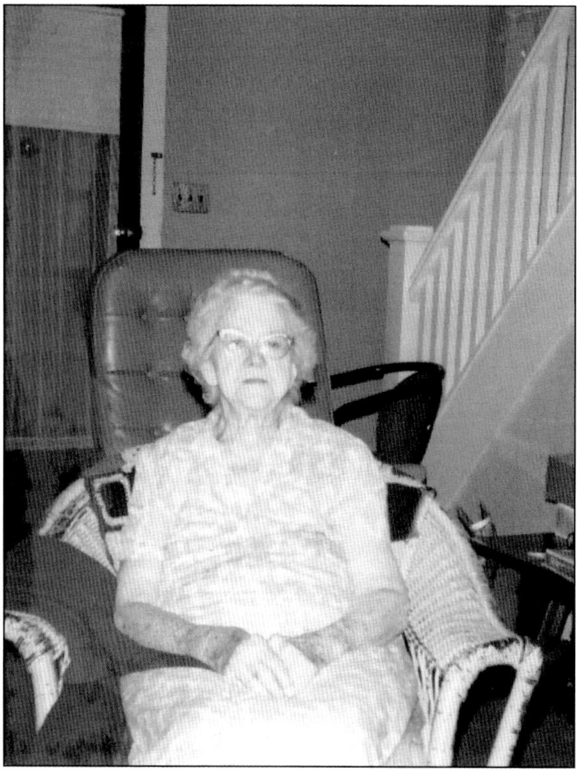

Florence "Aunt Florence" Sloan Dunfee, was the cook at the Chatsworth School for many years. She was the wife of Elmer Dunfee, who for many years was the clerk of Woodland Township. The lunchroom was added to the Chatsworth School in 1938. (Courtesy of Amelia Green collection.)

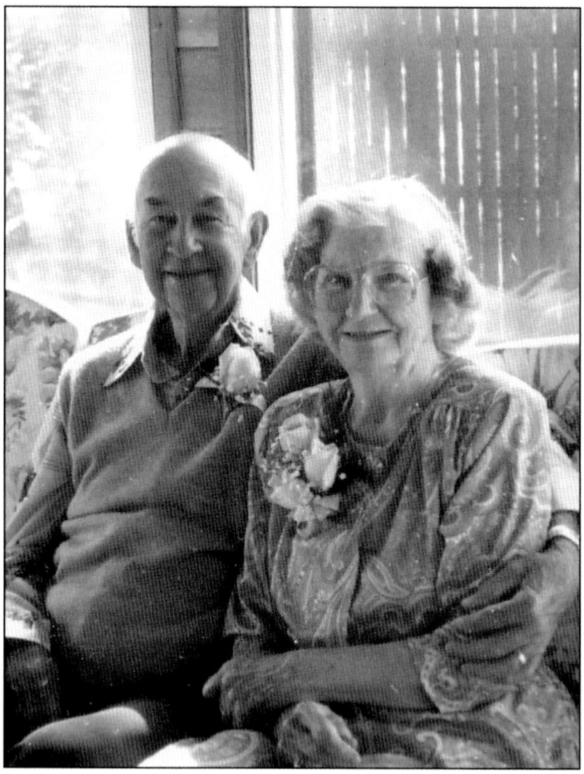

Charles and Alberta Applegate were two active citizens who gave of their time and talents to serve the community. Alberta, a beloved teacher at the Chatsworth School, taught grades five and six. Her husband, Charles, served as the custodian at the school, while also serving as a school bus driver. (Courtesy of Charles Applegate collection.)

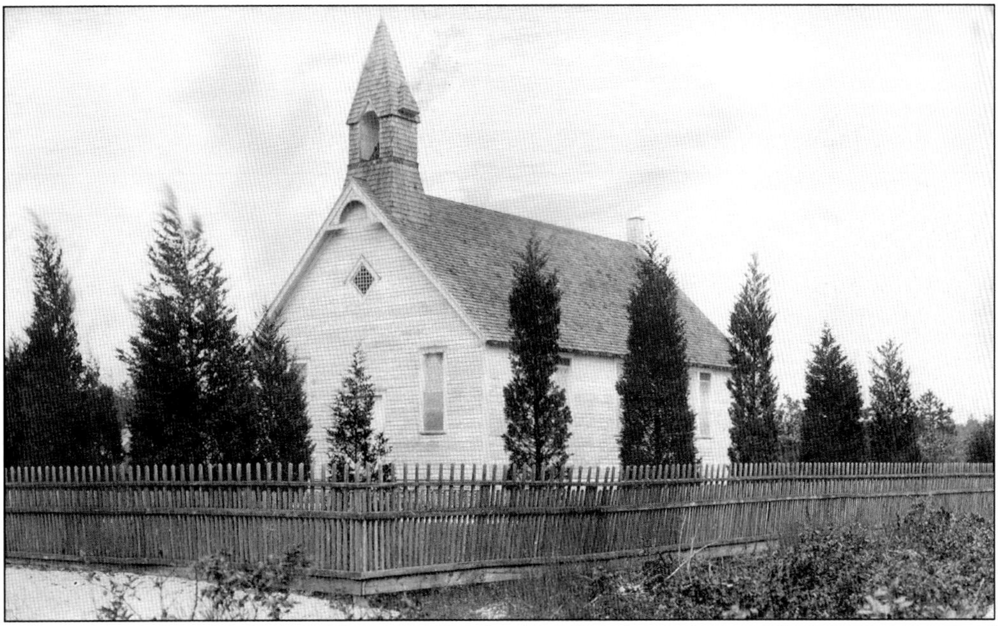

A Presbyterian church organized in 1873 was the first church in Chatsworth. Services were held in the school until 1875, when a church building was erected. In 1893, the structure was destroyed in a fire caused by lightning. The new church was constructed on the old foundation and was deeded to the trustees of the Chatsworth Methodist Episcopal Church on January 6, 1909. This photograph is taken from a postcard mailed in 1908. (Courtesy of Stan and Maureen Worrell.)

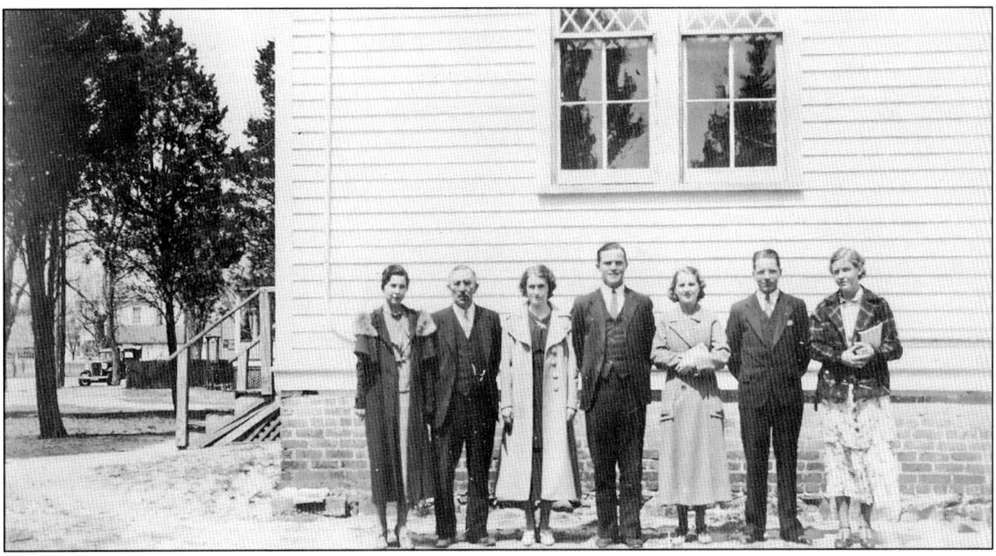

The leaders of the Chatsworth Methodist Church assembled for this 1935 photograph. They are, from left to right, Ruth Haines, Fred Dunfee, Verna Pepper, Stanley Worrell, Mary Ella Pepper, Rev. Robert Howe, and Amelia Green. Worship services would be held at 6:30 p.m. each Sunday. A special service was always held on Christmas Eve. (Courtesy of Stan and Maureen Worrell.)

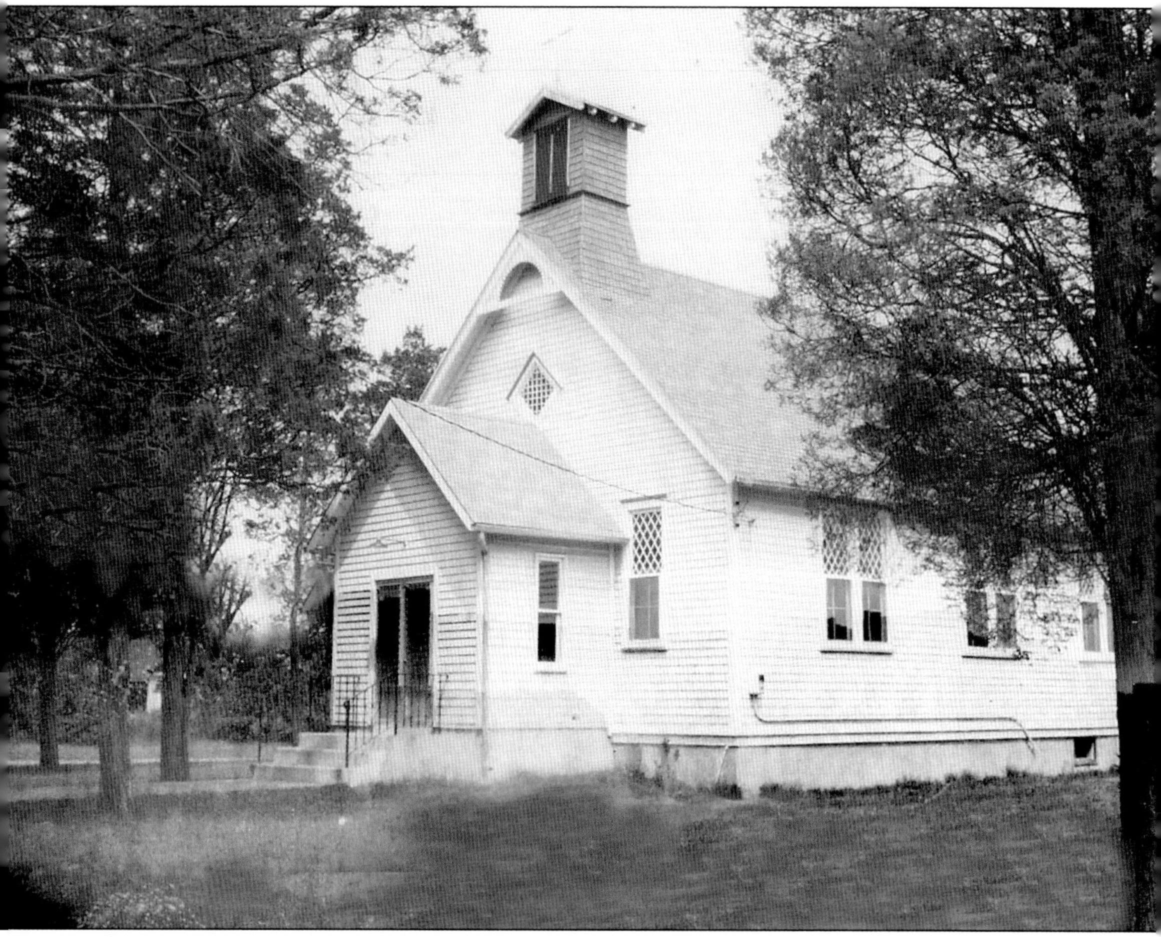

This 1960 photograph of the Chatsworth United Methodist Church on Main Street shows two major improvements to the building, a new roof and new steeple, work that was completed by Harold Stevenson. In 1956, a total renovation of the interior of the sanctuary was completed by volunteer labor at a cost between $2,500 and $3,000. The Reverend Clarence Woodmansie, who served the church in earlier years, returned 14 times in the later years to serve the people of Chatsworth. From its beginning to the present, the church has been a vital part of the community. In 1916, Mary Davis started a Sunday school at Johnson Place. The next year she accepted a commission as a church missionary of the Pine Belt of New Jersey with the Presbyterian Synodical Home Missions. A church was erected on Mary Davis's property, which for many years was the center of many religious and social activities at Johnson Place. Additionally, Catholic services were held in the White Horse Inn (Shamong Hotel) in Chatsworth prior to ownership of the inn by the Stevenson family. (Courtesy of Vera Topham.)

Three

Industry and Agriculture

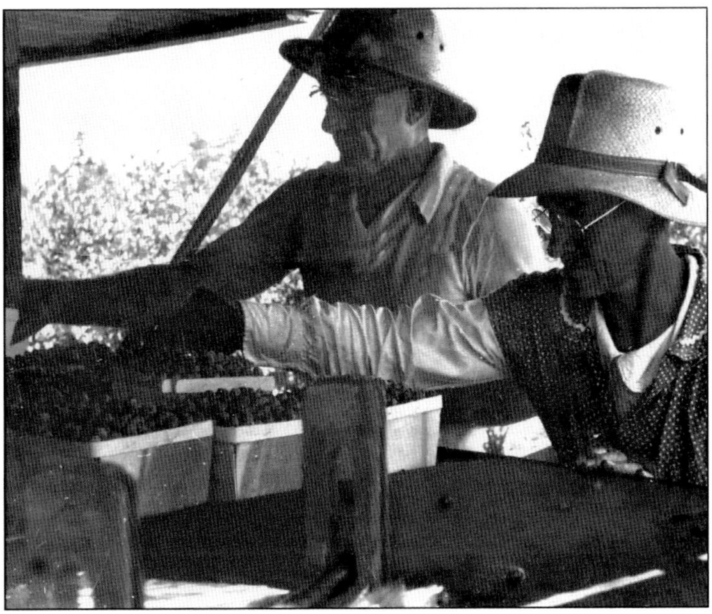

Blueberry workers bring picked berries to the packinghouse during the summer of 1940. Jesse Messler and Annie Applegate, both with hats to withstand the hot summer sun during blueberry harvest season, bring the berries they picked by hand to the packinghouse where they are prepared for shipment to market throughout the country and abroad. Blueberries were the dominant crop in June and July. (Courtesy of Maureen and Stan Worrell.)

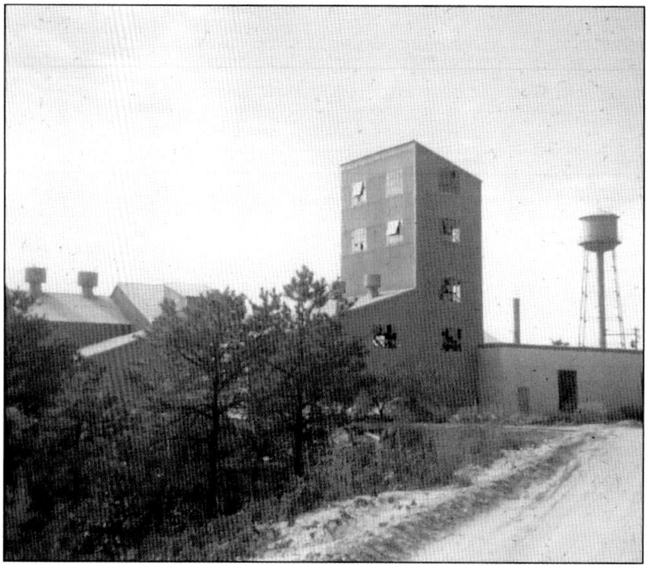

The Zinc Plant was a facility built in Chatsworth in 1939 by the New Jersey Zinc Company as a wartime project. The plant was equipped with underground storage tanks and an elaborate network of tunnels, floodgates, passages, and piping. A tower building stood over 60 feet above the ground. Pioneer Smelting Company purchased the plant in 1972. In 1973, the plant processed and refined nonferrous metals, aluminum drosses, copper residues, and other metal residues at this location. (Courtesy of Sooy family.)

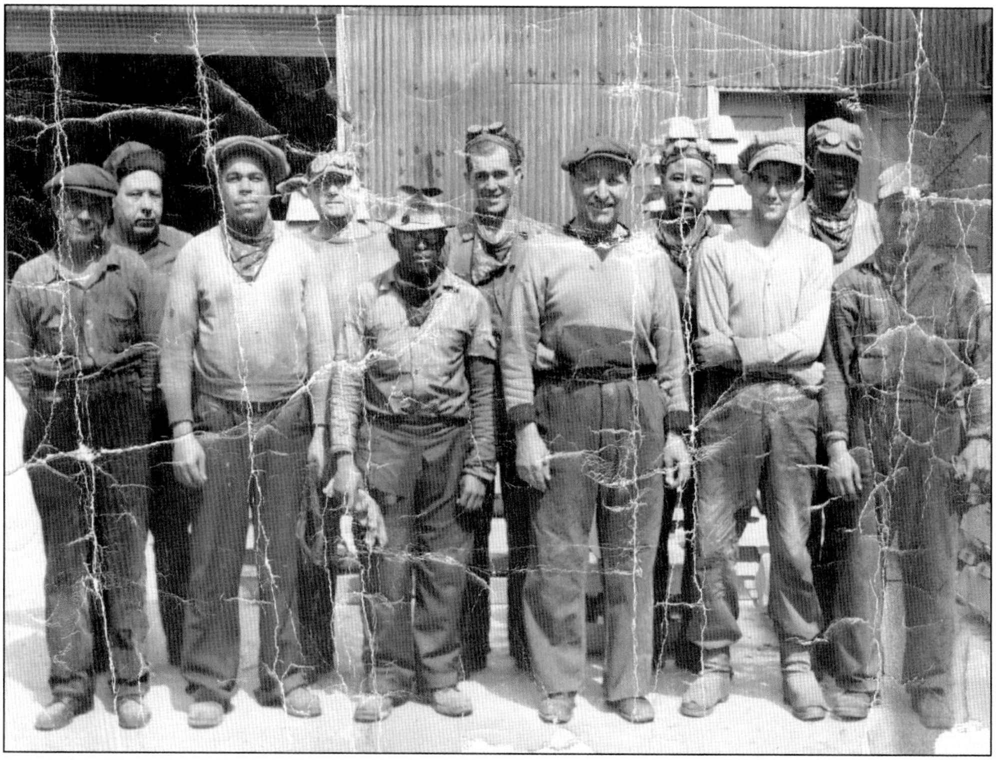

Many local residents found employment with Pioneer Smelting Company as can be seen by this picture. The third person from the left in the front row is Hector Nicholson, and the third man from the left in the second row is Charles Leek. Both men lived in Chatsworth. The facility was abandoned in 1996, and in 2003–2004, the Environmental Protection Agency and its contractors completed an environmental demolition of the buildings and cleanup of the site. (Courtesy of Charles R. Leek family.)

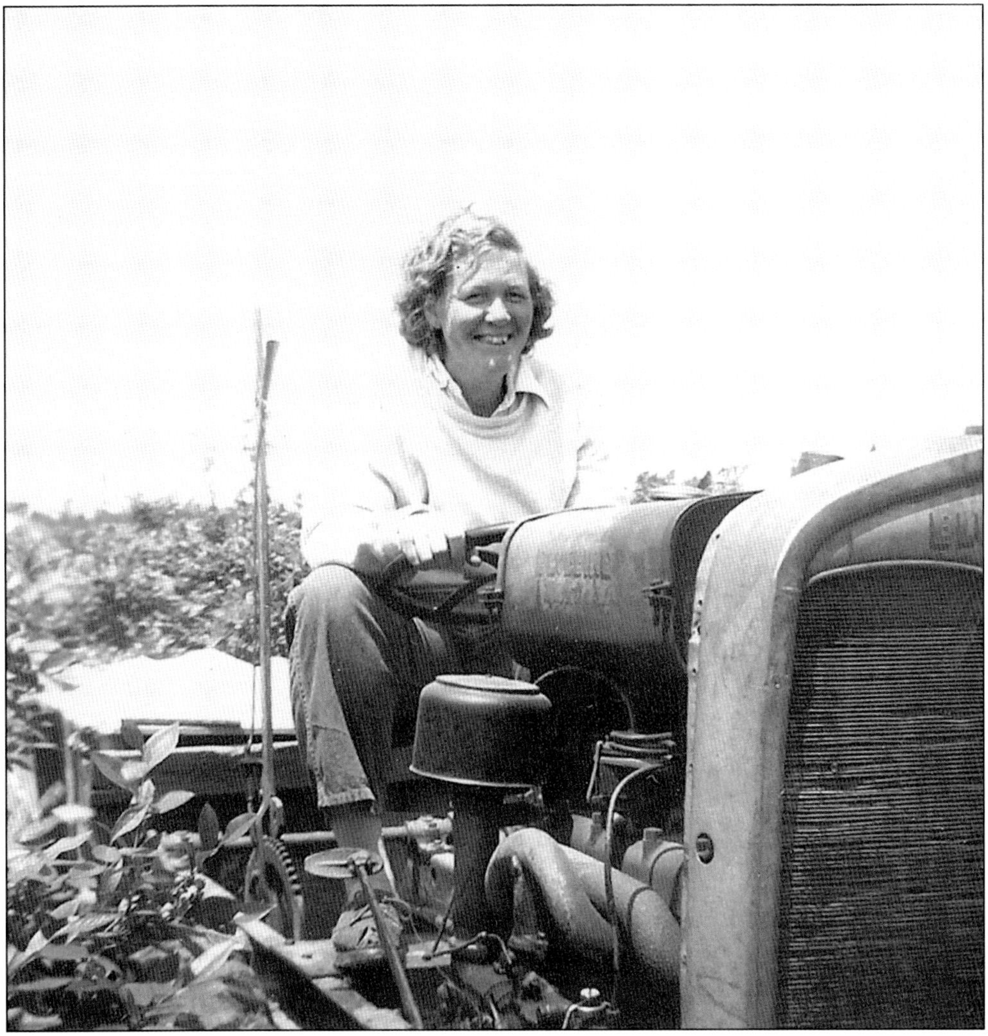

Shown operating a tractor in her blueberry field in 1950, Amelia "Mid" Stevenson Green was one of Chatsworth's most prominent citizens. Known for her kindness, generosity, and her genuine compassion for others, she made numerous significant contributions in so many ways to her community and to others, especially her leadership role for over 30 years in the education of children. She literally touched and enriched the lives of countless numbers of her fellow citizens. Her legacy of excellence in human relationships continues to be cherished by all who were privileged to know her. Among the many blueberry growers at this time were Akers Blueberries, Albert Ammon, David Applegate, Russell Anderson, Edward Brower, Peter T. Brower, Walter Brower Sr., Anthony DeMarco, J. Russell Dunfee, Francis Estlow, Richard Green, William S. Haines Sr., Joseph Holloway, Stephen Lee, Albertus Pepper, Albert Prickett, Bill Sloan, Alfred Stevenson, and Stanley Worrell. (Courtesy of Amelia Green collection.)

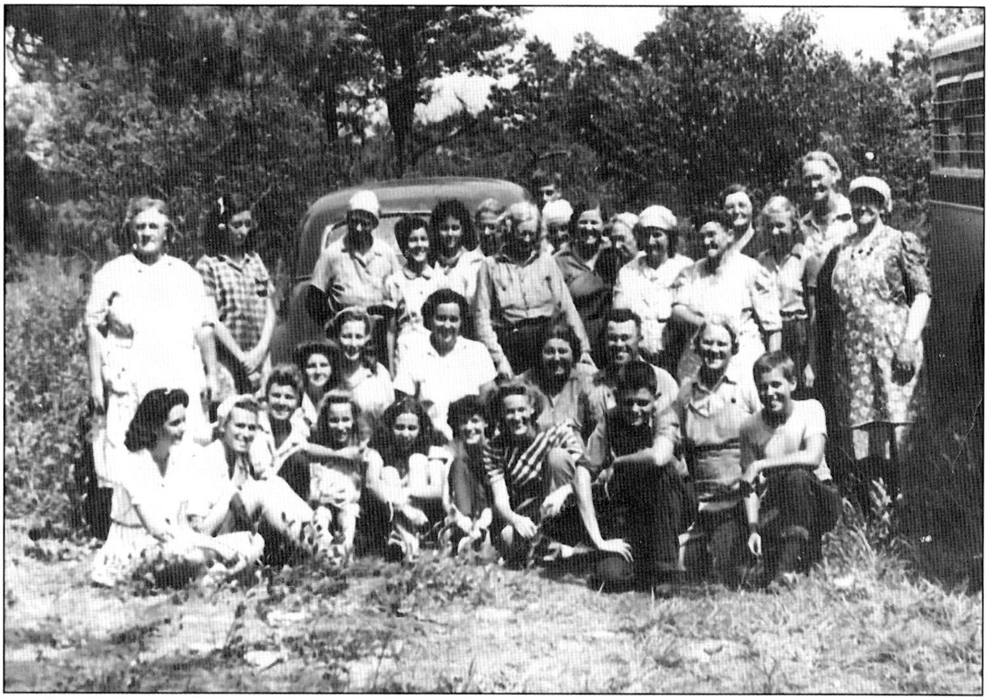

Gathered with other blueberry pickers at Akers field for this camera shot in 1935 are Addie Holloway (far left) and Bill and Pearl Dunfee (kneeling second row right). Berries were picked by hand, and pickers often earned as much as $10 in one day. (Courtesy of Sooy family.)

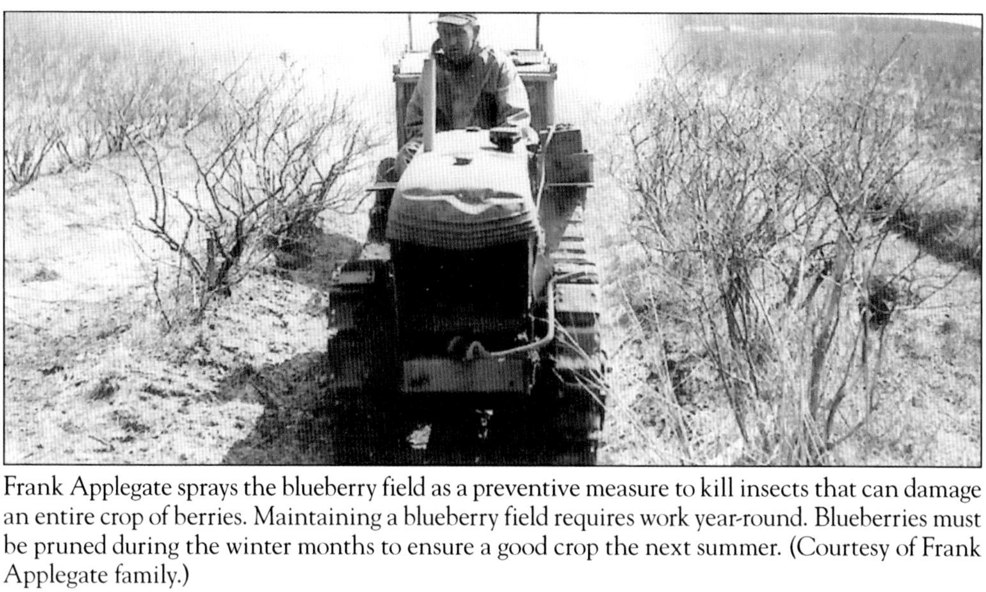

Frank Applegate sprays the blueberry field as a preventive measure to kill insects that can damage an entire crop of berries. Maintaining a blueberry field requires work year-round. Blueberries must be pruned during the winter months to ensure a good crop the next summer. (Courtesy of Frank Applegate family.)

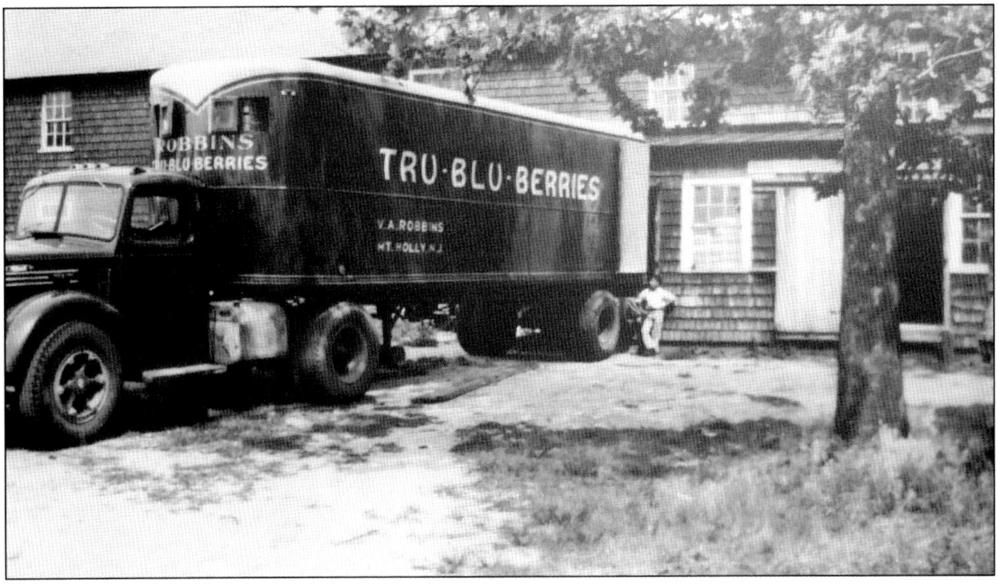

A daily visitor to Chatsworth during the blueberry season was the Tru-Blu-Berries truck that each afternoon would park on Main Street to receive from the local growers the harvested blueberries to begin the journey to market. The Tru-Blue-Berries Cooperative was formed in 1928 to aid local growers in selling the berries in markets not only in New Jersey but in nearby states as well. (Courtesy of William S. Haines Sr. family.)

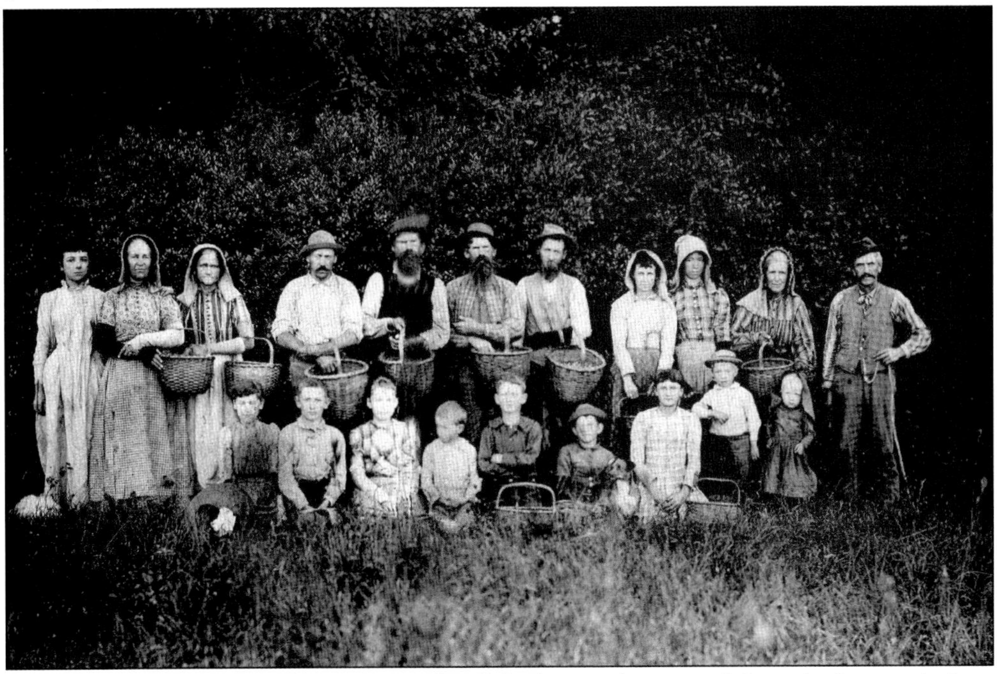

This group of cranberry pickers, equipped with baskets and protected from the hot sun by hats and long sleeves, is ready for a day of cranberry harvesting. The second woman standing at left is Jane Lee, who was married to the first Stephen Lee in the area. Lee Brothers farm remains in existence today. The names of the other pickers are unknown, and the photograph is from the early 1900s. (Courtesy of Charles Applegate collection.)

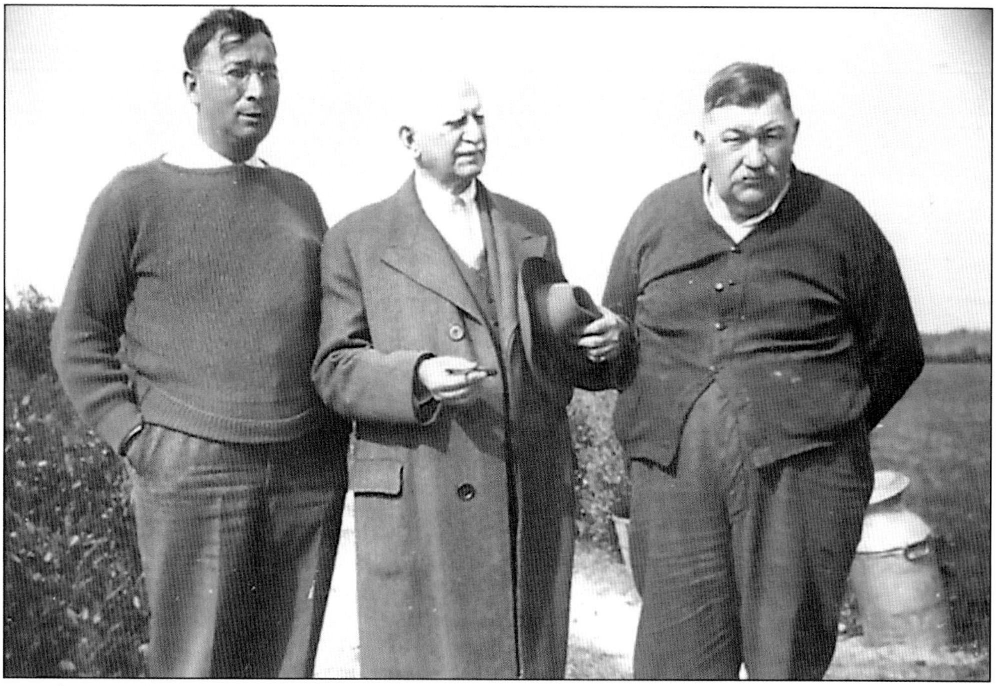

Jonathan Godfrey (center), a cranberry bog owner, would make periodic visits to Chatsworth. He is shown in this 1930 photograph meeting with Anthony DeMarco and Alfred Stevenson, who oversaw the bogs and the processing of the berries. Godfrey lived in Connecticut and Philadelphia but visited in this area often. (Courtesy of Vera Stevenson Topham.)

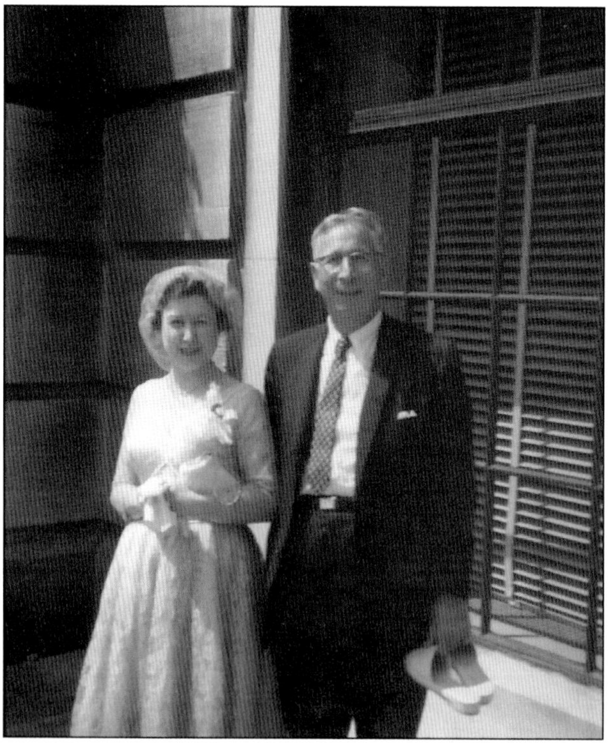

Anthony and Gladys Alloway DeMarco were married on June 28, 1930. Gladys Alloway was a teacher in the Chatsworth School from 1927 until 1930. When school was dismissed in June 1930, she married Anthony DeMarco, who was the owner of cranberry bogs in the Chatsworth area and employed many local workers. (Courtesy of J. Garfield DeMarco.)

J. Garfield DeMarco, who took over the management of A. R. DeMarco Enterprises (Chatsworth Cranberry Company) and developed it into a large producer of cranberries, is shown here. Local men worked in the cranberry bogs, and women sorted cranberries in the cranberry house on Route 532 in Chatsworth. (Courtesy of J. Garfield DeMarco.)

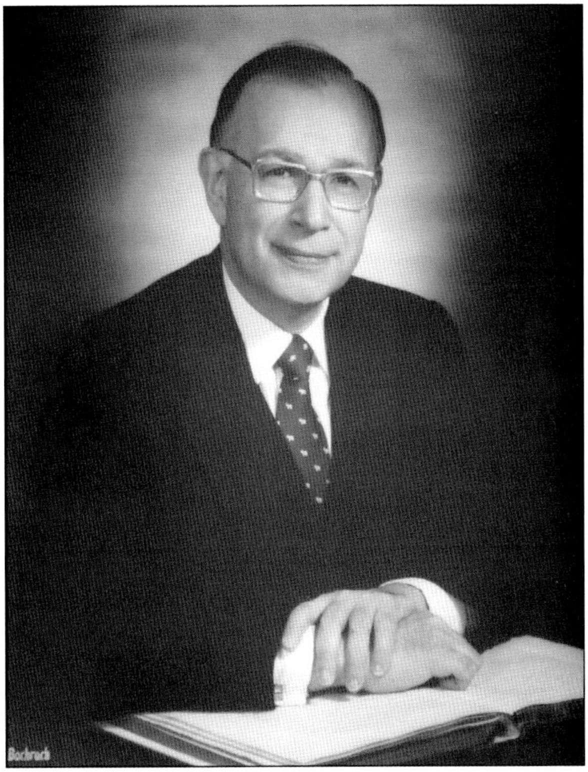

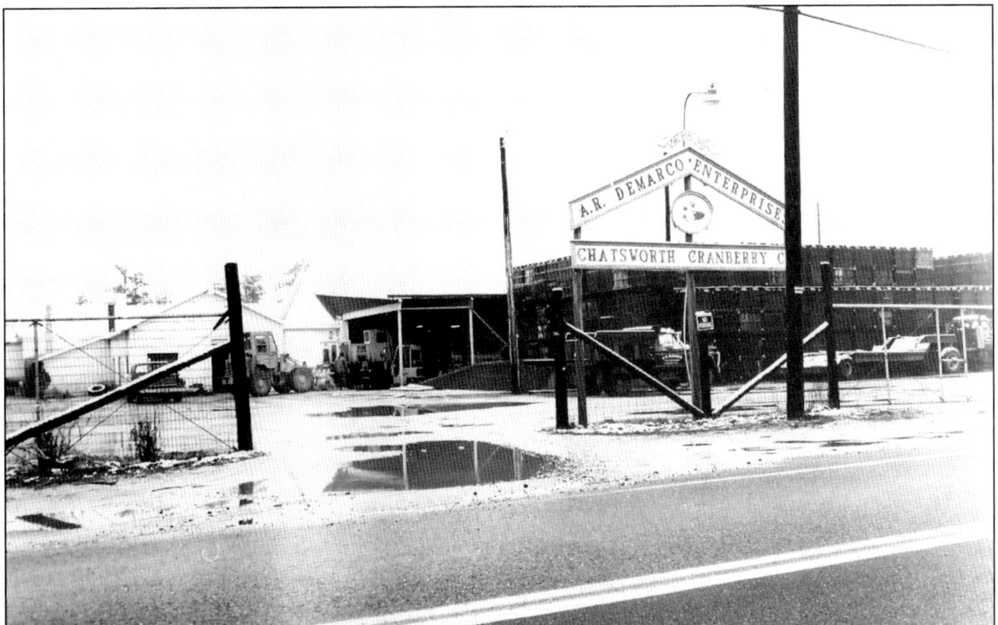

The heart of operations for A. R. DeMarco Enterprises was on Route 532 in Chatsworth. It housed not only the sorting and packinghouse, but also machine and repair shops for maintenance of equipment. Some workers were also housed at this facility. (Photograph by and courtesy of Stan Fayer.)

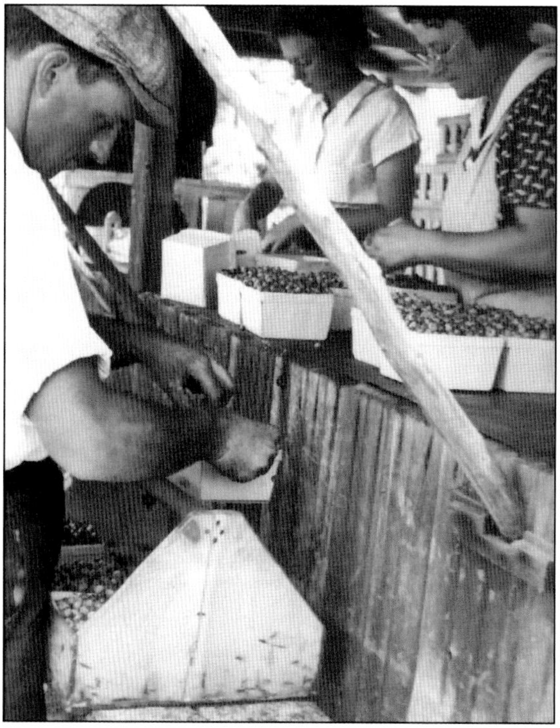

Ben Ranalli, Louise Brower, and Anna Shinske (Choroccynski) Alloway sort berries in the DeMarco packinghouse. During the harvest season, residents of the town worked many long hours harvesting, sorting, and packing the berries for shipment to other areas of the country. (Courtesy of J. Garfield DeMarco)

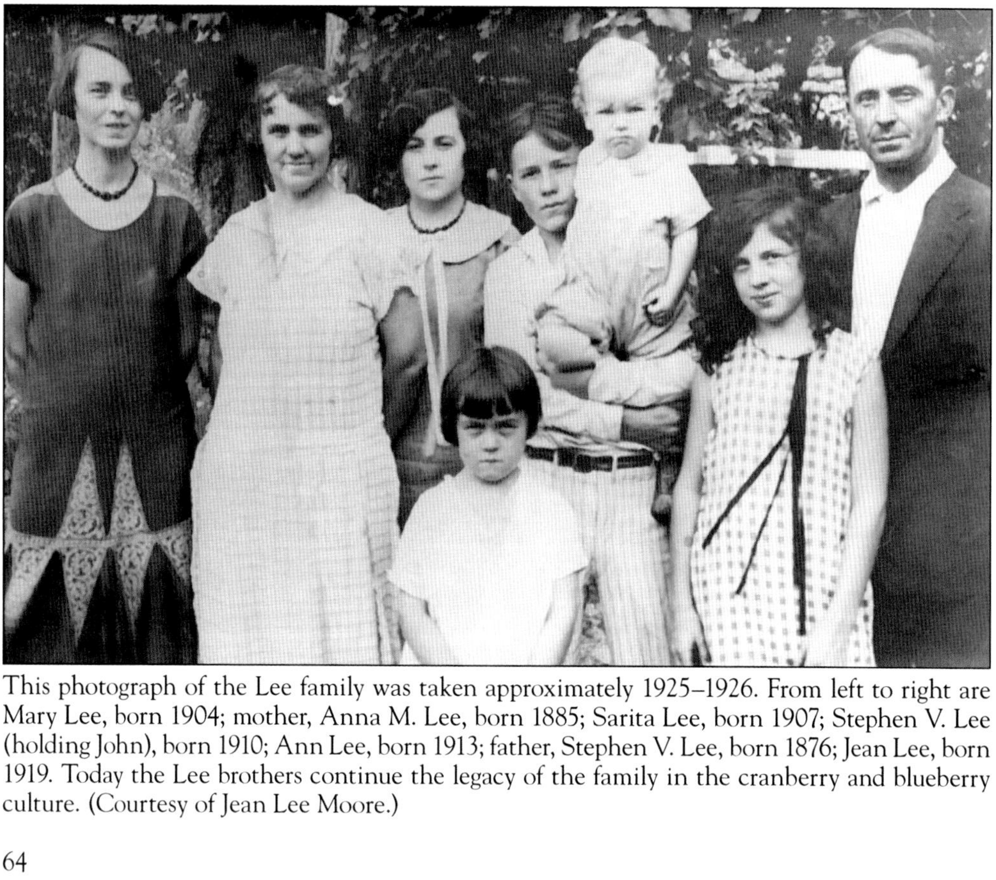

This photograph of the Lee family was taken approximately 1925–1926. From left to right are Mary Lee, born 1904; mother, Anna M. Lee, born 1885; Sarita Lee, born 1907; Stephen V. Lee (holding John), born 1910; Ann Lee, born 1913; father, Stephen V. Lee, born 1876; Jean Lee, born 1919. Today the Lee brothers continue the legacy of the family in the cranberry and blueberry culture. (Courtesy of Jean Lee Moore.)

William S. Haines Sr., the largest cranberry grower in New Jersey, is shown demonstrating the use of a "dibble," a tool that was used to prepare a furrow and then push the cranberry vines into the soil. Haines later donated this interesting and useful tool to the Woodland Township Historical Society for their museum. (Courtesy of Stan Fayer.)

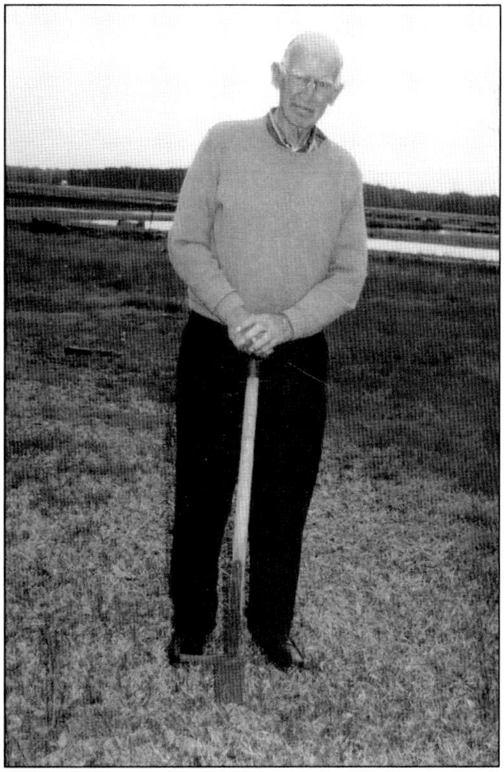

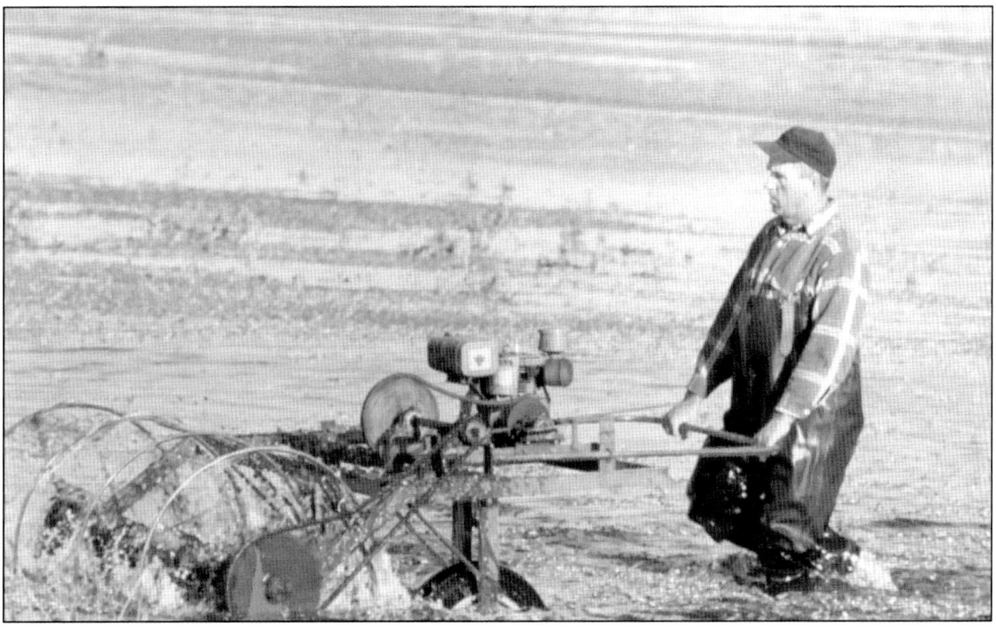

Alison "Possum" Sooy guides a "cranberry beater" through a flooded cranberry bog during the fall harvest. This method of harvesting the berries originated in New Jersey, the third largest cranberry state in growing this luscious berry. After the berries are harvested, they are taken to the Ocean Spray facility in Chatsworth to be washed before they are taken to Ocean Spray in Bordentown, New Jersey, for processing. (Courtesy of Sooy family.)

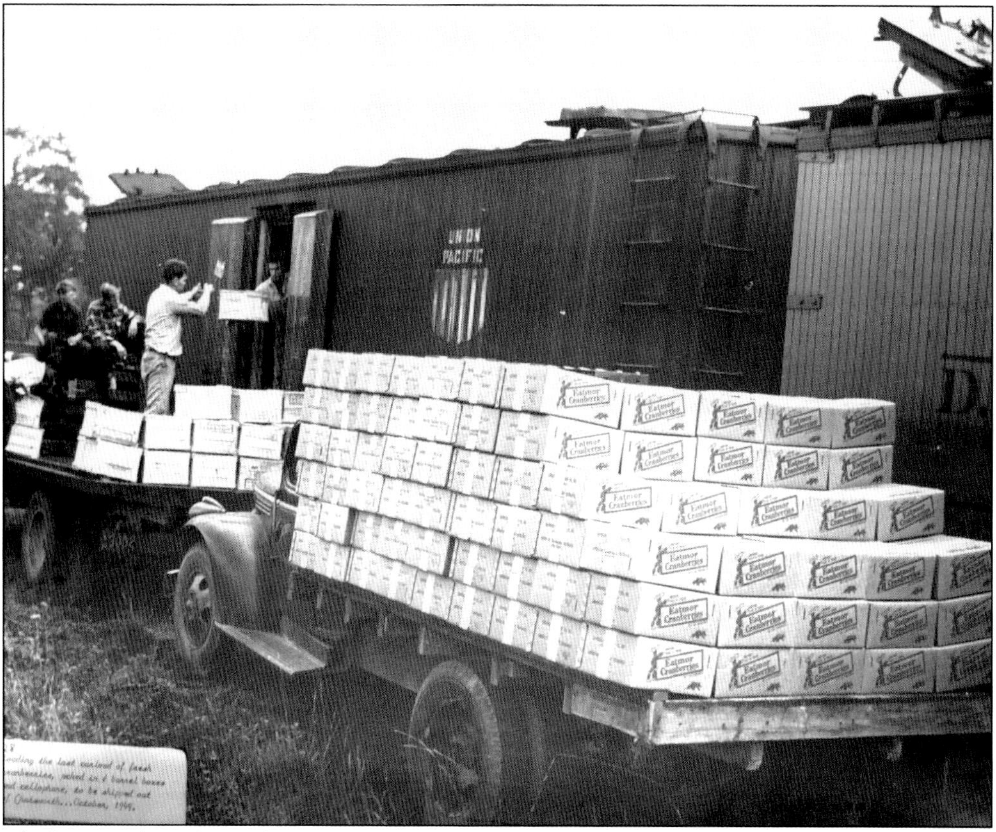

The harvested cranberries have been prepared for shipment to market by freight train in Chatsworth. Standing inside the railroad car is William S. Haines Sr., being handed a packed box of cranberries by John Lee. This was the last shipment of cranberries by rail from Chatsworth in 1949. Others in the photograph are unidentified. (Courtesy of William S. Haines Sr. family.)

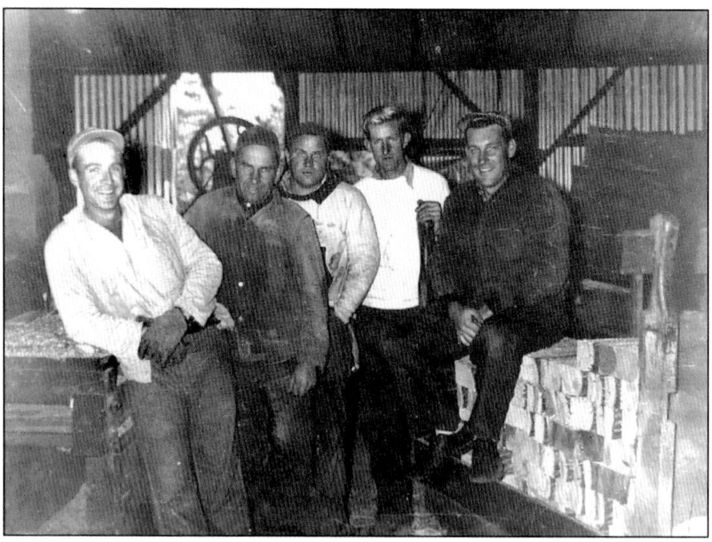

From left to right, Richard Stewart, Frank Applegate, Russell Dunfee, Walter Littler, and Robert Dunfee pause from their work in the Applegate Sawmill to pose for this picture. Sawmills in Chatsworth were popular in the 1930s, 1940s, and 1950s and provided work for many men in the community and surrounding area. (Courtesy of Frank Applegate family.)

One of the many sawmills that existed in Woodland Township was the Lebanon Sawmill. It was located off Route 40 (now Route 72) in the 1920s. Small villages sprang up at the site of a sawmill, and when the lumber was cut off, the houses were moved to the next operating site. One such village was Coon Hill, which is now nonexistent. (Courtesy of Lynch family.)

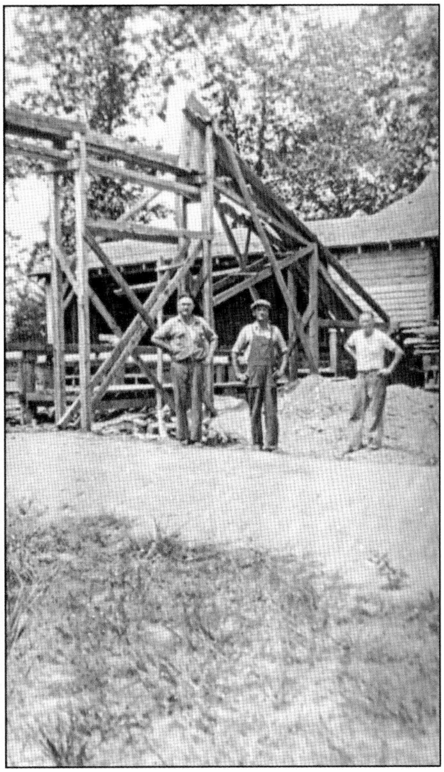

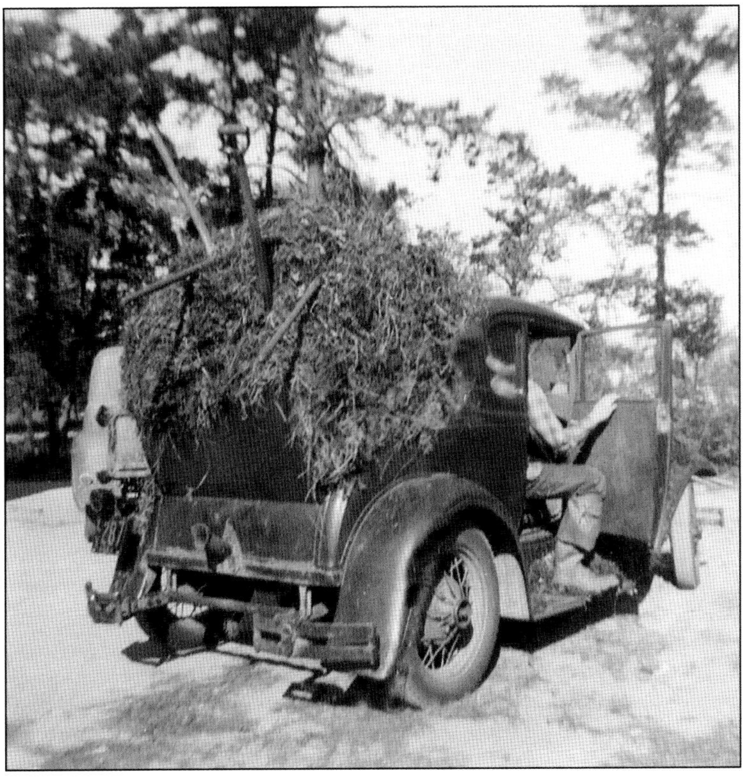

Gathering sphagnum moss was the livelihood of early settlers in the area. The moss was pulled from the ground with pitchforks or homemade grapnels, spread out for drying in the sun, later baled, and shipped to florists in New Jersey and other areas. John "Jackie" Wills is sitting in the truck around 1950. The rumble seat is packed with moss ready to be spread for drying. (Courtesy of Sooy family.)

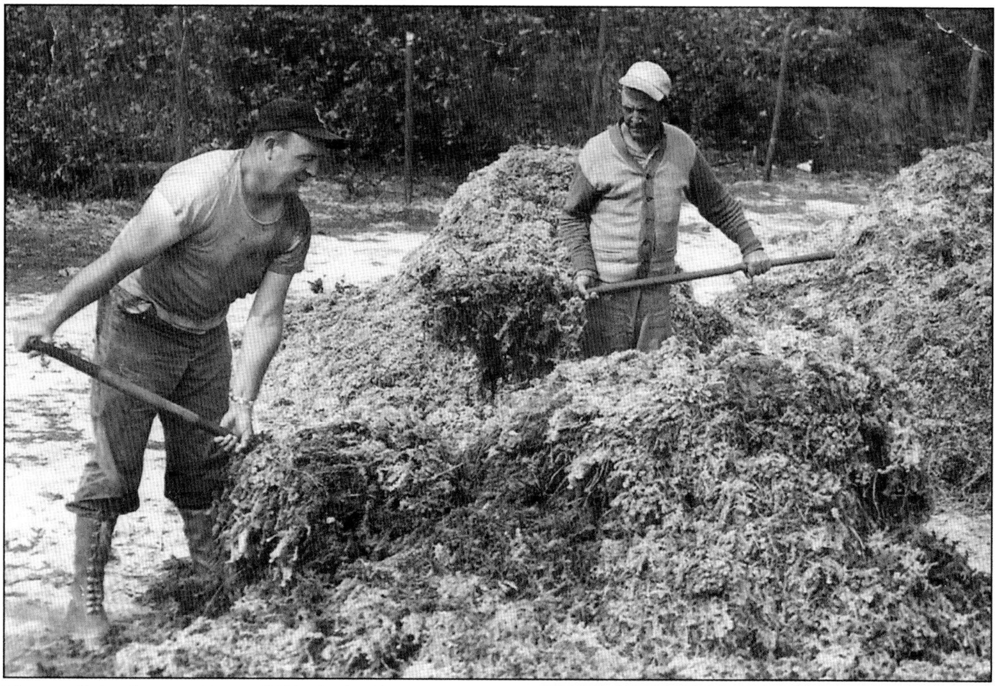

Howard Anderson Sr. and Herb Anderson are spreading sphagnum moss to be dried. The moss was very heavy when wet, and it was hard work gathering and spreading it before it could be put into bales and shipped to florists. Many residents of Chatsworth were involved in gathering the moss. (Courtesy of Joyce Anderson.)

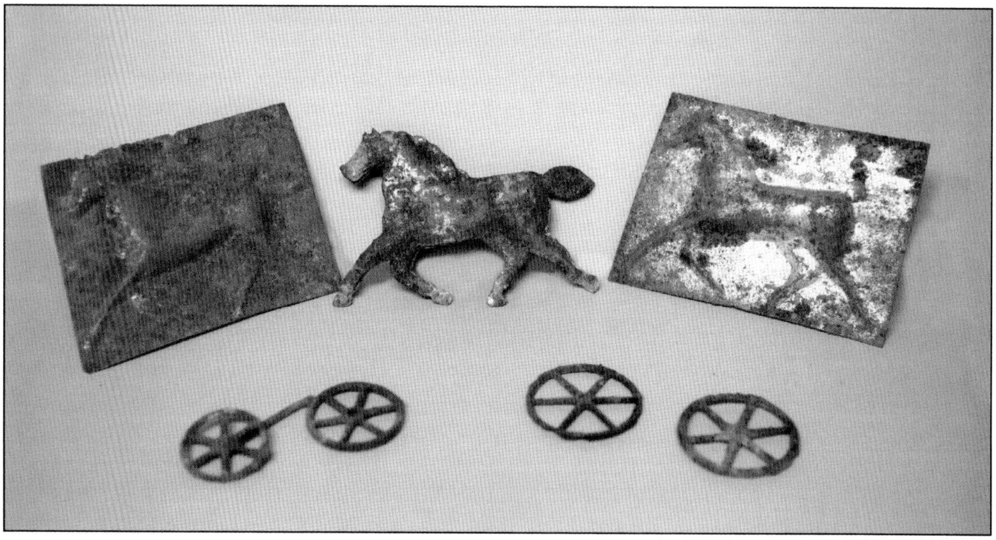

In the early 1900s, Chatsworth was the home of the Akers Toy Factory, the maker of children's toys. The above photograph provides a sample of some of the products the factory produced. Each mold made half of the horse, then they were put together to form a whole. The toy factory continued in business but only for a short period of time. There were other businesses in Chatsworth for which there are no photographs. There was a mattress factory, a shoe factory, and a factory that made uniforms for soldiers during World War I. When the war ended, the factory ceased to exist, and the owners moved away. (Courtesy of Stan Fayer.)

Four

THE CHATSWORTH CLUB

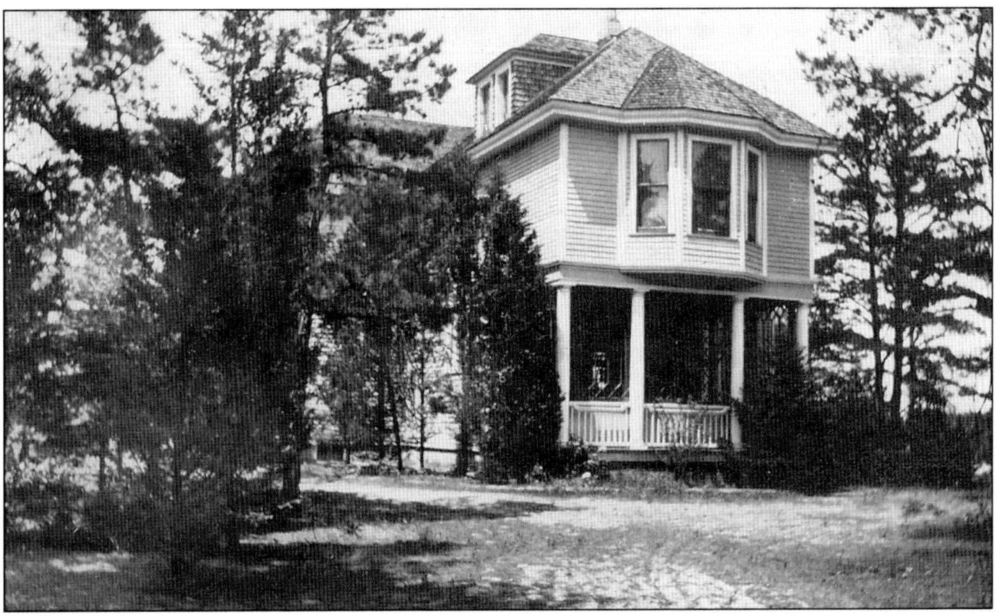

In 1893, Prince Mario Ruspoli de Poggio-Suasa, an attaché at the Italian embassy in Washington in the 1890s, married one of the daughters of Joseph Beers Curtis, a land speculator who owned over 25,000 acres of land in South Jersey. The couple built a villa on the shore of Lake Shamong, now Chatsworth Lake. The adjacent Chatsworth Club was named after the Chatsworth House, the countryseat of the Duke of Devonshire, who was a friend of various members of the syndicate. (Courtesy of Burlington County Library.)

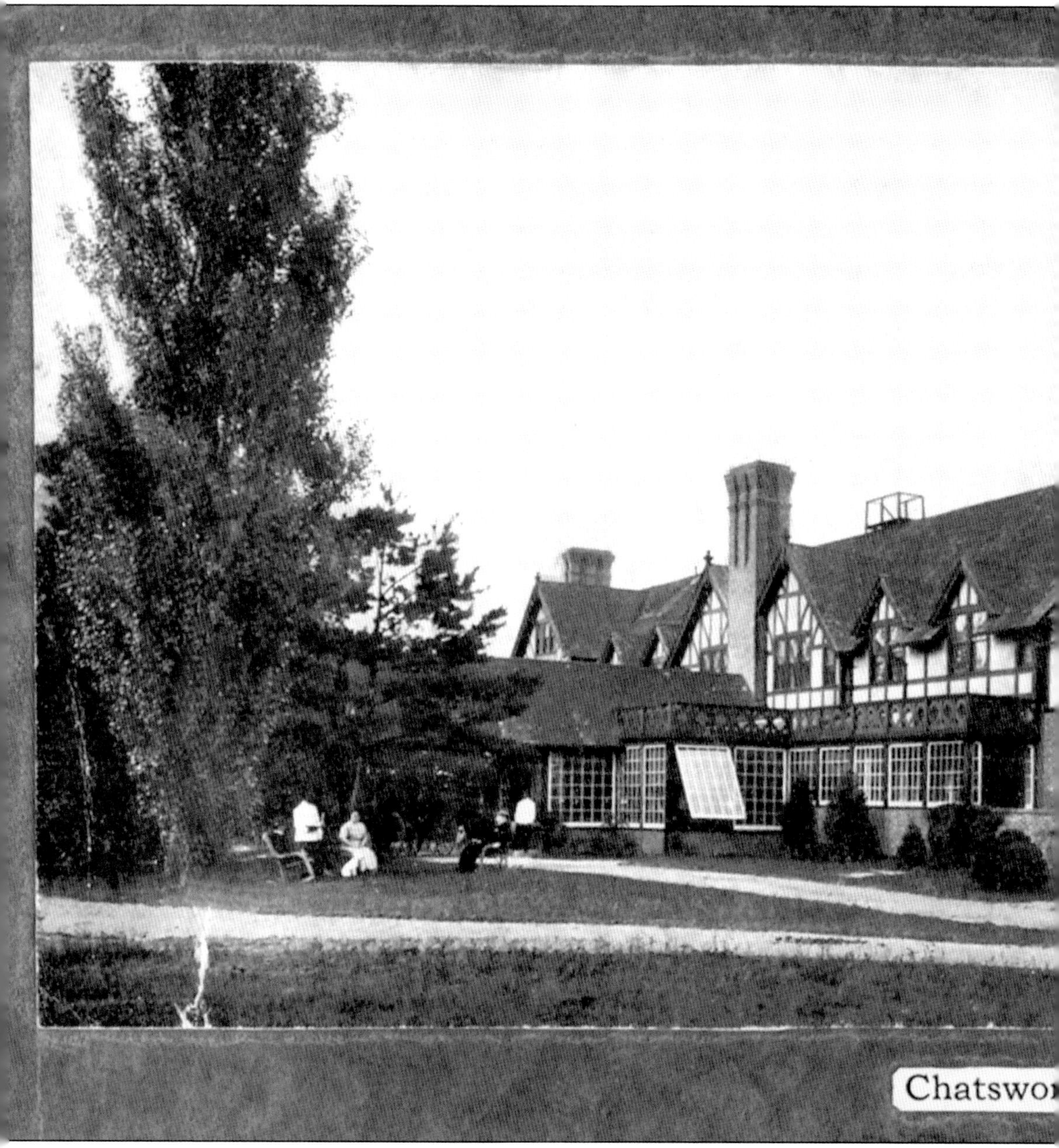

The Chatsworth Club, a Tudor-style building (c. 1897) located at the Chatsworth Lake, had members from throughout the country who came to enjoy the beautiful surroundings and fresh air of the New Jersey Pines. The purpose of the club was "for the mental and physical cultivation of its members." Its members arrived by train and were transported from the railroad station to the club by horse-drawn carriages. In 1904, the year the club was incorporated, the membership

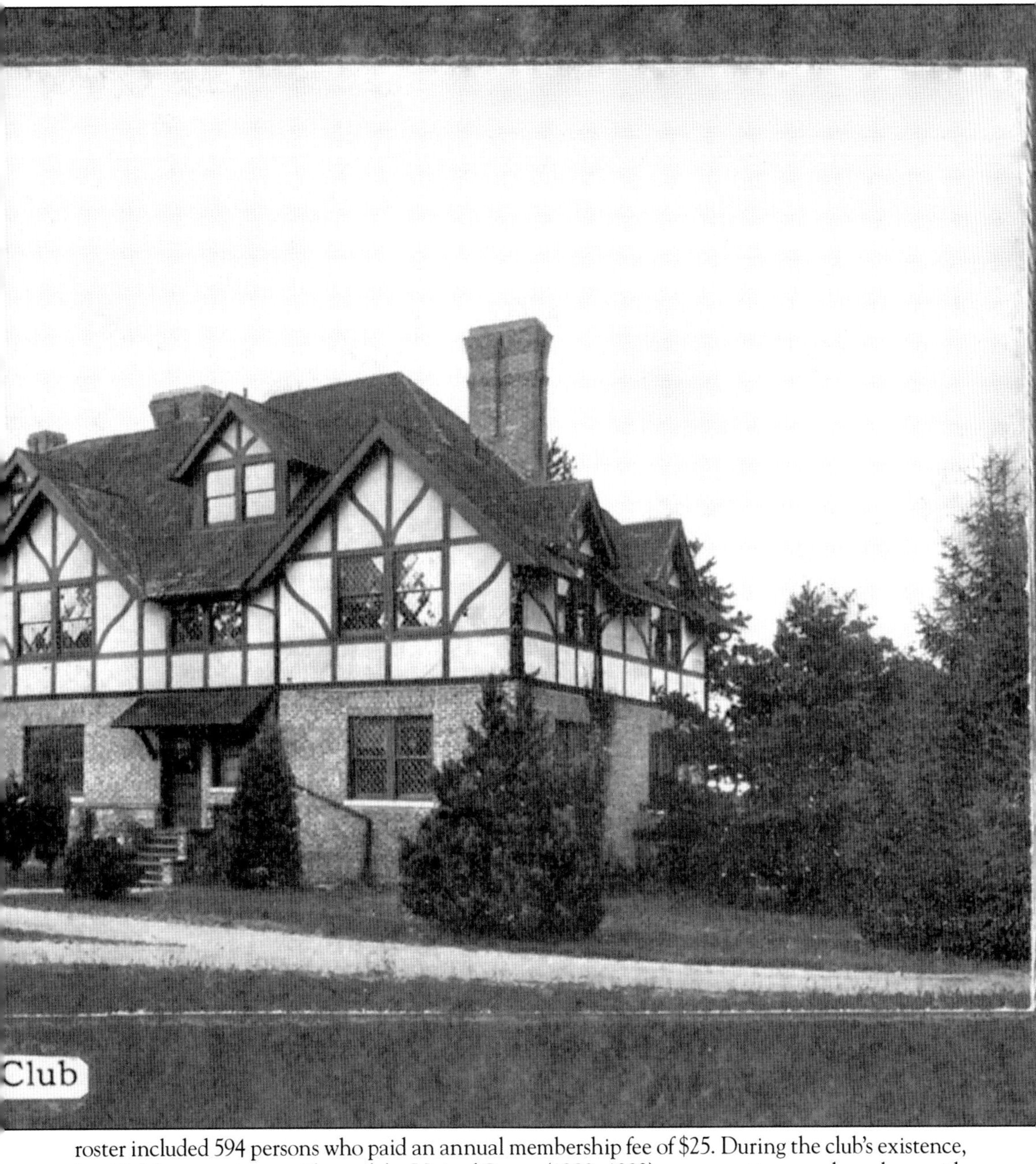

roster included 594 persons who paid an annual membership fee of $25. During the club's existence, Levi P. Morton, vice president of the United States (1889–1893) was an active member, along with members of the Biddle, Gould, Drexel, Astor, and Vanderbilt families. (Courtesy of Burlington County Library.)

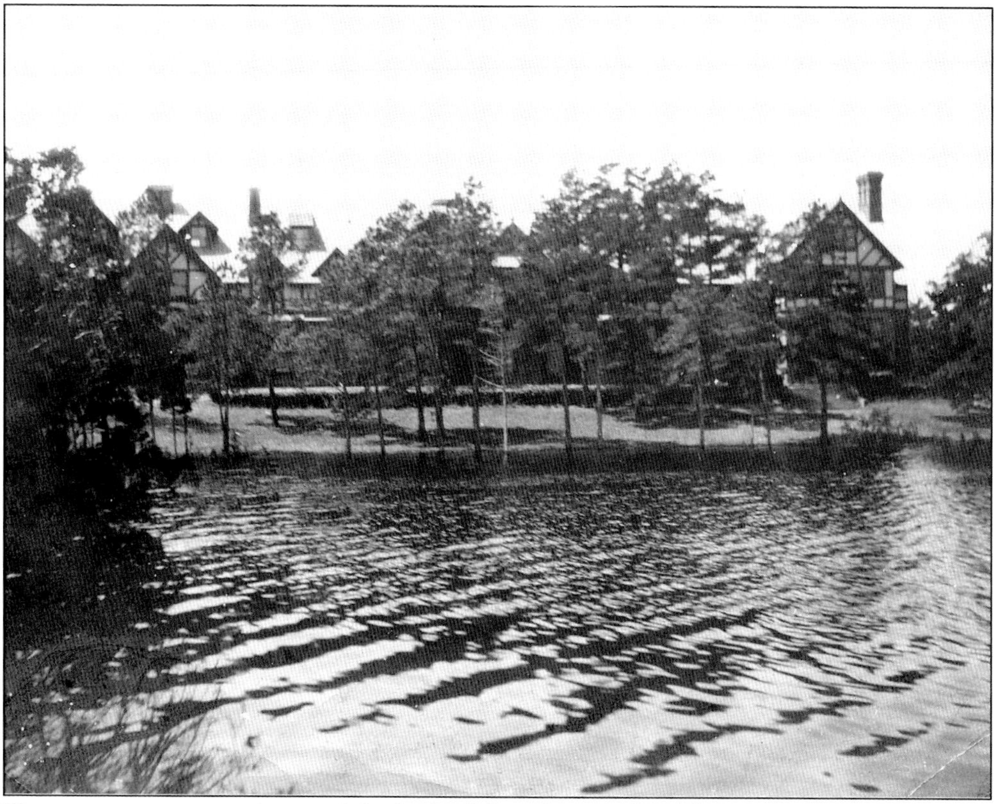

Shown is a most unusual view of the back of the Chatsworth Club located at the Chatsworth Lake, providing a view of the well-kept landscaping that added to the attractiveness of the club and its surroundings. Several of the five chimneys appear through the trees. (Courtesy of Stan and Maureen Worrell.)

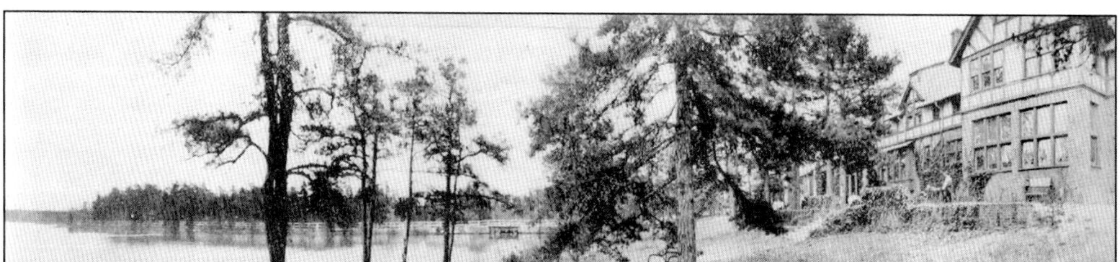

This view of the Chatsworth Club facing south reveals the proximity of the club to Chatsworth Lake and shows the wooden fencing along the road leading to Tabernacle. The windows are Gothic period, except for those in the sunroom. Several guests appear to be relaxing or socializing in front of the club. (Courtesy of Burlington County Library.)

Shown here is the living room of the Princess House, built by Prince Mario Ruspoli de Poggio-Suasa on the shores of Chatsworth Lake. The baby prince was born in this house. It has been said that the wallpaper was red-watered silk, and the house was handsomely appointed, as shown in this photograph. Many older residents of Chatsworth can remember playing on the wide stairway when the house stood deserted in the 1930s. (Courtesy of Amelia Green collection.)

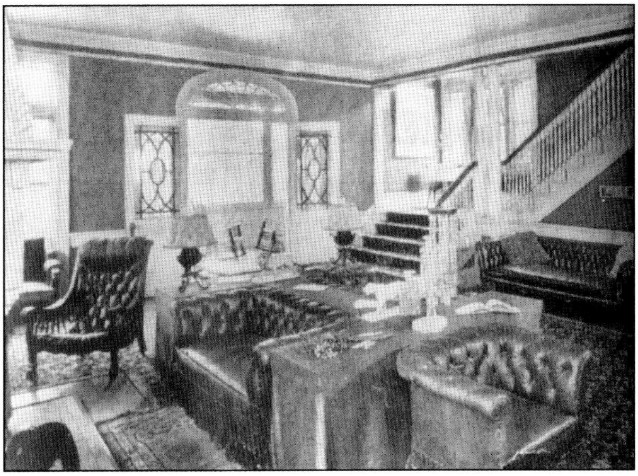

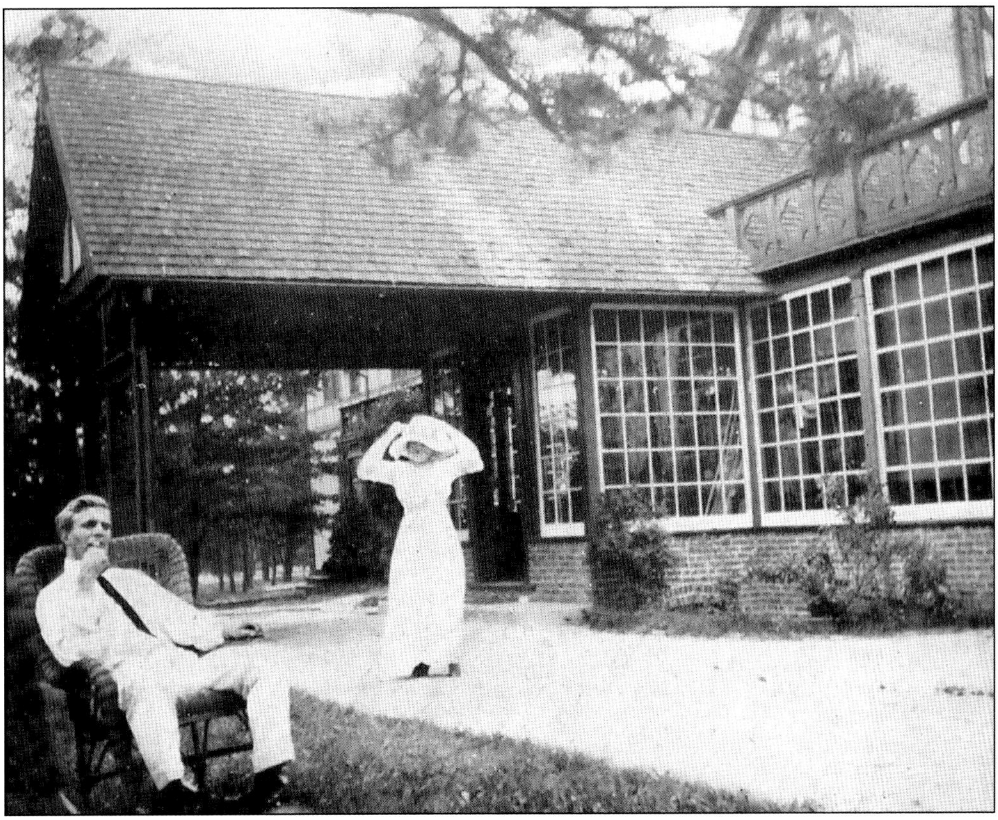

A lady emerging from under the portico secures her large hat, while her companion relaxes in a wicker chair before joining her for a stroll around the club gardens. Note the grand windows in the sun parlor of the club, the wide driveway, and the manicured lawn. (Courtesy of Burlington County Library.)

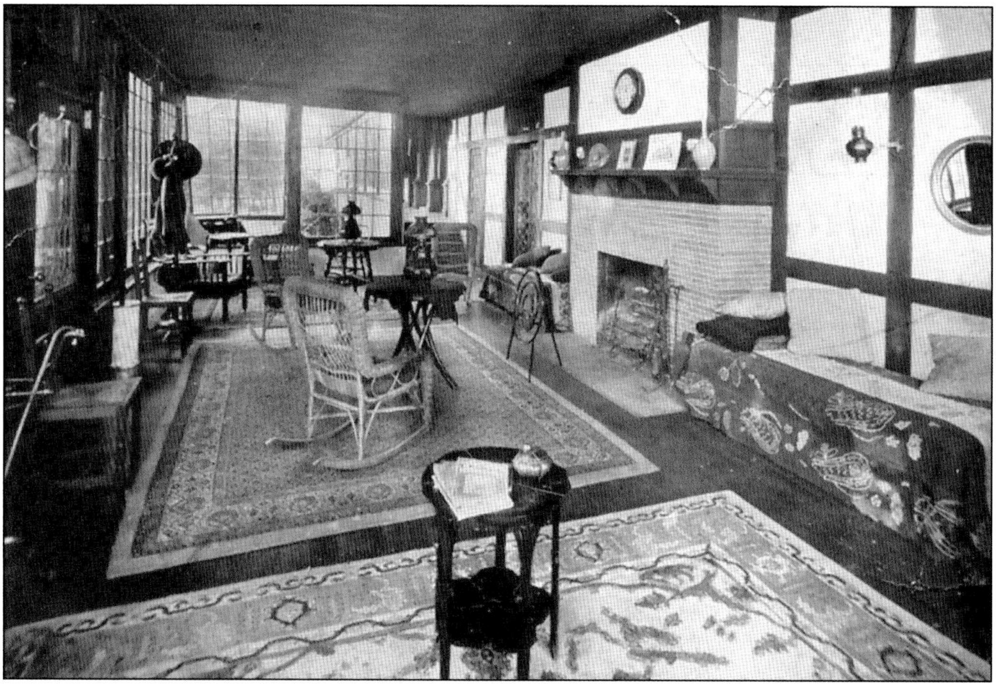

The elegance of the Chatsworth Club is highlighted by these two rooms that were undoubtedly popular with the members of the club—the sunroom (above) and the poolroom (below). Outside activities enjoyed by the members were golfing, hunting, trap shooting, ice hockey when the lake was frozen, and horseback riding through the sweet pine woods. (Courtesy of Burlington County Library.)

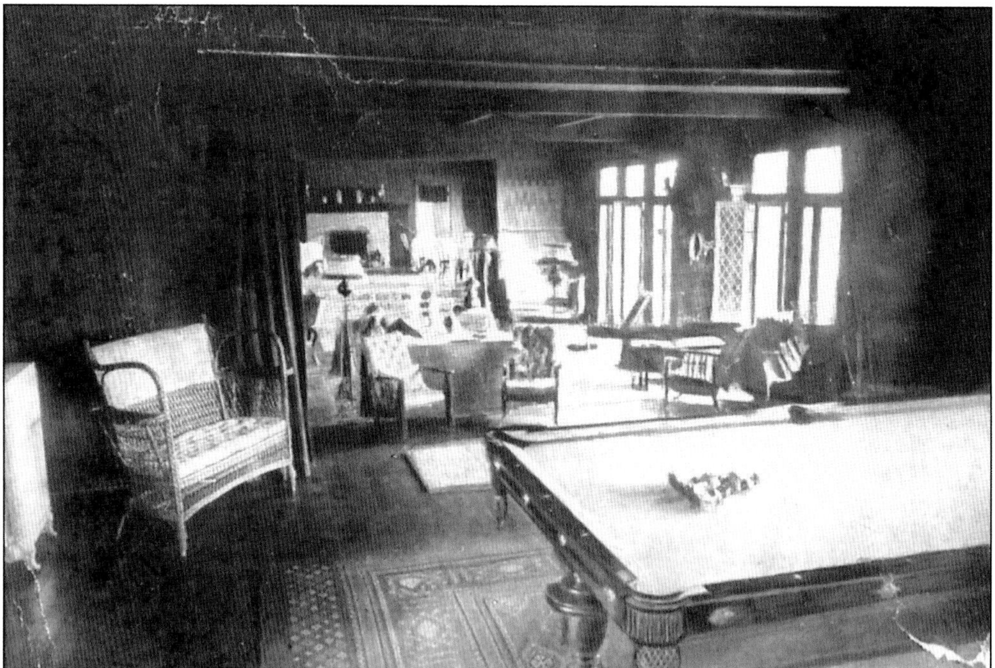

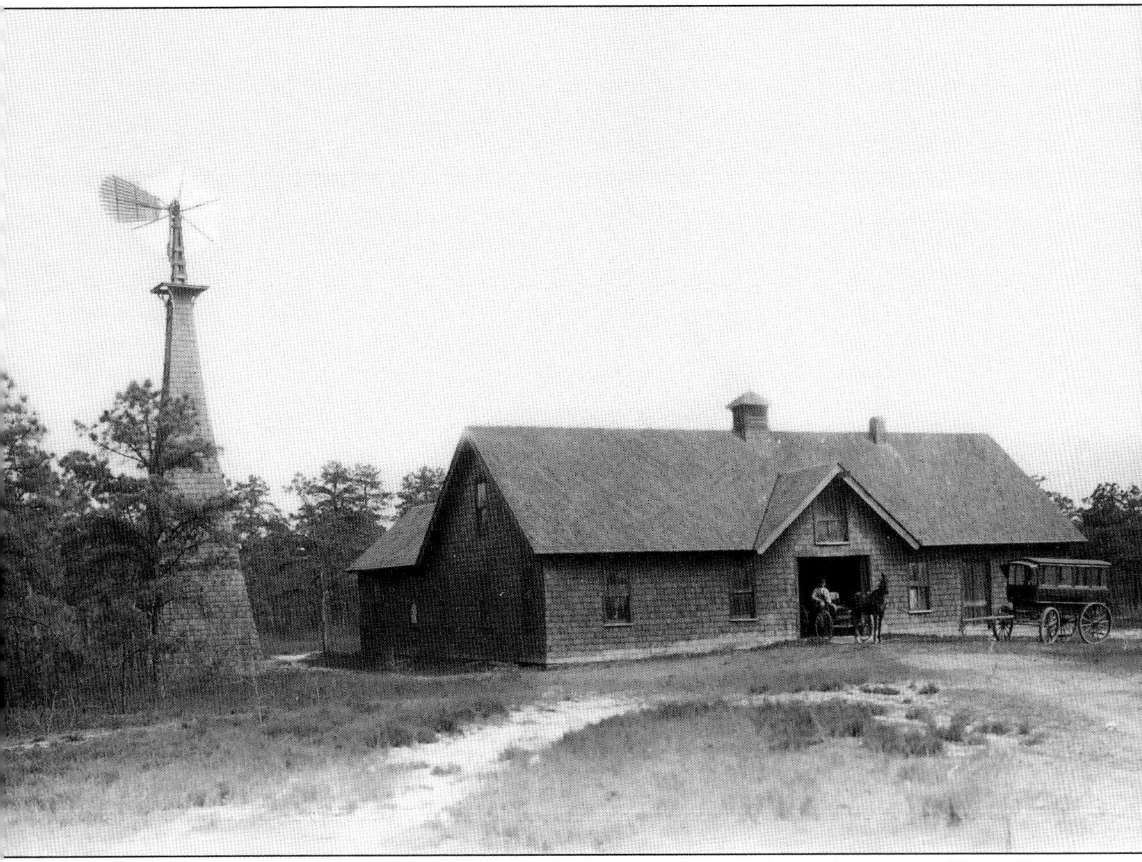

The barn at the Chatsworth Club, where horses and carriages were housed, is pictured here. Early in the history of the club, the barn housed at least nine horses that were used to provide guests with rides throughout the nearby pine woods. They were also used to pull the carriages that transported guests to and from the railroad station. (Courtesy of Amelia Green collection.)

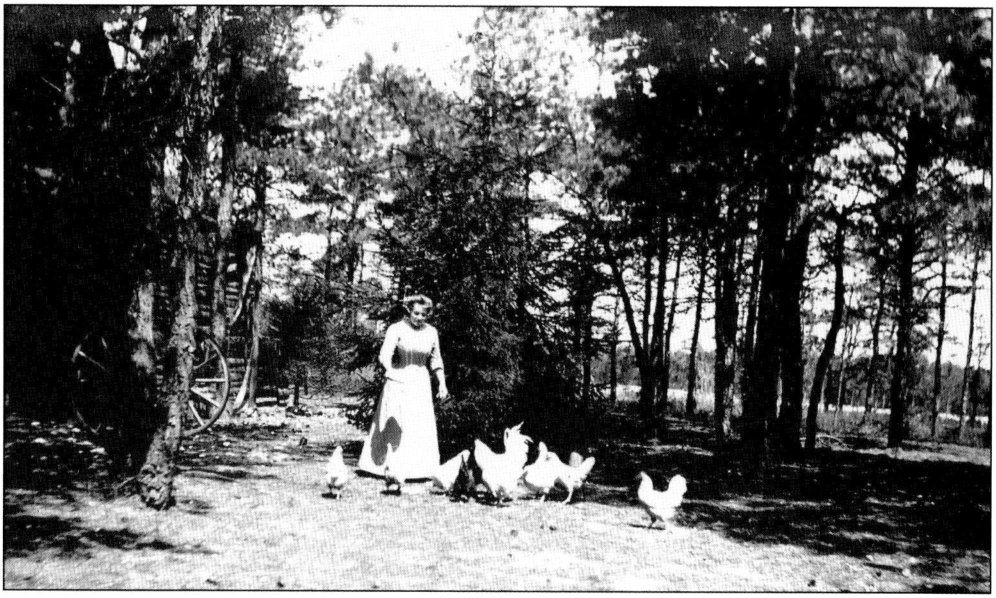

A member of Prince Ruspoli's staff feeds chickens in the barnyard of the mansion. The Ruspolis entertained on a grand scale. Residents of Chatsworth were employed at the Chatsworth Club to perform indoor and outdoor services to assist in the care of the wealthy and pampered guests. (Courtesy of Stan and Maureen Worrell.)

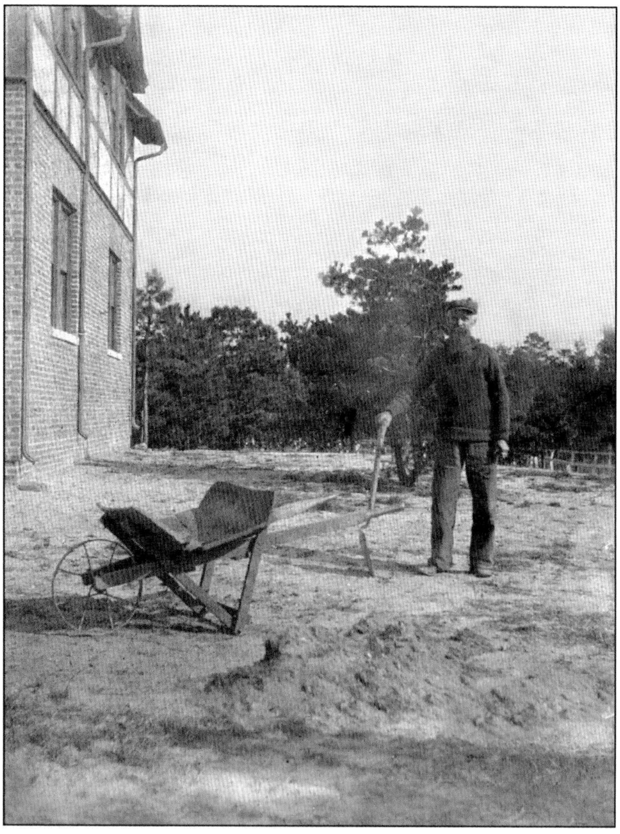

Alfred Adams was one of several Chatsworth residents who worked at the Chatsworth Club to aid in the maintenance of the buildings and their surroundings. This photograph appears to have been taken before the planting of grass and shrubbery. Several residents of the area were also employed during the construction of the Chatsworth Club. (Courtesy of Stan and Maureen Worrell.)

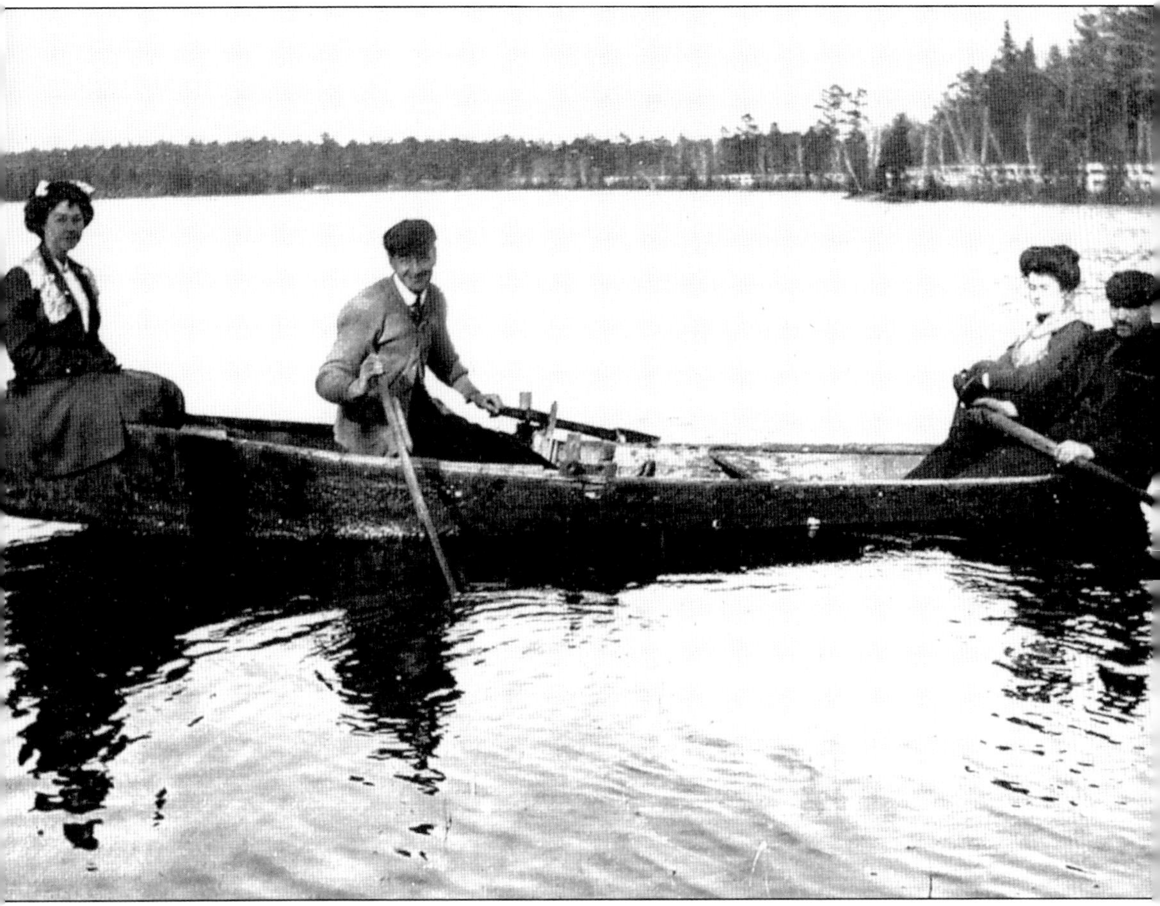

Visitors to Chatsworth enjoyed the beauty of the woods and the sweet pine-scented breezes. Relaxation time at the Chatsworth Club included, among other things, canoeing on the lake and gathering for conversation on the boardwalk. Sailboats were also kept at the club for use of the members. Tennis courts were available for matches. Note that the attire of the early 1900s for canoeing appears to be different from what would be worn today. Many club members traveled from New York aboard Jersey Central passenger trains running through rural Monmouth and Ocean Counties to Chatsworth. (Courtesy of Stan and Maureen Worrell.)

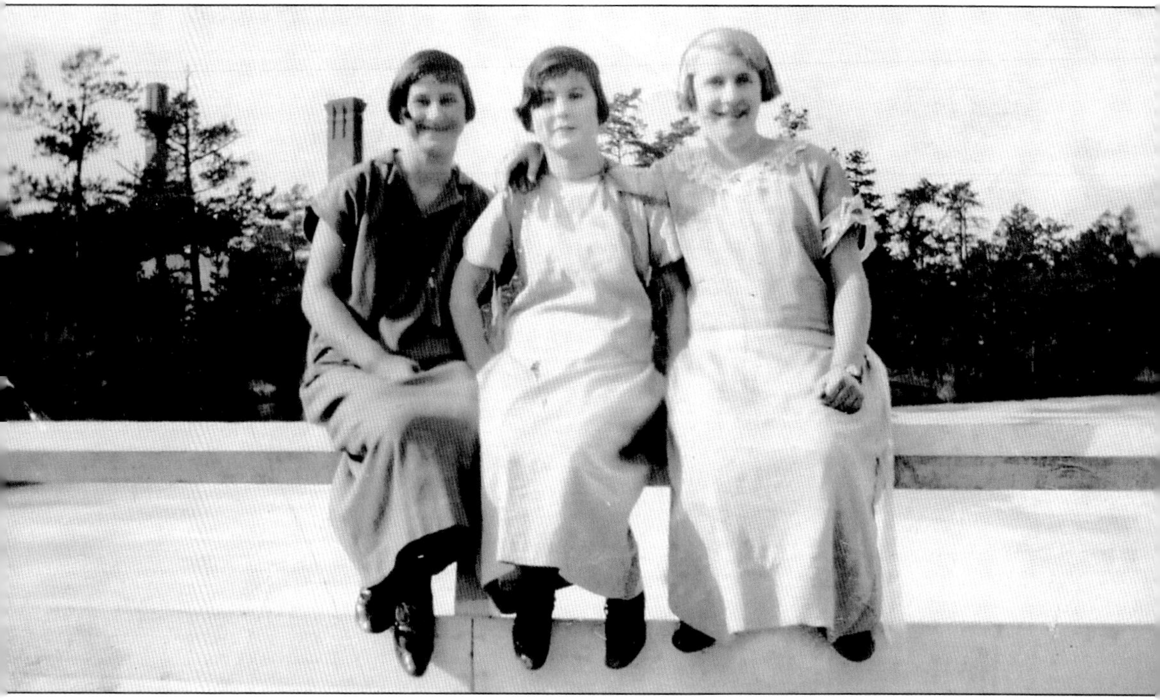

Three Chatsworth young ladies, Florence Wills, Ruth Haines, and Nettie Applegate, gather at the bridge at Chatsworth Lake for this 1920s photograph. Their long dresses are the style of the 1920s. Two chimneys of the remains of the once opulent and luxurious Chatsworth Club are seen in the background. (Courtesy of Charles Applegate collection.)

Five

MEMORABLE EVENTS

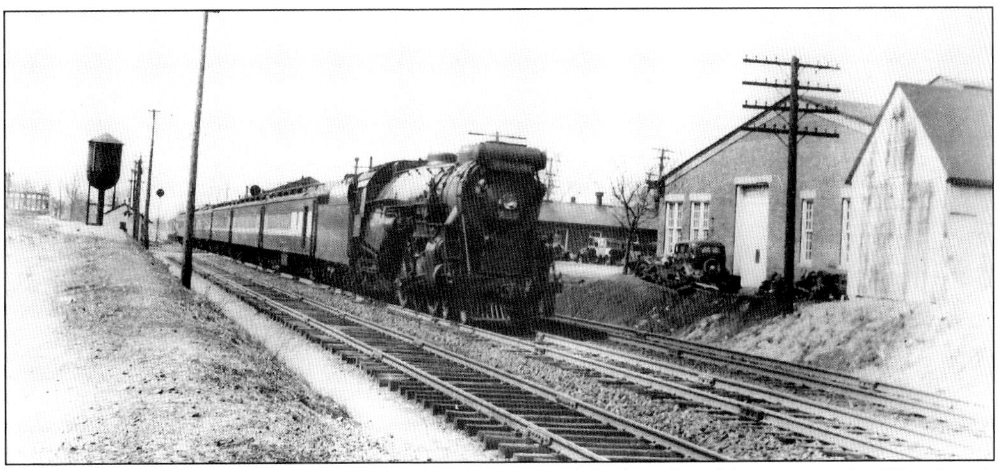

For 12 years, the Blue Comet, operated by the Central Railroad and known as the "Seashore's Finest Train," was very much a part of the Chatsworth community. From its first run, February 21, 1929, local citizens were proud that the nation's first all-coach, reserved-seat, deluxe express train passed through the village each day to and from Jersey City and Atlantic City. (Photograph by Herbert and Edith Gerber; courtesy of Robert Gerber Jr.)

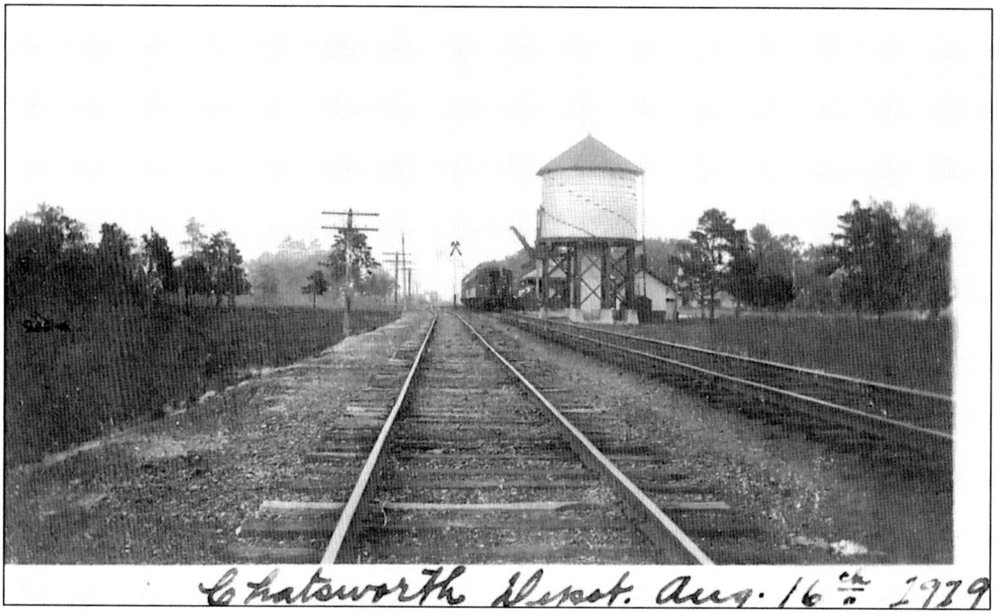

An eastbound train stands at the Chatsworth Station in August 1919. The left track was a passing siding used in the early 1930s because of the frequency of trains, including the Blue Comet, during that period. Special note is made of the large water tower near the station that, in 1913, replaced a smaller tank. The citizens of Chatsworth took advantage of the excellent train service affording travel to Bridgeton and Atlantic City. (Courtesy of Frank Applegate family.)

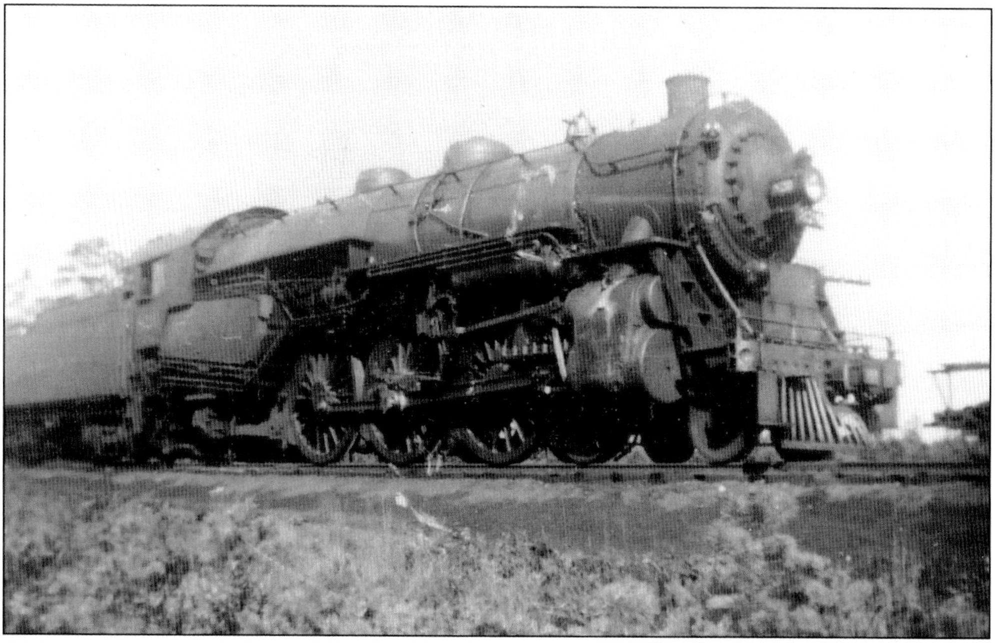

Although not a regularly used Pacific Class G-3 engine of the 831 series, Engine No. 820 was assigned to the Blue Comet on its ill-fated day. The regular engines had a headboard (BLUE COMET) and a distinctive whistle that sounded like that of an ocean liner. They were painted royal and packard blue with gold striping and lettering. (Photograph by Herbert and Edith Gerber; courtesy of Robert Gerber Jr.)

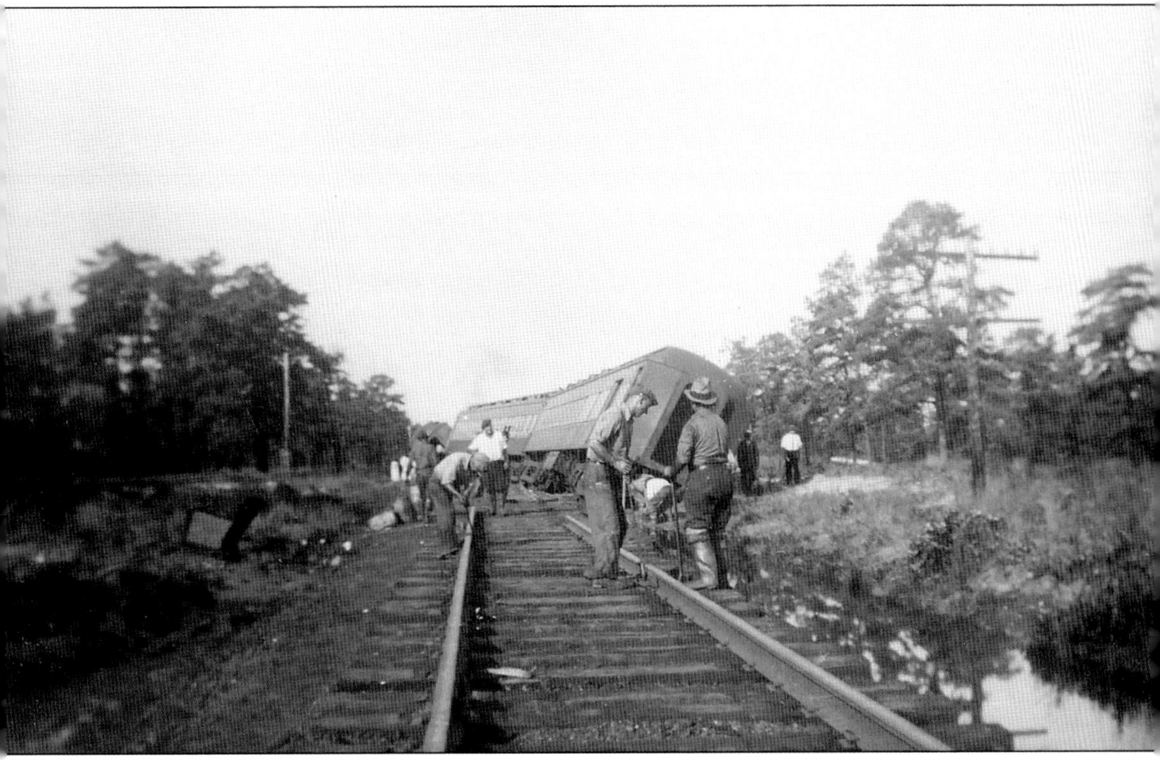

The Blue Comet was a special train that caught the interest and attention of people throughout South Jersey and beyond. People would drive to Chatsworth and park trackside to catch a glimpse of this magnificent train, which would pass at 70 miles an hour. Saturday, August 19, 1939, was an ill-fated day for the Blue Comet. Fifteen inches of rain with periodic cloudbursts fell, causing widespread flooding throughout the area. The train left Atlantic City a few minutes late that afternoon. John Thomas was the engineer, Anthony Cinque was the fireman, and Joseph Welch the conductor. When the train (No. 4218) reached Winslow Junction, about 19 miles west of Chatsworth, engineer Thomas received an order to proceed cautiously because of the heavy rains. He complied and reduced the train's speed to about 35 miles an hour. A mile west of the Chatsworth Station where the roadbed had washed away, the rear wheels of the engine's tender left the tracks at Milepost 86, and the five cars were scattered on the ground. (Photograph by Herbert and Edith Gerber; courtesy of Robert Gerber Jr.)

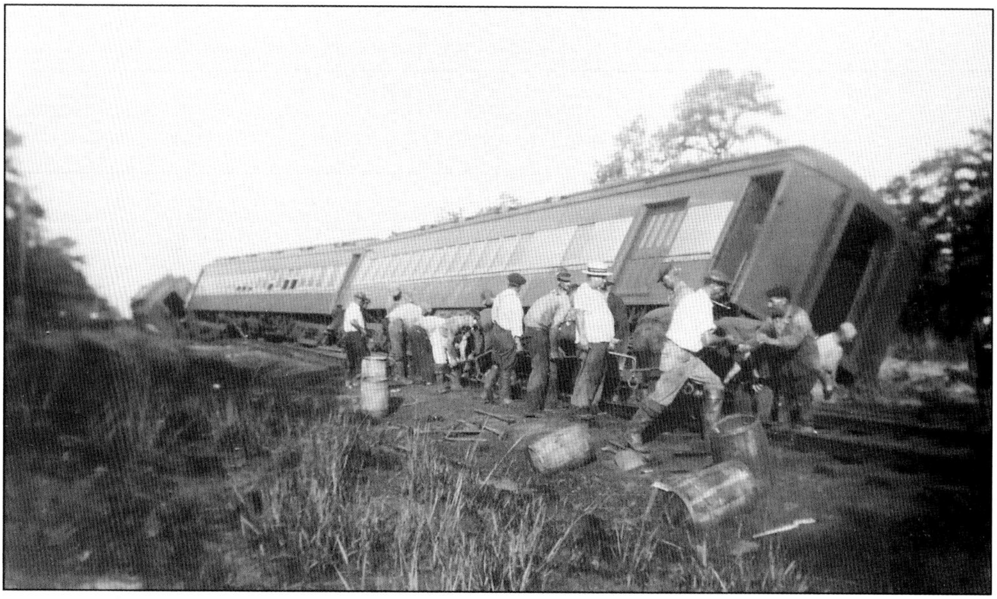

Citizens of Chatsworth, police, emergency squads, and medical personnel from Burlington County and South Jersey rushed to the scene to aid the passengers needing assistance. The wreck occurred in an area with no accessible roads, making it difficult for rescuers to reach the wreck. People walked along the tracks from Chatsworth to reach the scene of the derailment. The next morning, railroad work crews prepared the damaged track and five Blue Comet cars for removal. (Photograph by Herbert and Edith Gerber; courtesy of Robert Gerber Jr.)

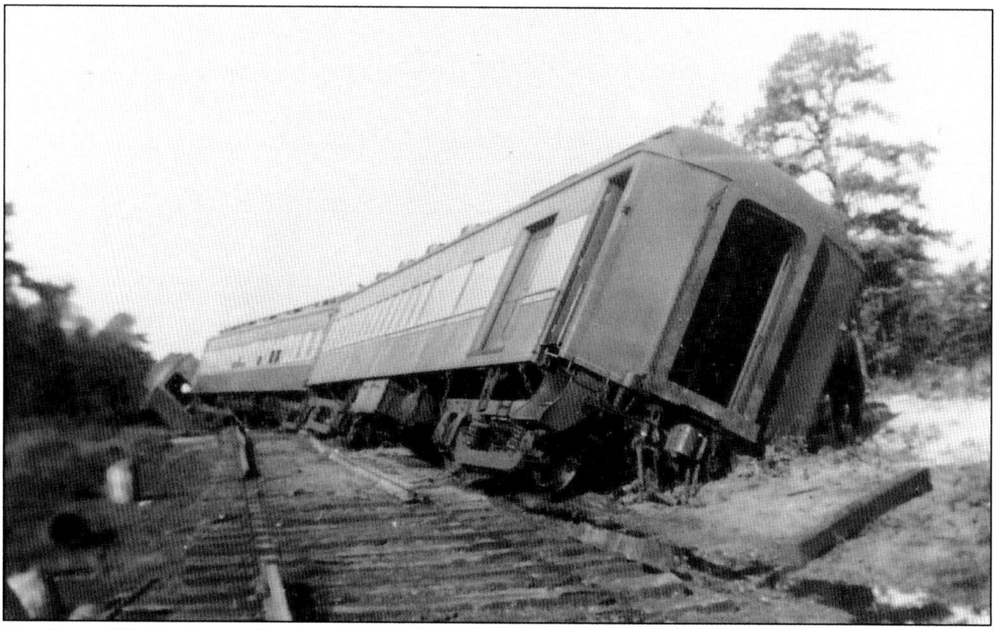

Combine "Halley" was the first car of the train. It is from this car of the speeding train that the daily newspapers were delivered to Chatsworth. The city had no newspapers until the Blue Comet began operation. The *Camden Courier* and the *Philadelphia Bulletin* were securely wrapped and pushed out of the car of the speeding train. Rarely were they ever damaged by the impact of hitting the ground. (Courtesy of Buzby collection.)

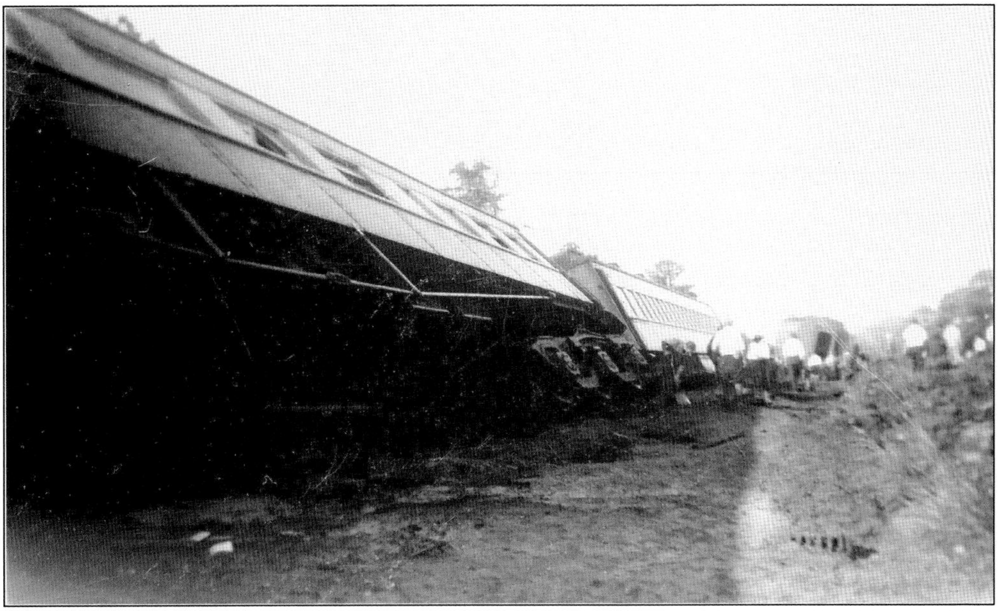

The dining car "Gracobini" seated about 35 persons and was known for its food and beauty. Blue was the dominant color in this well-designed car—blue carpeting, table linens, lights, china, and even glasses with a touch of blue. Waiters in white uniforms with blue accents served blue platter lunches for 75¢ and a full-course dinner, including appetizer, a choice of seafood, charcoal broiled steak or double lamb chops, and dessert for $1.25. (Photograph by Herbert and Edith Gerber; courtesy of Robert Gerber Jr.)

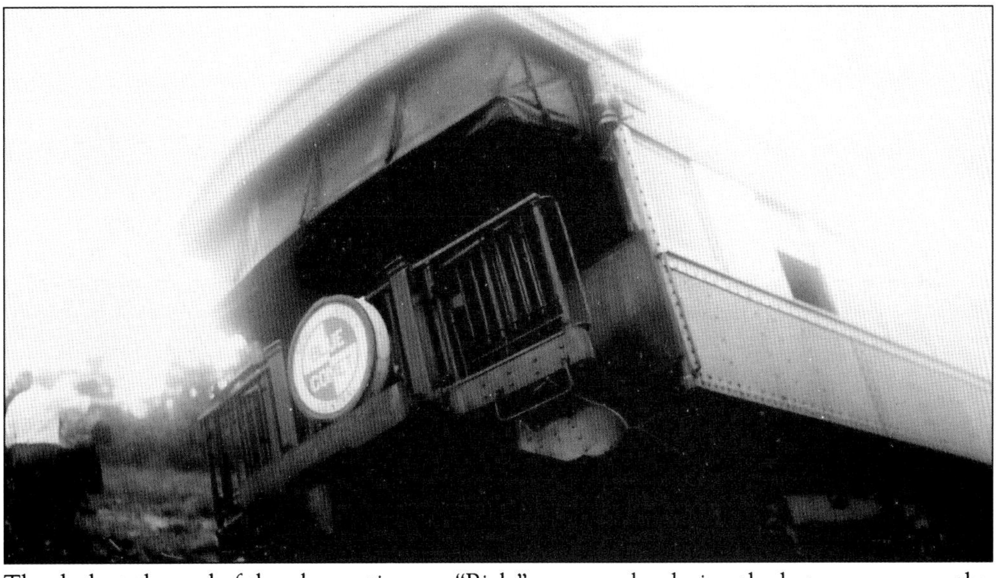

The deck at the end of the observation car "Biela" was popular during the hot summer months. Passengers were often seen sitting on the deck observing the beauty of the New Jersey Pinelands through which the train traveled from Winslow Junction to Lakehurst. The passengers would often wave to those local citizens who might be at the Chatsworth Station or located near the tracks. (Courtesy of Margie Wills Hall.)

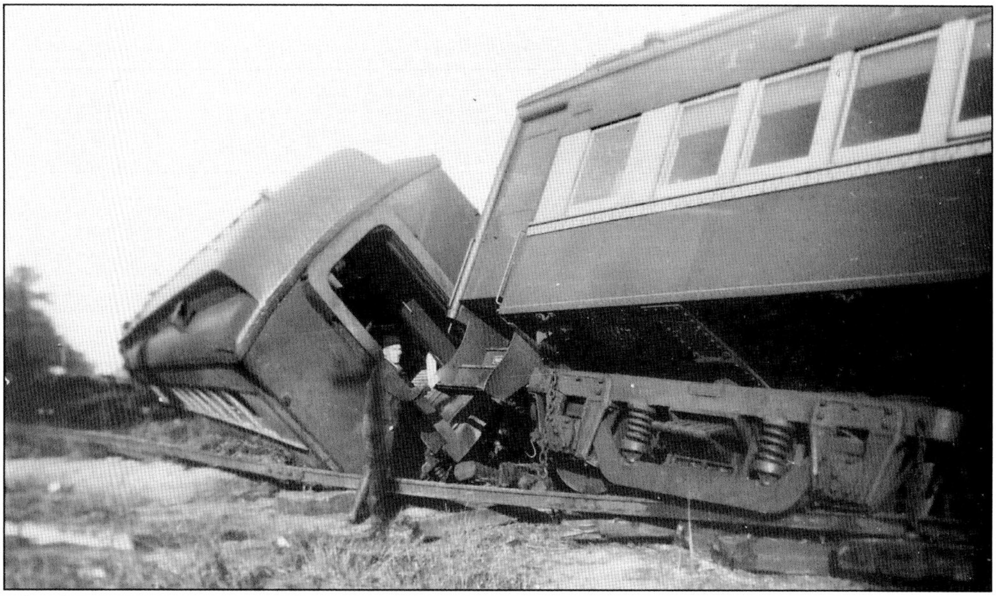

The five cars were painted blue and cream, and each was named for a comet—the combine "Halley," coach "D'Arrest," coach "Winnicke," the dining car "Gracobini," and the observation car "Biela." The observation car had comfortable wicker chairs placed along each side of the car that also had an outside deck platform with chairs. The carpeting and upholstery throughout the train featured the blue and cream pattern. (Photograph by Herbert and Edith Gerber; courtesy of Robert Gerber Jr.)

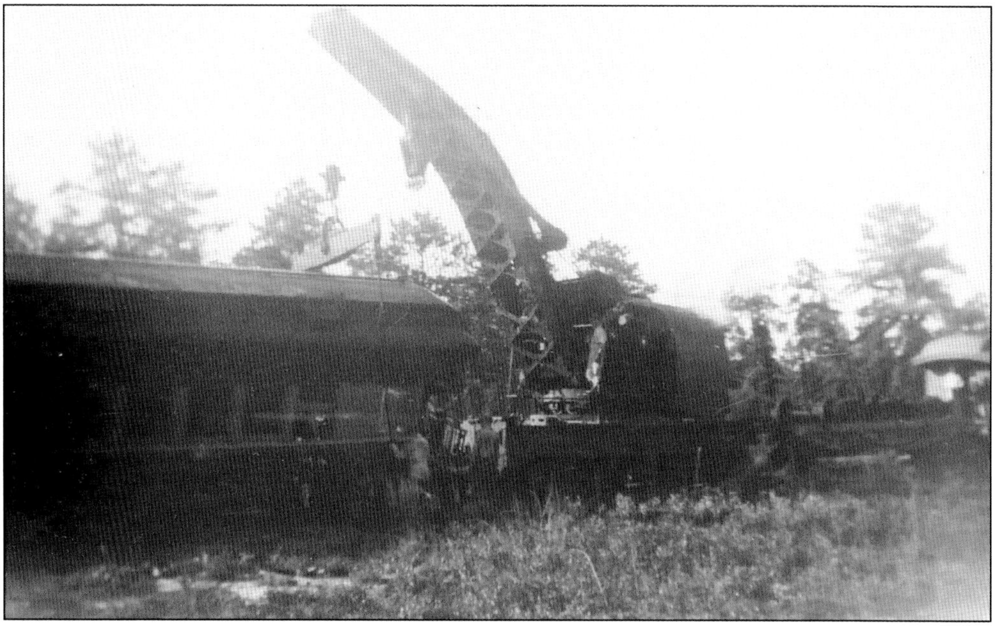

The local Chatsworth citizens marveled at the strength of the derrick used to lift the cars of the train and place them on the repaired roadbed. It was not unusual for members of the Chatsworth community to walk to the scene of the wreck to observe the hard work of the railroad crews in doing what was required to repair the tracks and lift the cars from their overturned positions. (Photograph by Herbert and Edith Gerber; courtesy of Robert Gerber Jr.)

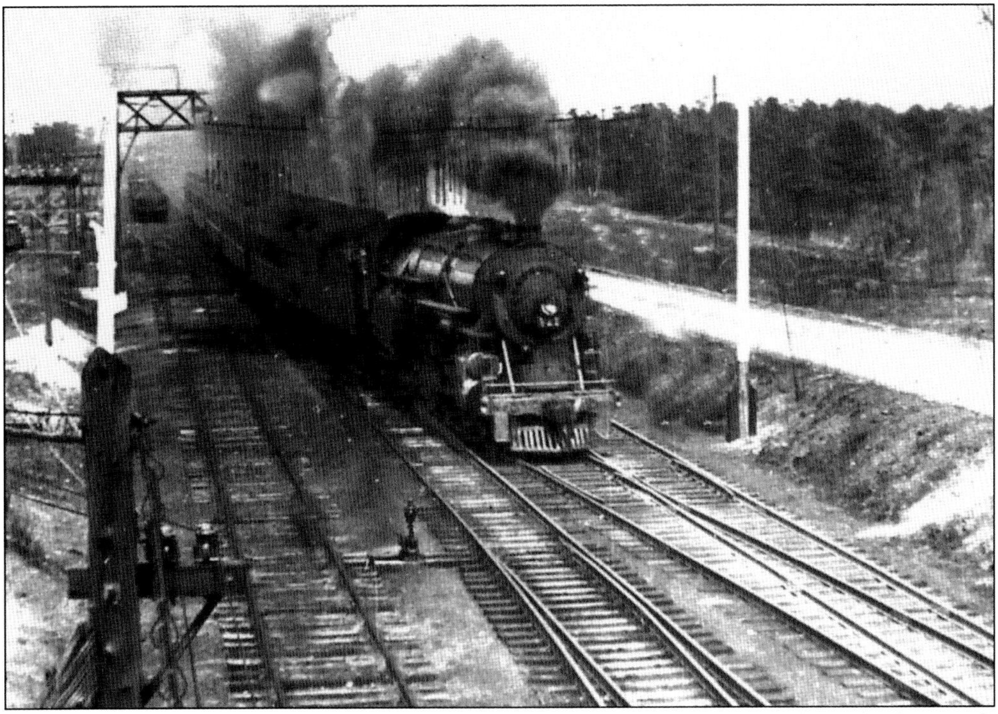

The Blue Comet (No. 4203) is shown arriving at Winslow Junction after passing through Chatsworth on April 25, 1940, on its way to Atlantic City. It is switching from the tracks of the Central Railroad of New Jersey to enter the tracks of the Pennsylvania-Reading Seashore Lines to proceed to Atlantic City. Pennsylvania-Reading Seashore Lines was created in 1933 by combining the Pennsylvania Railroad and Reading Railroad that served Atlantic City from Camden/Philadelphia. (Courtesy of Robert Kilpatrick family.)

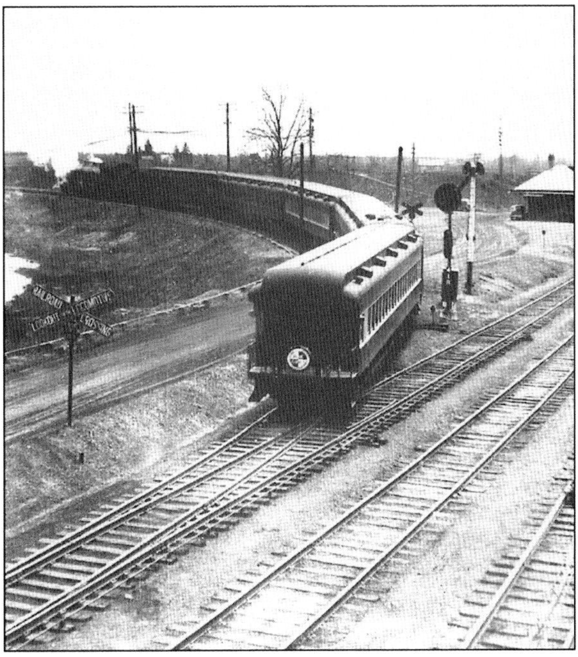

Only a few days passed and the Blue Comet was back in operation. It continued service until Saturday, September 27, 1941, when it made its last run. Although seven decades have passed since that derailment, residents of Chatsworth speak of their memories of the Blue Comet—its beauty, its speed, and all that it meant to have this unique and exclusive first-class passenger train pass their way each day. (Courtesy of Robert Kilpatrick family.)

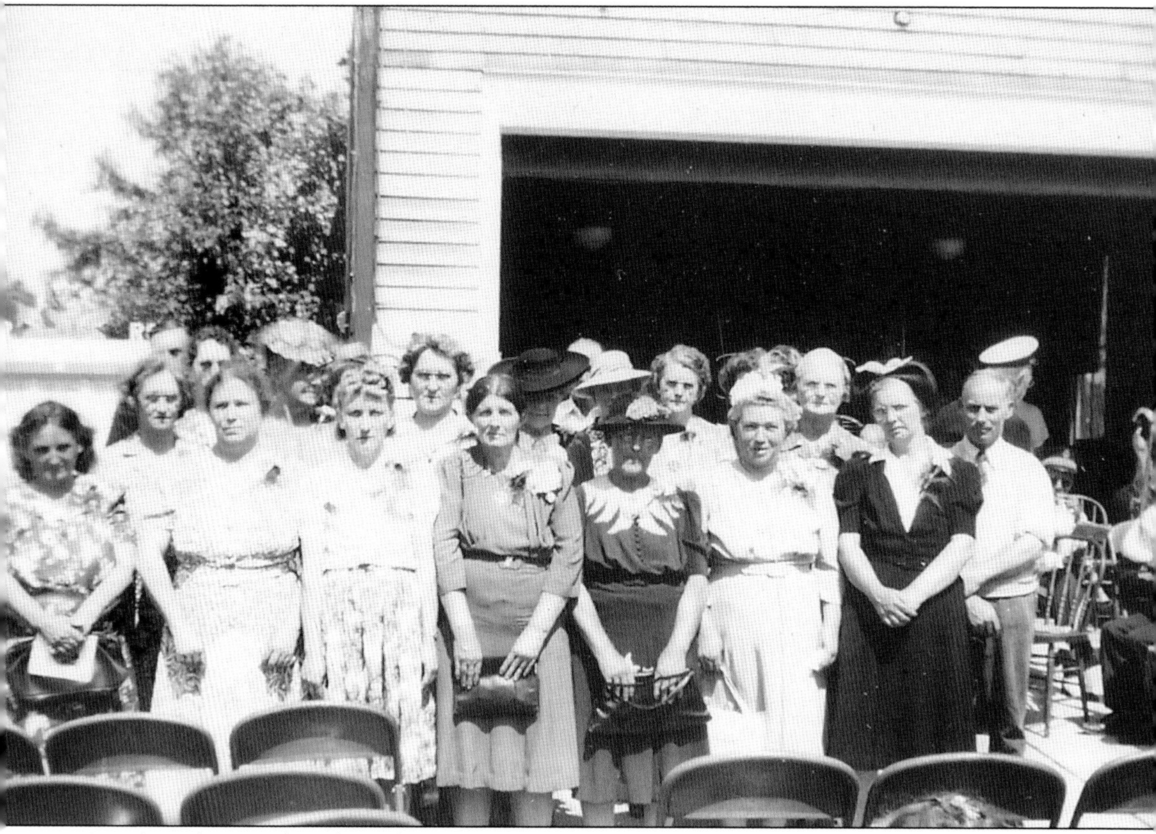

Local residents gathered Sunday afternoon, May 21, 1944, for the dedication of the honor roll bearing the names of servicemen from Chatsworth and throughout the township who were serving in the armed forces during World War II. The honor roll, made available by the Burlington County Highway Department, was unveiled by Lena Bates, the mother of Charles Bates, who died in service. The dedication ceremony, planned by Walter Brower Jr. and Helen Wills, brought together a grateful community to say thank you to those who had answered their country's call to military duty. (Courtesy of Walter A. Brower Jr.)

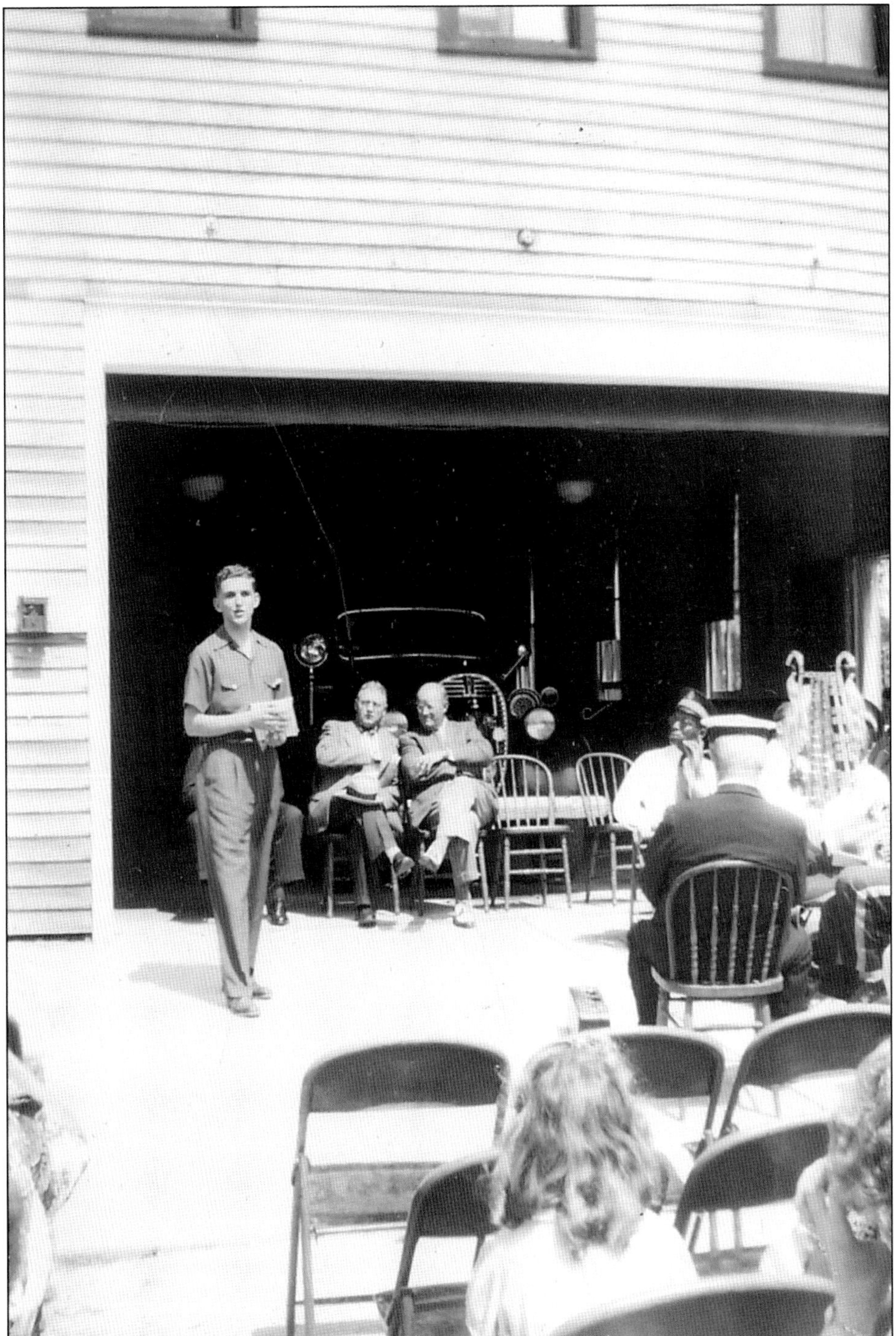

Walter Brower Jr. addresses the relatives and friends of 50 local citizens who served in the military service during World War II on May 21, 1944. Brower and Helen Wills planned the ceremony. A large plaque containing the names of the servicemen was unveiled by Lena Bates, whose son Charles died while serving in the U.S. Army. (Courtesy of Walter A. Brower Jr.)

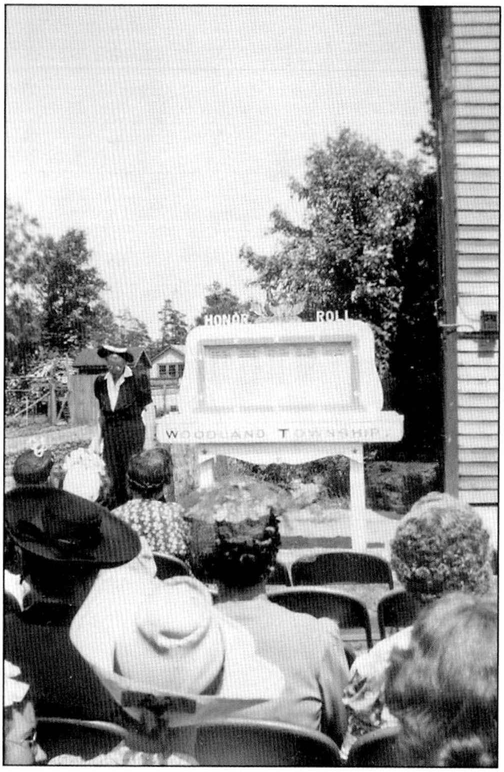

Lena Bates, the mother of Charles Bates, who died in action just one month prior to the dedication, unveiled the honor roll. Nearly the entire town turned out to witness the unveiling of the honor roll, and it remained as a reminder of all those who gave so unselfishly of themselves during World War II. (Courtesy of Walter A. Brower Jr.)

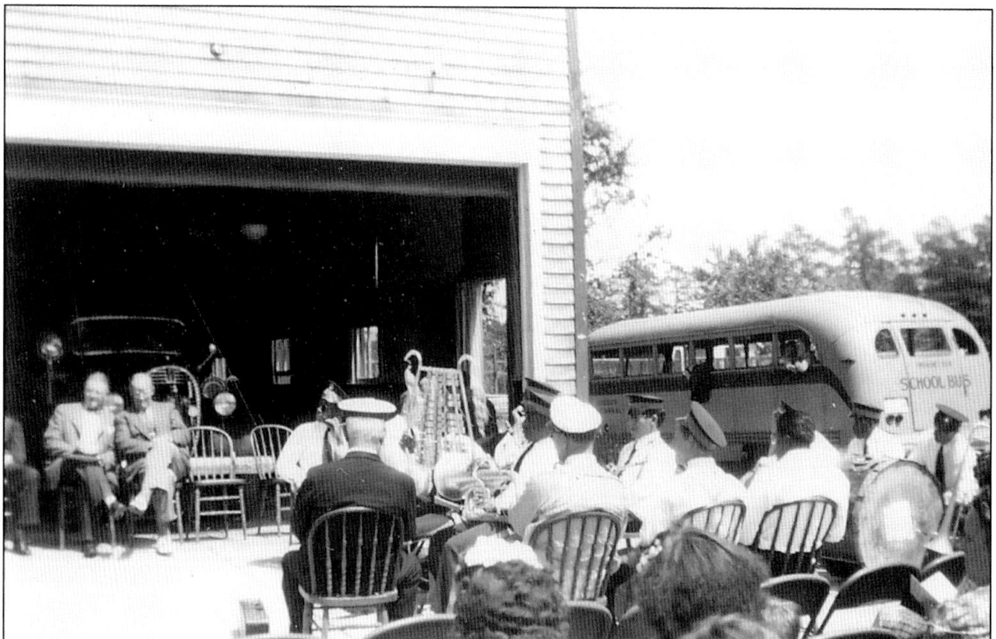

The New Jersey State Colony Band performed at the ceremony for dedication of the honor roll that was held at the firehouse on Main Street in Chatsworth on May 21, 1944. The ensemble offered up patriotic songs for all branches of the service, which were enjoyed by all. (Courtesy of Walter A. Brower Jr.)

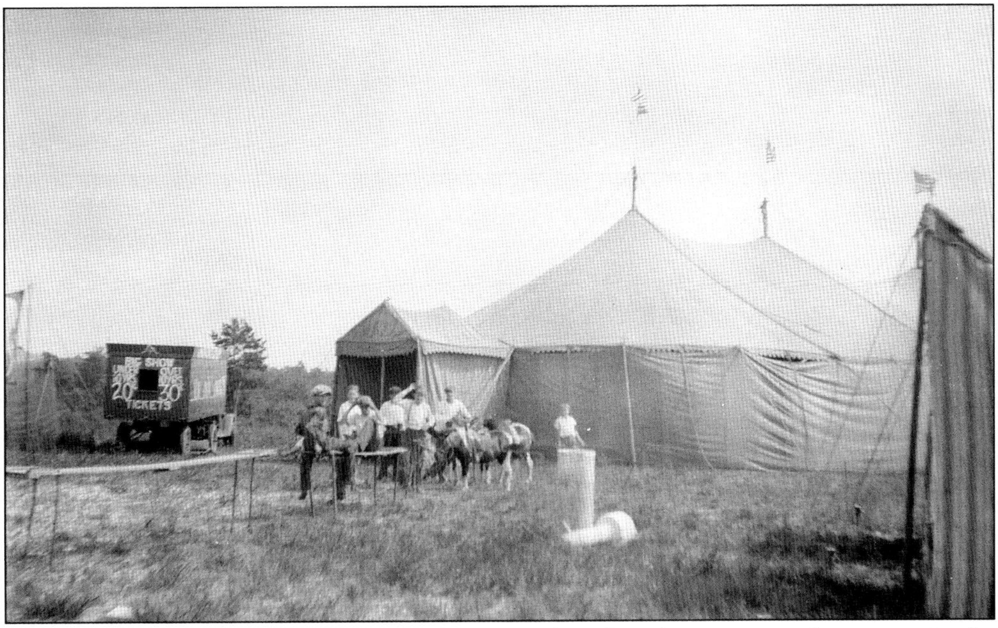

The circus came to town in 1935. It was an exciting day when the circus crew began to raise the big tent. Many of the town's children gathered at the Chatsworth School's playground to witness what was probably the only circus to find its way to the remote village. A few of the children helped to carry water from nearby homes for the horses. (Courtesy of Buzby collection.)

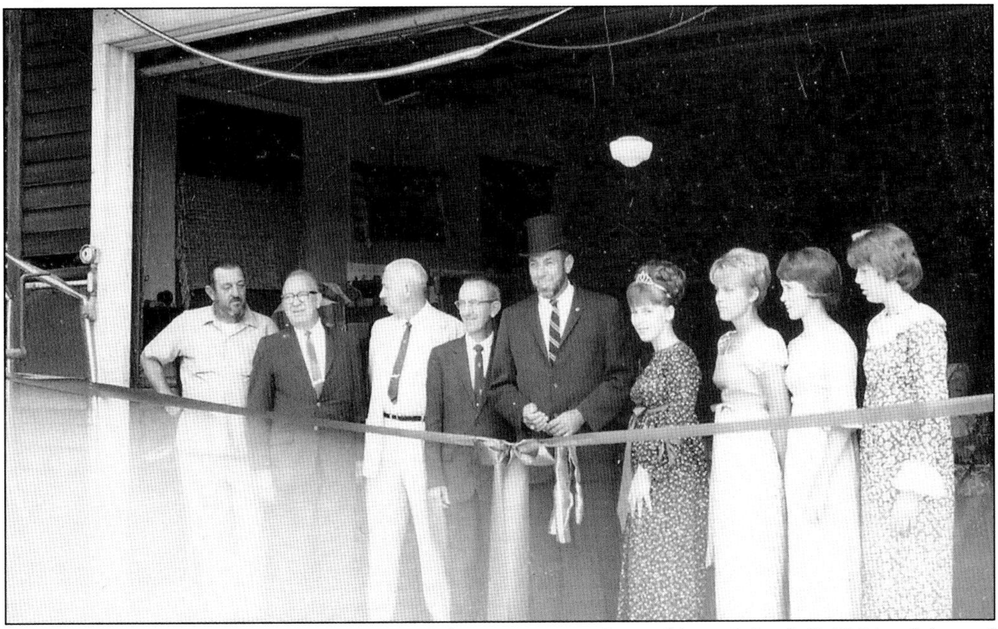

Woodland Township, created by an act of the New Jersey Assembly on March 7, 1866, celebrated its 100th anniversary on August 26–28, 1966, with three days of parades, luncheons, dinners, dances, an antique show, and special church services. Cutting the ribbon to signal the beginning of the festivities are, from left to right, Alfred "Junior" Stevenson, Eugene Minks, Francis Russell, Rev. William Stockton, Mayor Peter Brower, Linda Bowker, Cathy Dunfee, Sandy Dunfee, and Beth Brower. (Courtesy of William S. Haines Sr. family.)

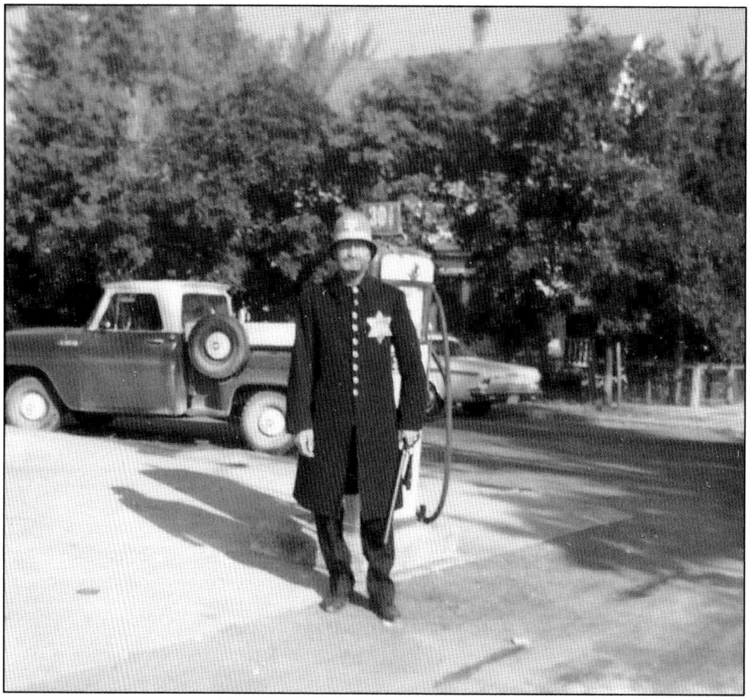

A proclamation was issued by the mayor decreeing that males will remain unshaven until the conclusion of the celebration. Tommy Anderson, the 1966 celebration "Constable" stands ready to make his first arrest of the first male who has not complied with the mayor's decree. (Note the gas tank showing that gasoline was 30.09¢ a gallon in 1966.) (Courtesy Margie Wills Hall.)

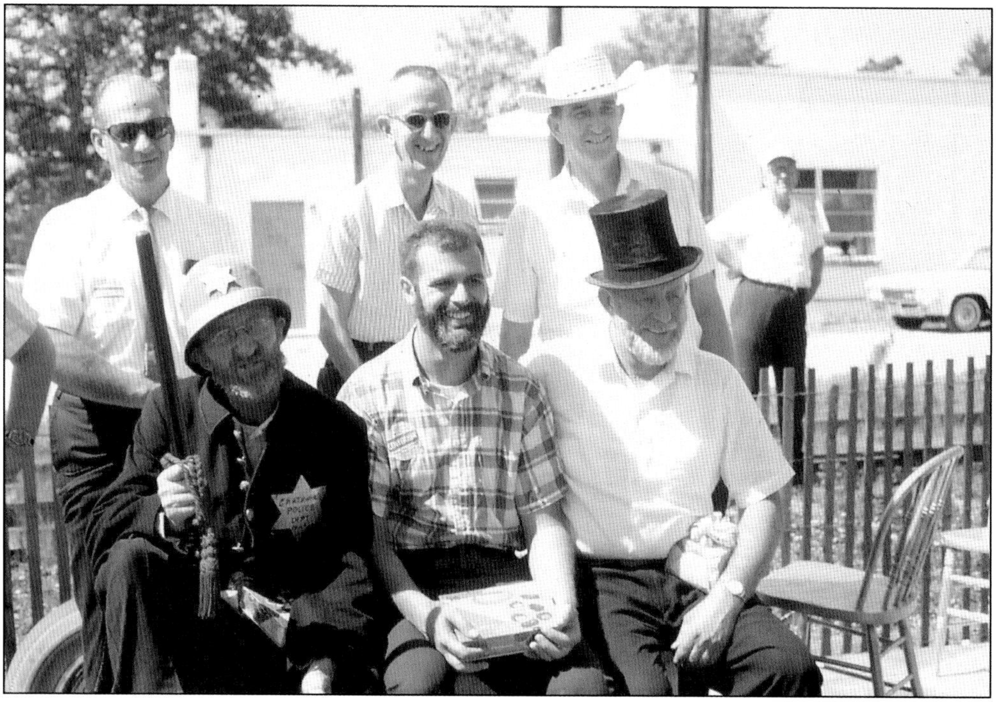

The beard-growing contest, part of the township's centennial celebration, sought to identify the best and the worst beard. The winners were, from left to right (first row) Tom Anderson, the worst beard; Al Morison, the second-best beard; and Richard Green, the best beard. The judges for the contest were (second row) Benjamin Ranalli, Rev. William Stockton, and freeholder Donald F. MacBride. (Courtesy of William S. Haines Sr. family.)

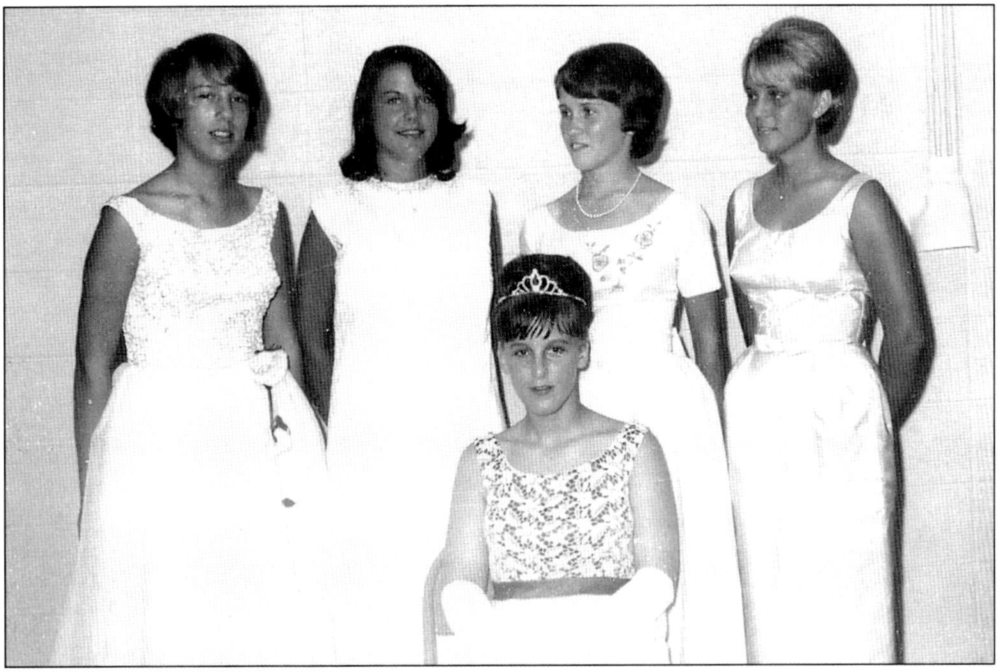

The judges for the queen of the centennial celebration had a difficult job before them. The contestants gather for a photograph shoot prior to the judging. They are, from left to right, (seated) Linda Bowker; (standing) Beth Brower, Patsy Estlow, Sandy Dunfee, and Cathy Dunfee. Linda Bowker was crowned Teen Queen. (Courtesy of Vera Topham.)

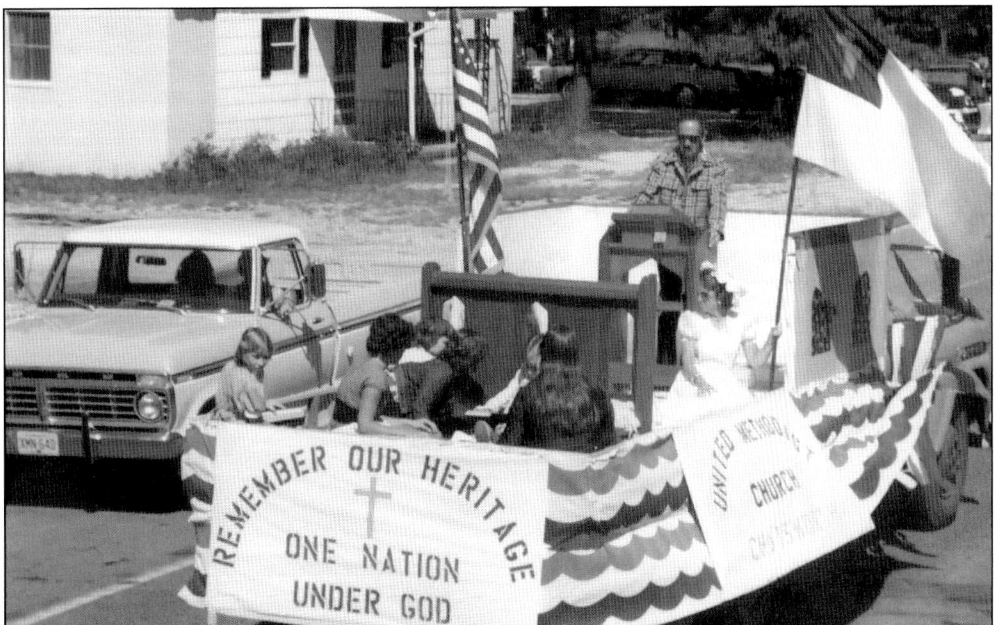

Rev. Raymond Carter, at the pulpit, and his wife, Betty, wearing a white ruffled cap, ride on the float of the United Methodist Church of Chatsworth during the 1966 centennial celebration. Open convertibles brought dignitaries from county government to participate in the parade that filled Main Street. (Courtesy of Vera Topham.)

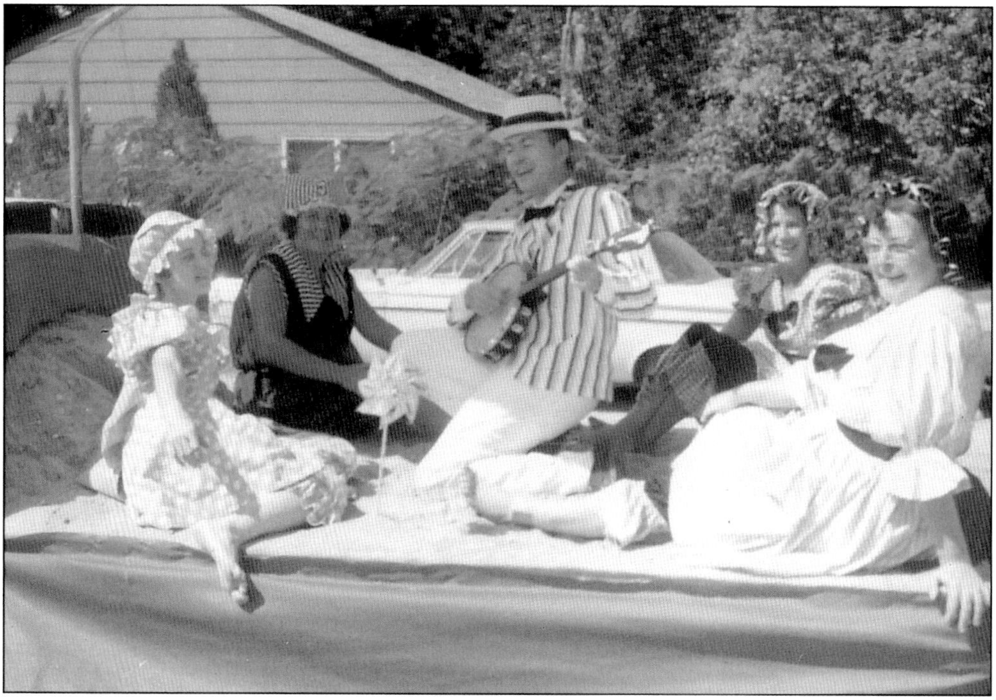

Four Chatsworth bathing beauties, decked out in their most daring swimming attire, enjoy the croons of banjo-strumming George Barringer during the centennial parade. They are, from left to right, Mae Barringer, Marcella Stevenson, centennial chairman Natalie Kennedy, and Ethel Brower. A good time was had by all. (Courtesy of Vera Topham.)

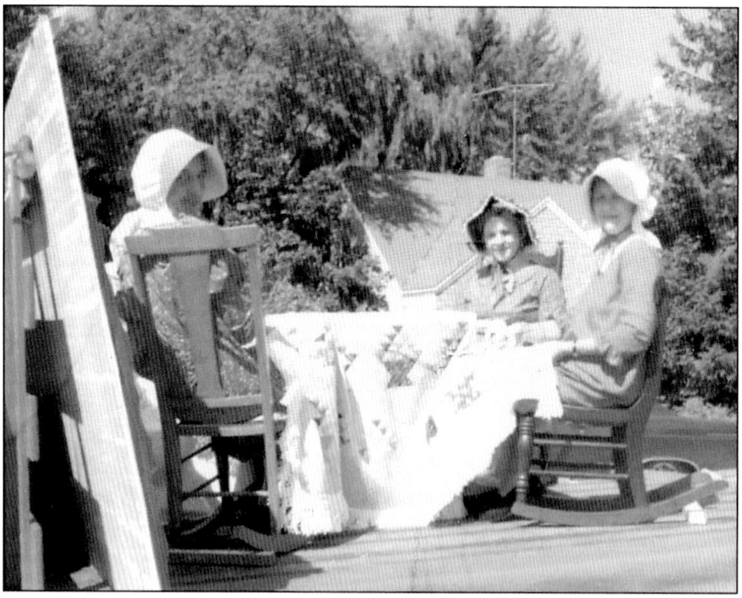

And here comes another float. Dressed in distinctive garb of the earlier years, the women of the Ladies Auxiliary of the Chatsworth Fire Company, Sylvia Sloan, Shirley Morison, and Vera Topham, depict a quilting bee typical of bygone days as they participate in the 1966 centennial parade. (Courtesy of Vera Topham.)

Riding through town with Mayor Peter Brower in a flashy automobile operated by Vinnie Henrich are Bertha Dunfee, the oldest citizen, and Sarah Applegate, who was 81 years young. The weather seems to be cooperating, and there are smiles on every face. (Courtesy of Frank Applegate family.)

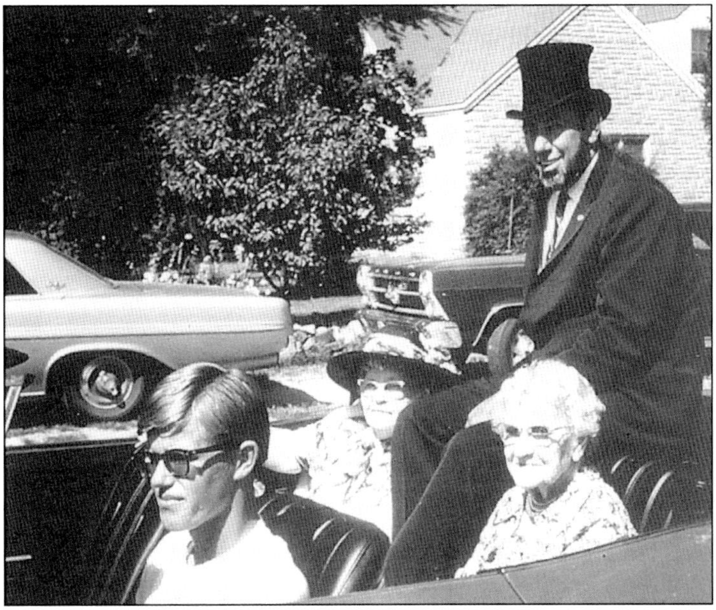

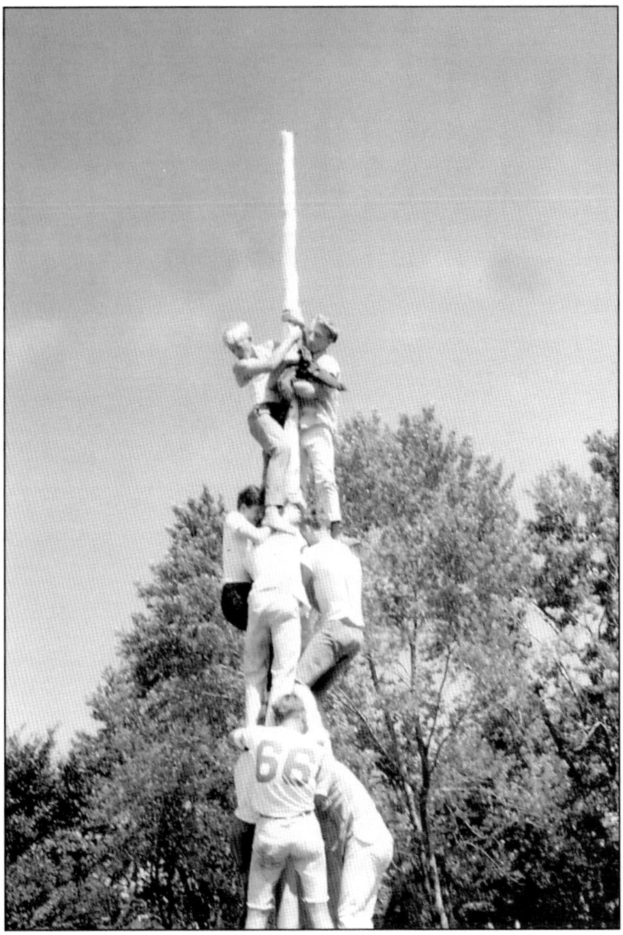

After several of his buddies failed to climb all the way up the pole to get the $20 bill at the top, Al Henrich, with the help of several of his friends, successfully reaches the summit and wins the prize. The event was part of the township's centennial festivities. (Courtesy of William S. Haines Sr. family.)

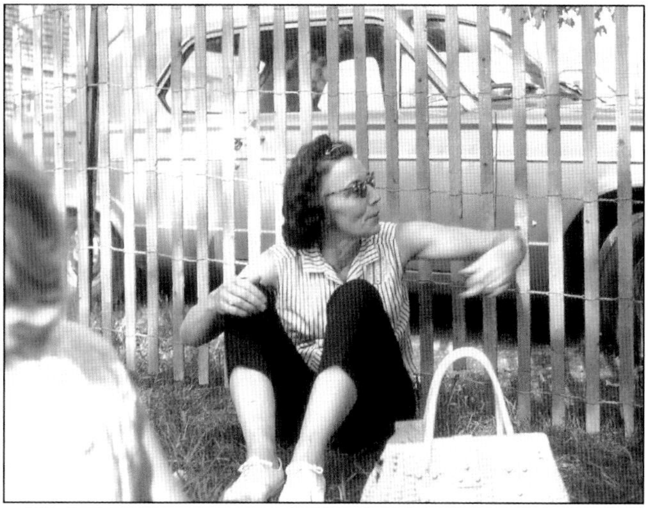

Sally Haines (Mrs. William S. Haines Sr.) appears to be enjoying herself at the 1966 centennial celebration parade. A prominent citizen in Burlington County, Sally Haines and her husband were longtime cranberry growers in the Chatsworth area. Today William S. Haines Jr. oversees the cranberry operation that is known as Pine Island Cranberry Company, Inc. (Courtesy of William S. Haines Sr. family.)

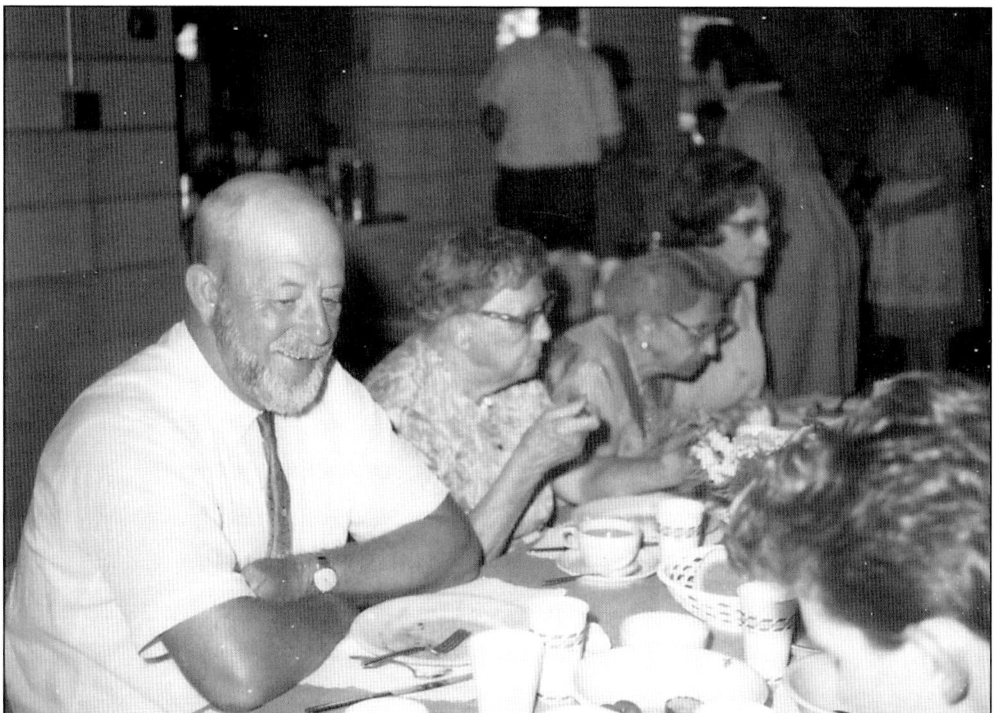

An important part of the centennial festivities was the plentiful food that was available to all. Shown in this photograph taken in the firehouse are Richard "Ty" Green, Martha Stevenson, Ella Hewitt, and Margaret "Peg" Kerchner, who are enjoying the meal together. After the meal of barbequed chicken, a dance was held in the firehouse. (Courtesy of Vera Topham.)

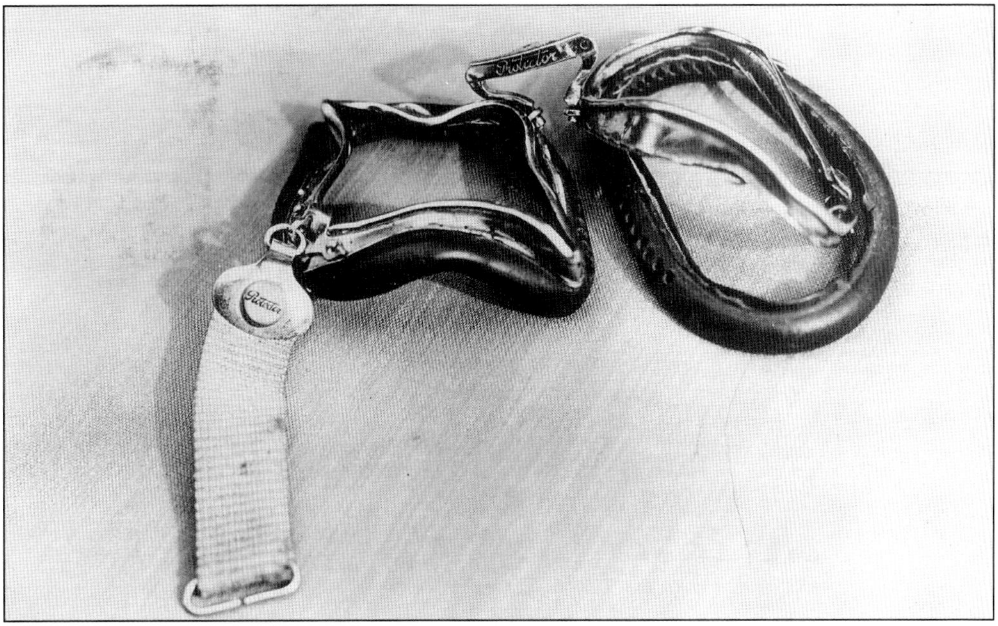

Capt. Emilio Carranza, a Mexican aviator, made a goodwill flight to the United States in 1928. The 23-year-old pilot left Roosevelt Field in New York to return to Mexico on the evening of July 12 and encountered severe electrical storms that caused him to crash in the heavily wooded area known as Sandy Ridge, near the village of Tabernacle. Chatsworth resident John Henry Carr discovered the plane's wreckage and Carranza's body on July 13, 1928. This picture shows Carranza's flight goggles, which were found at the scene of the crash. (Courtesy of Buzby collection.)

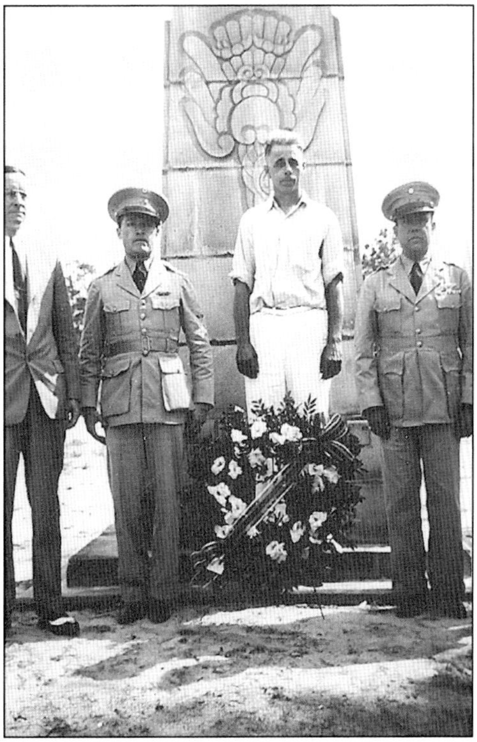

Pictured with representatives of the Mexican embassy at the Carranza Monument in the New Jersey Pine Barrens in July 1942 is John Henry Carr (in all white) of Chatsworth. In recognition of his service in finding the body of Capt. Emilio Carranza, Carr was given a check for $500 by the Republic of Mexico on July 18, 1928. (Courtesy of Amelia Green collection.)

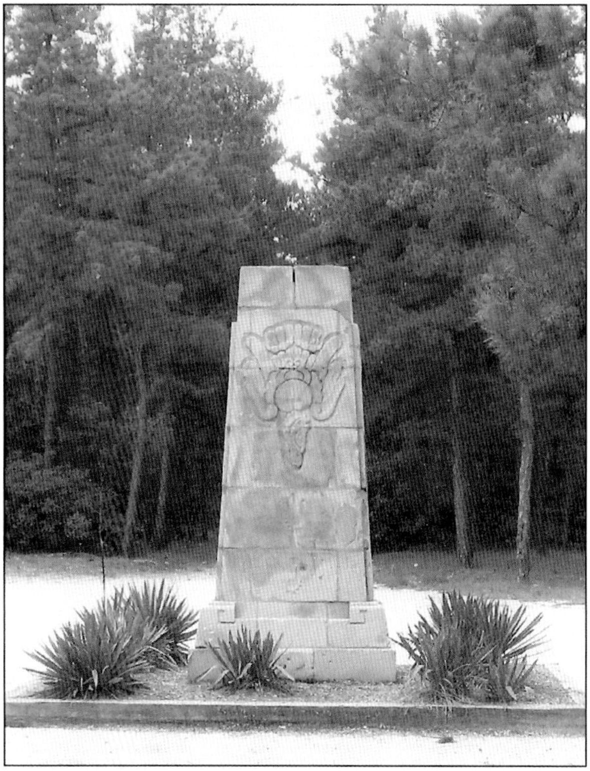

Pictured is the monument erected in the early 1930s at the site of Captain Carranza's plane crash. The monument, made possible by Mexican children saving pennies, is 12 feet high and made of limestone. An Aztec falling eagle stands out in relief on one side, and Spanish words are on the other. The historical marker was placed at the site by the Tabernacle Historical Society. Through the years, the American Legion Post 11 in Mount Holly has held an impressive memorial service in July at the site of the crash. There have been as few as two people at the service and as many as 2,000. Dignitaries from Mexico and family members of the aviator attend the service each year, as well as local and state police, politicians, U.S. armed forces, civil air patrol, and dozens of American Legion posts. (Both, courtesy of Walter A. Brower Jr.)

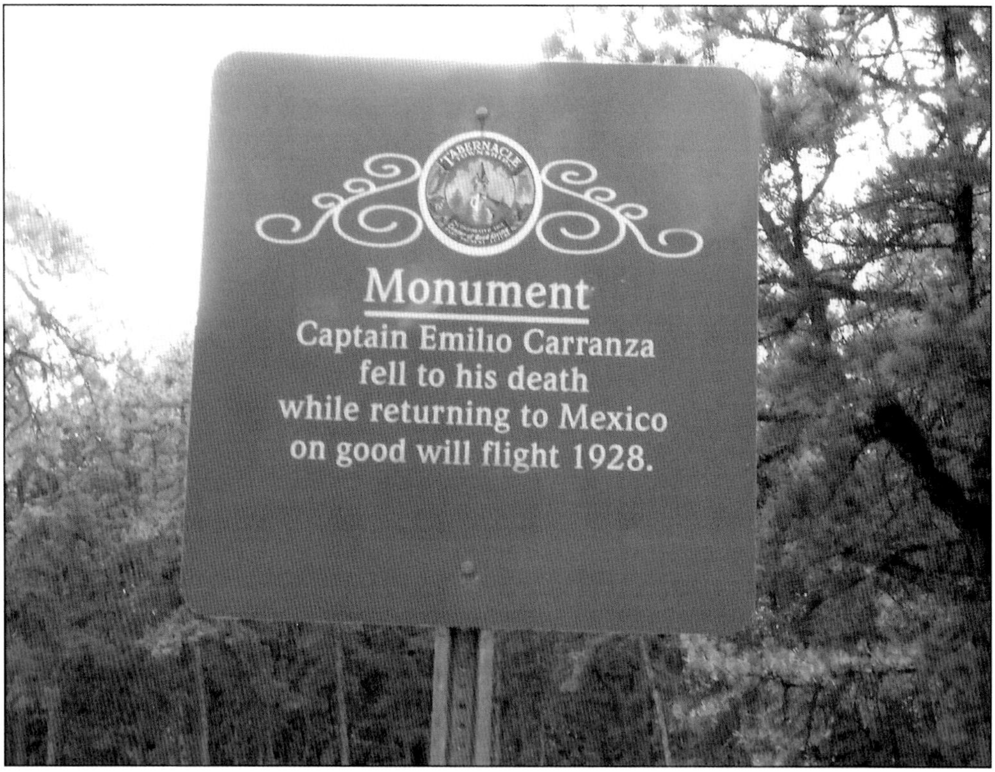

Six

Fire and Police Protection

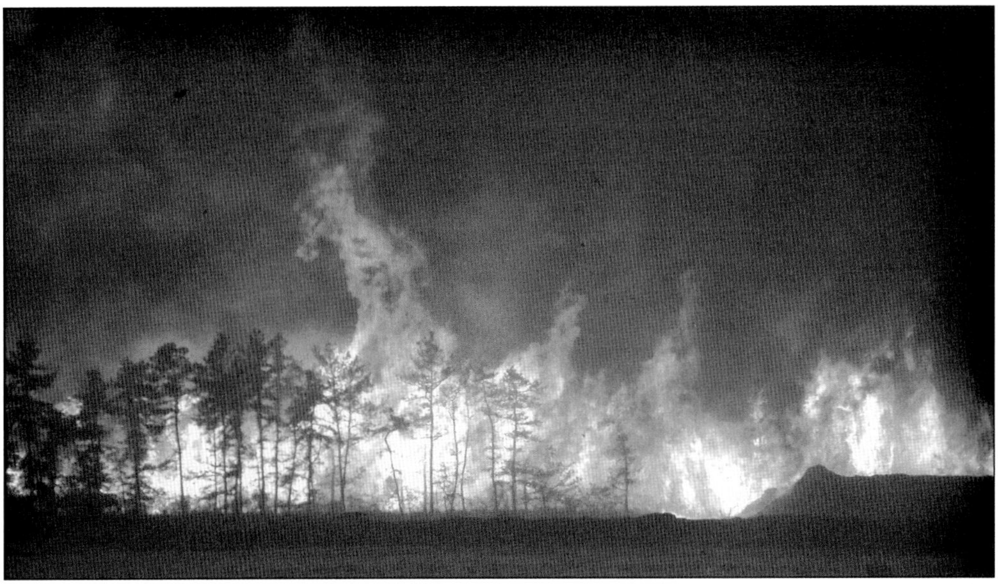

The local citizens of Woodland Township quickly learned that fires were quite common in the Pine Barrens. Whether caused by lightning in the dry forest, by sparks from the engine of a passing railroad steam engine, by the carelessness of a motorist having discarded a lighted cigarette, or an improperly extinguished campfire, fires were frequent, especially in the hot summer months. (Courtesy of New Jersey Forest Fire Service.)

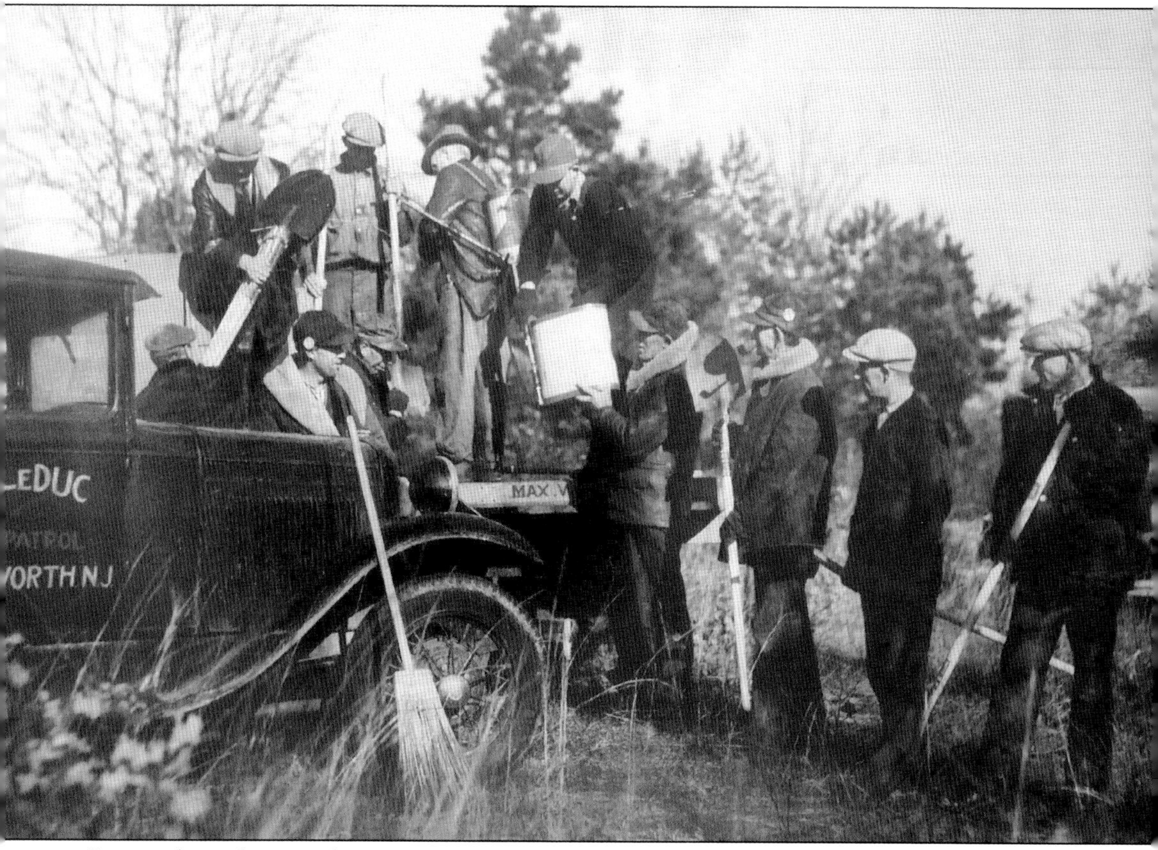

During the early years there was no organization responsible for fighting fires. When a fire was detected, every able-bodied male would—with shovels, rakes, brooms, and buckets—attempt to extinguish the fire. Sand was often used to smother the fire. It was not until 1899 that Gifford Pinchot, a consultant to the state geologist, initiated discussions concerning the need to control forest fires in New Jersey. As a result of his efforts, the New Jersey Legislature enacted a law in 1906 establishing the forest fire service. Now over 100 years old, the forest fire service continues to perform an important role in the life of the citizens of the New Jersey Pines. These early firefighters are identified as follows: (first row, sitting on truck) three unidentified; (second row, standing on truck) Vince Pepper, Ed Brower, Jack Ritzendollar, and unidentified; (third row, standing on ground) unidentified, Sam Leek, Raymond Leek, Bill Anderson, Jess Messler, and Jim Sloan. (Courtesy of Stan Fayer.)

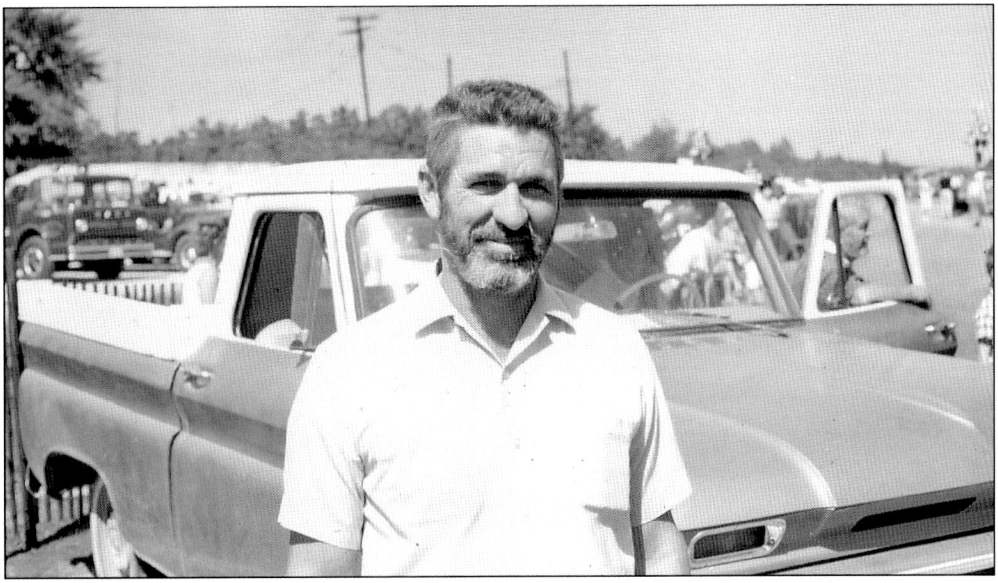

William "Billy" Sloan, a local cranberry and blueberry grower, served as a Section 2 fire warden with the New Jersey Forest Fire Service. This photograph was taken at the Chatsworth Centennial Celebration in 1966. The Sloan family lived in Chatsworth for many generations. (Courtesy of William S. Haines Sr. family.)

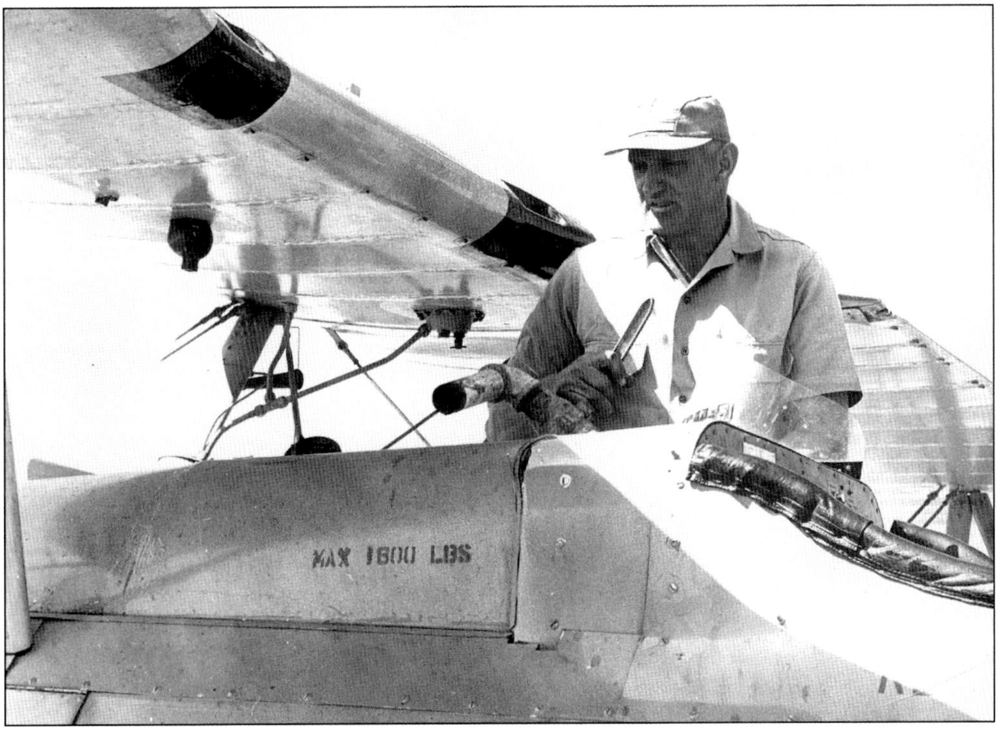

Irving "Diz" Mantell, a local resident, served as a section warden with the New Jersey Forest Fire Service. He is shown filling the tanks of a biplane with the chemical used to extinguish forest fires. The plane would fly over the fire and release the chemical on the fire below. (Courtesy of Stan and Maureen Worrell.)

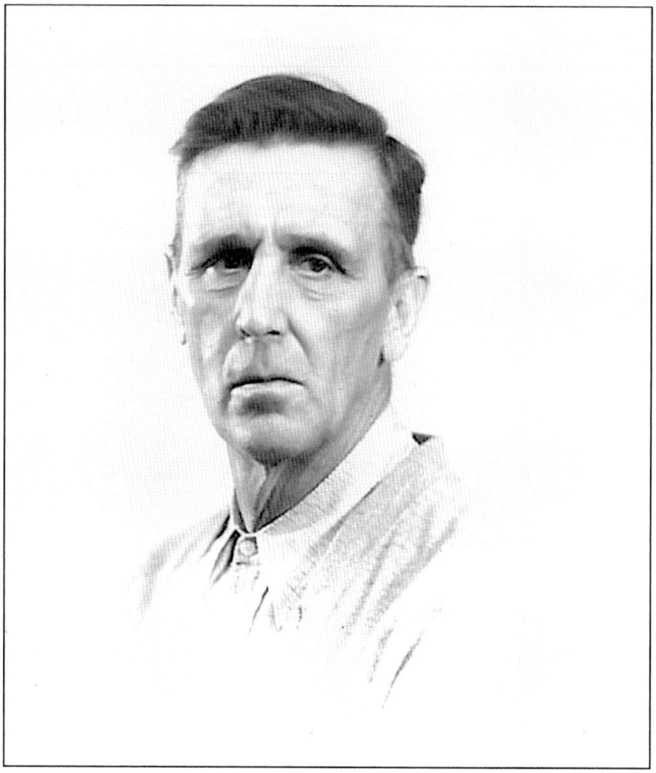

Joseph Holloway, a prominent local citizen, was a seasonal section warden for the forest fire service in the 1930s, in addition to his work for the Wharton Estate. He later worked for the A. R. DeMarco Cranberry Company. He and his family had resided in the area for over half a century. (Courtesy of Sooy family.)

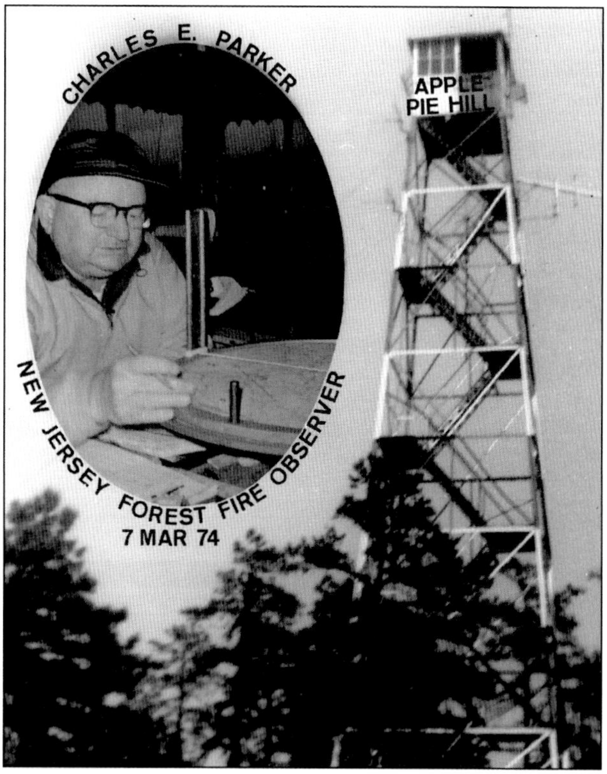

Charles "Eddie" Parker was a New Jersey forest fire observer. He could be found in the Apple Pie Hill tower during fire season. It was said that he could spot and pinpoint the site of a fire within several feet of its actual location. He also owned Parker's Bar and Gas Station on Route 40 (now Route 72). (Courtesy of Edward Kaufholz.)

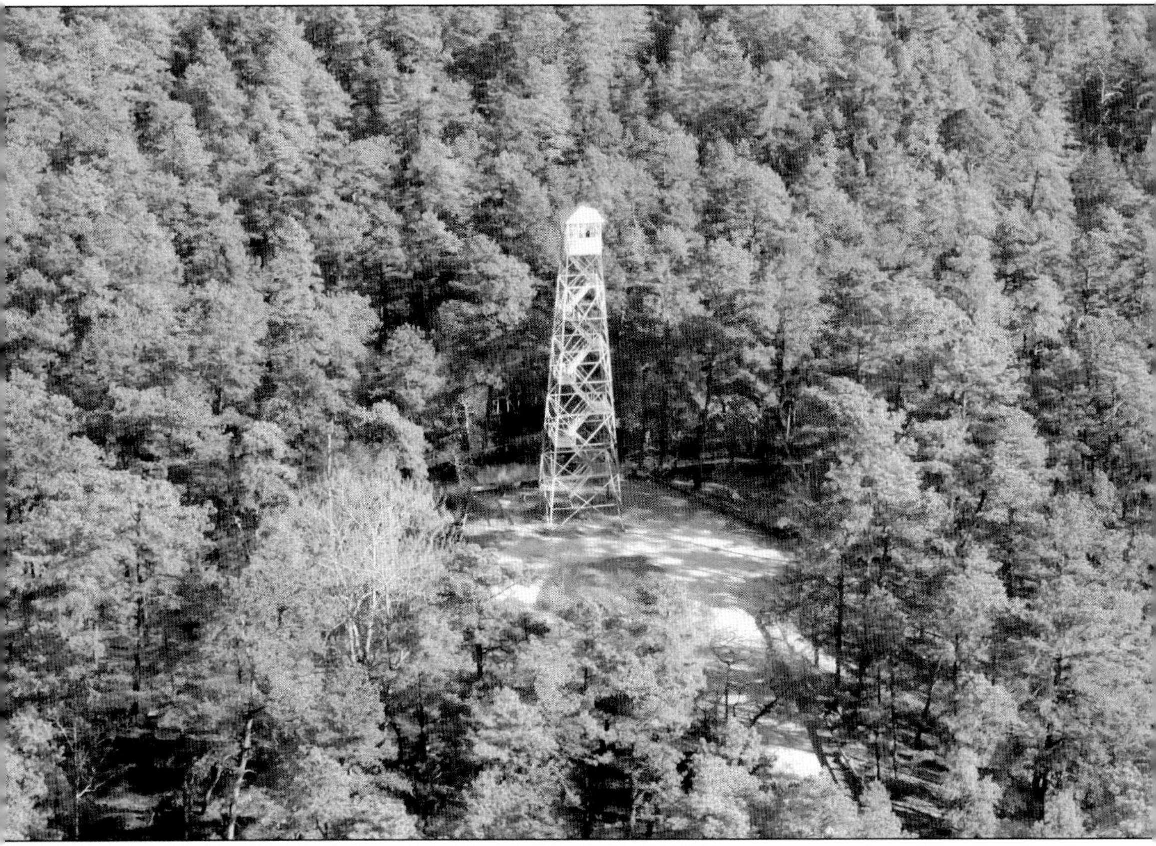

Located a short distance from Chatsworth is Apple Pie Hill, at a point where Woodland and Tabernacle Townships meet. Known as the highest elevation in the New Jersey Pinelands and in Southern New Jersey, its elevation, 210 feet above sea level, lends itself perfectly for the location of a lookout tower for the New Jersey Forest Fire Service. The tower, one of many in the state, is manned by personnel who search for miles around to discover fires in their early stages. Through the years, the Apple Pie Hill tower has been a vital component of the firefighting arsenal of weapons to end forest fires before they can inflict severe damage to the pinelands, to settlements, and to people in that area of the state. Apple Pie Hill has been known by that name since the early 1800s. A prominent New York physician built a home and a sanatorium at that location. (Courtesy of Stan Fayer.)

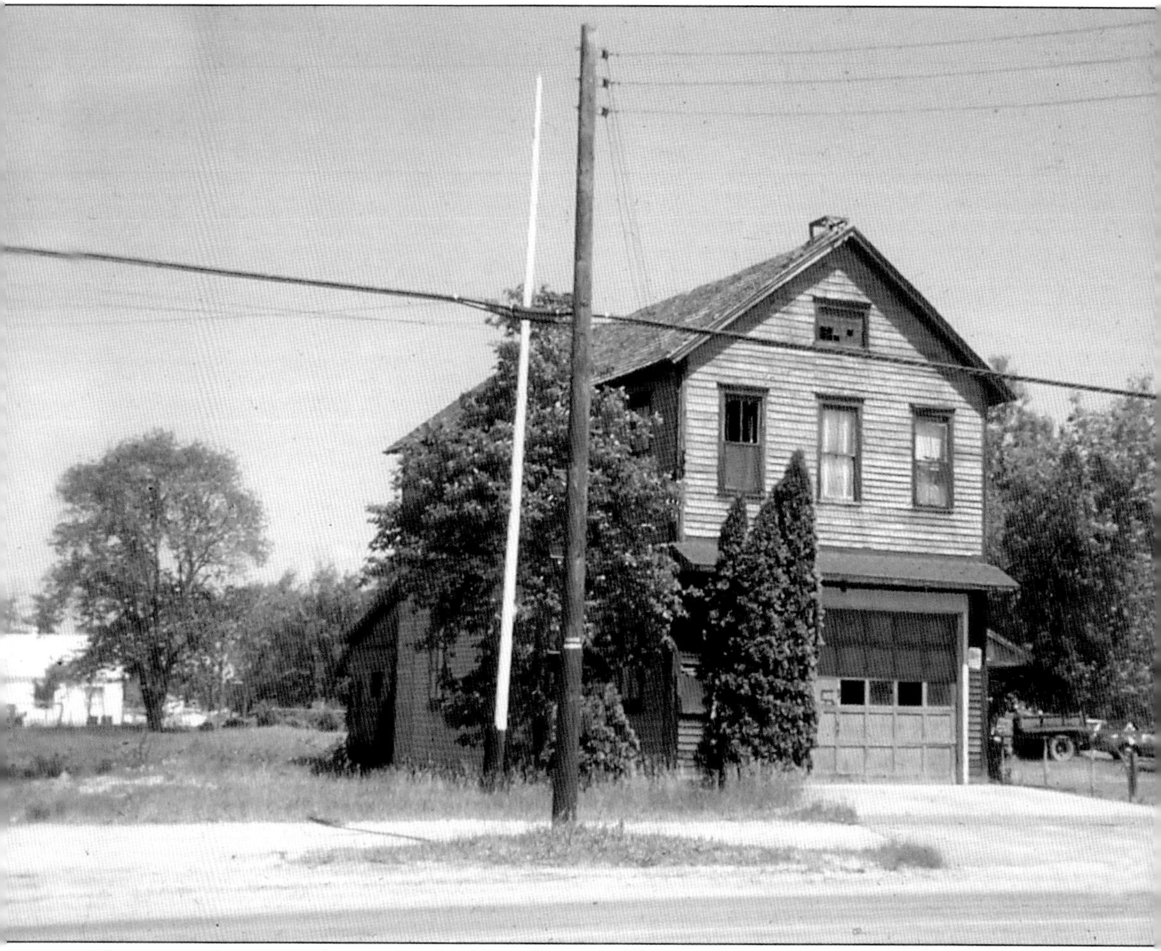

The original municipal township building (town hall) on Main Street was constructed early in the 1900s. While used for municipal offices and meetings, it also became a "Community Center" where dances were held. By the 1930s, movies were periodically shown on a Friday or Saturday night by a traveling entrepreneur who brought the movies to small towns. Those in attendance, mostly children, paid 5¢ and sat on wooden benches. The operator of the movies would have to stop to change reels throughout the showing. In the late 1930s, the building became the home for the first Chatsworth Fire Company. It was demolished in the 1970s. (Courtesy of Walter A. Brower Jr.)

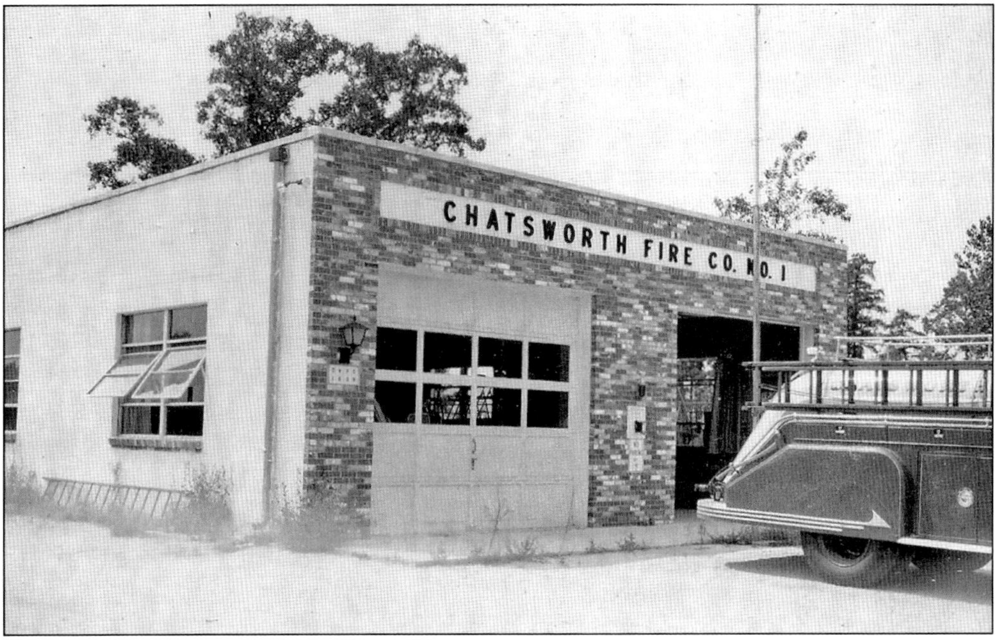

The Chatsworth Fire Company No. 1 is shown here on the occasion of the Centennial Anniversary of Chatsworth in 1966. The fire company was organized in April 1939. Harold Stevenson was elected president, and William Stewart was named chief. The original trustees of the fire company were Otto Katt, Harold Stevenson, William Stewart, Frances Estlow, and Walter Brower Sr. Twenty-five men from the local area joined the company. A 500-gallon pumping apparatus was made available to the fire company through the forest fire service. It was a forward step for the community, which never before had its own volunteer fire protection. (Courtesy of Vera Topham.)

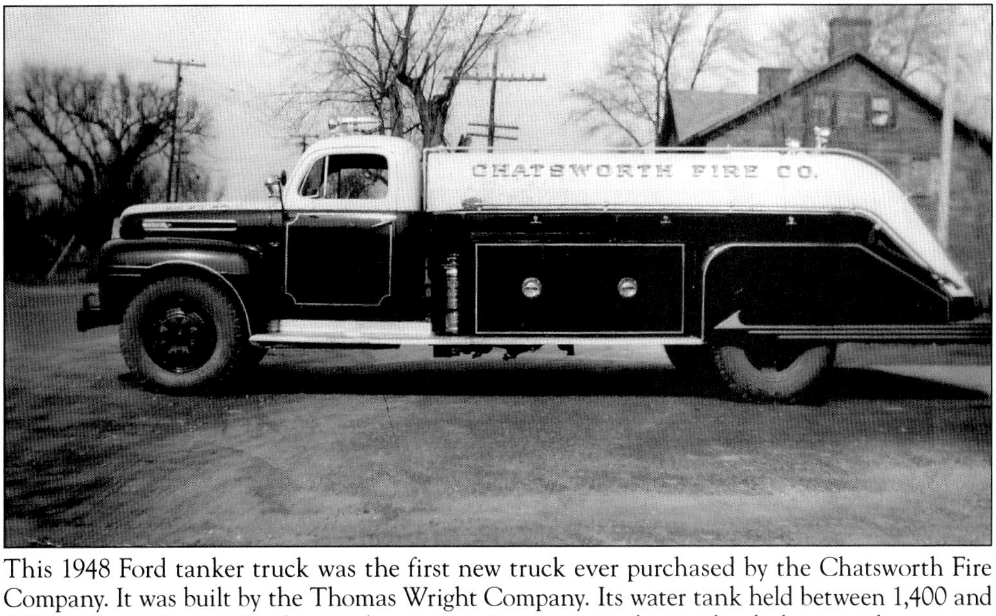

This 1948 Ford tanker truck was the first new truck ever purchased by the Chatsworth Fire Company. It was built by the Thomas Wright Company. Its water tank held between 1,400 and 1,600 gallons of water. Tanker trucks are very important in the pinelands, because there are no fire hydrants from which to obtain water. This truck was replaced in the 1970s by a used truck. (Courtesy of Charles Applegate collection.)

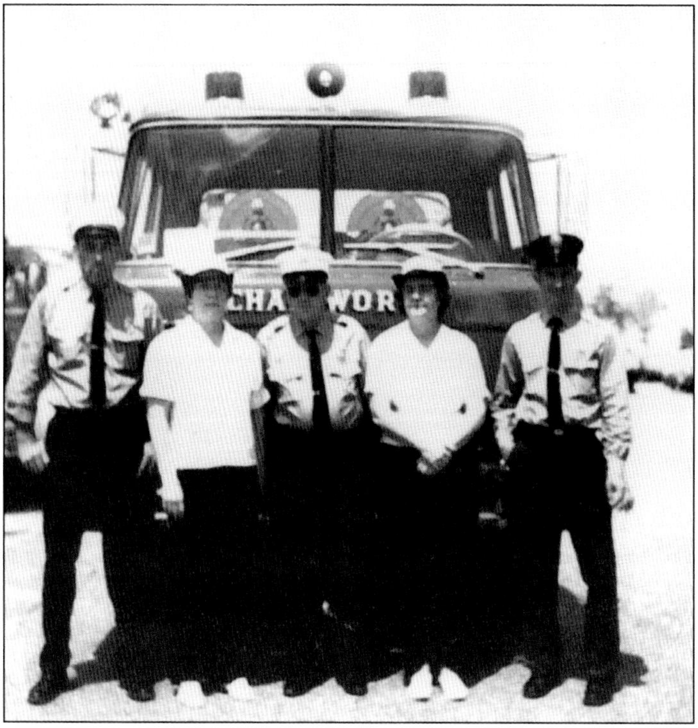

Buddy Leek, Marcella Stevenson, Fred Kennedy, Natalie Kennedy, and Herbie Wickward (left to right), representatives of the Chatsworth Fire Company and Ladies Auxiliary pause for this 1970 photograph taken with the fire truck in the background. Their dedicated service to the community remains as an example of the service rendered today by those who follow in their footsteps. (Courtesy of Kennedy family.)

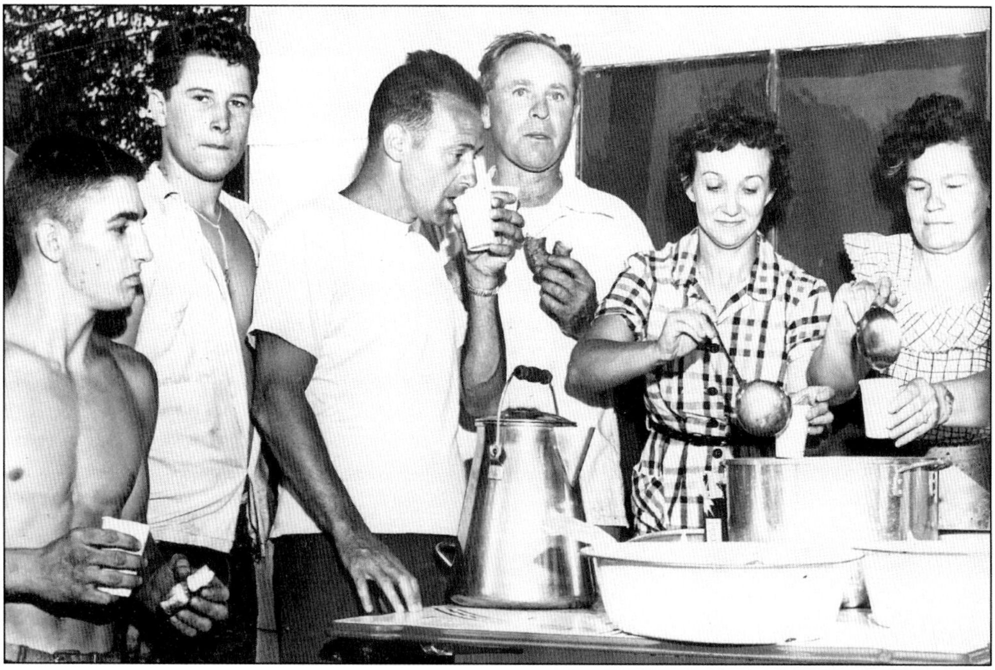

Albert Ranalli, Billy Miller, an unidentified man drinking, and Daniel Tice are local residents being served refreshments by Grace Brower Donnelly and Kathryn Stevenson Estlow. They are on the porch of the former Chatsworth Post Office on Main Street on the day of the July 1954 forest fire that surrounded Chatsworth but was extinguished by a rainstorm. (Courtesy of Walter A. Brower Jr.)

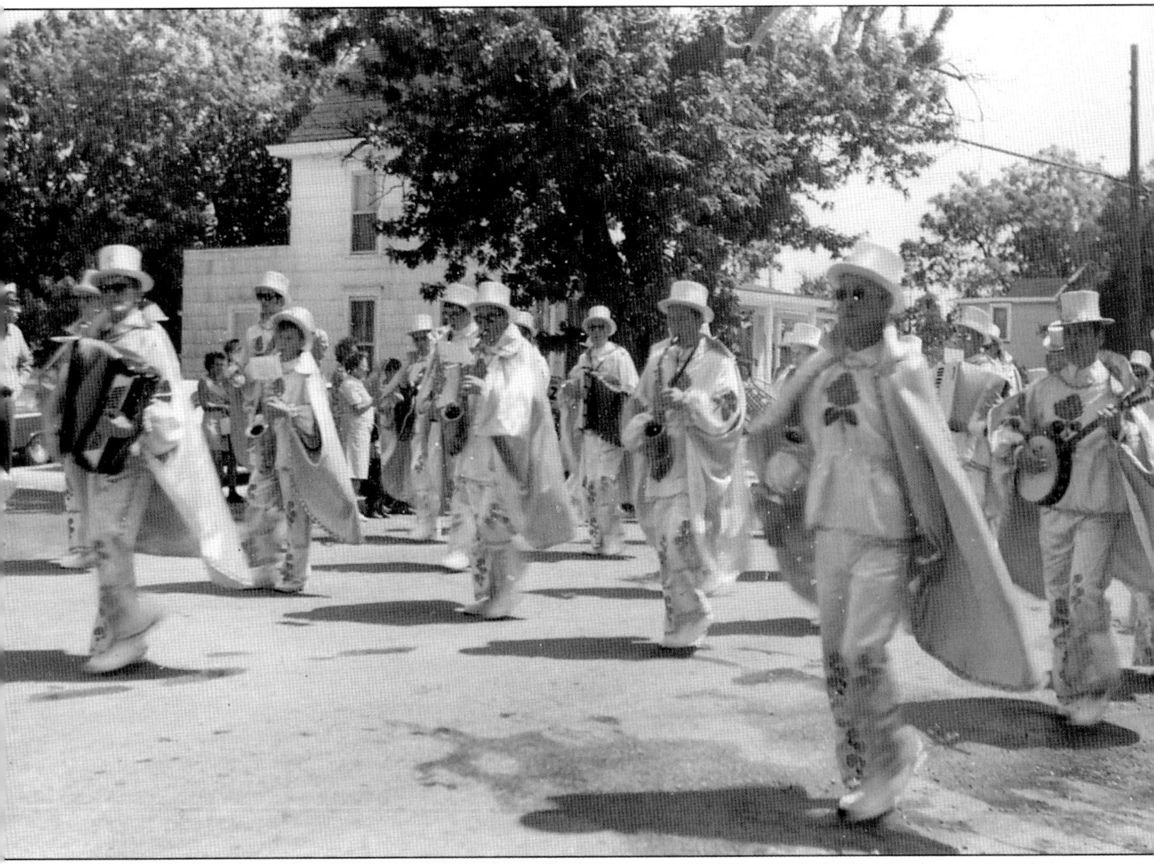

Saturday, August 23, 1969, was a big day of celebration in Chatsworth for the housing of the new fire truck and dedication of the firehouse. The firehouse was built by John Bowker, Jack Shaner, Fred Kennedy, Alfred Heinrich, Donald Estlow, and others who would assist from time to time. The officers of the fire company were John R. Shaner, president; John Bowker, vice president; Dominick J. Repici, secretary; Herbert Wickward, treasurer; Donald Estlow Jr., financial secretary; Fred Kennedy, fire chief; Clarence Leek Jr., assistant fire chief; Charles Applegate, engineer; and Ernest DiStefano, assistant engineer. The trustees were William Sloan, John Bowker, Charles Applegate, Donald Estlow Sr., and Charles Cooper Sr. People from throughout the area joined townsfolk and lined Main Street for the parade that saw fire companies from many communities, a color guard from Fort Dix, and a string band dressed in colorful gold-and-red costumes, for the dedication of the firehouse. Representatives of Good Will Fire Company in Pemberton and America Hose Company of Mount Holly were present for the celebration. (Courtesy of Robin Shaner Hollingshead.)

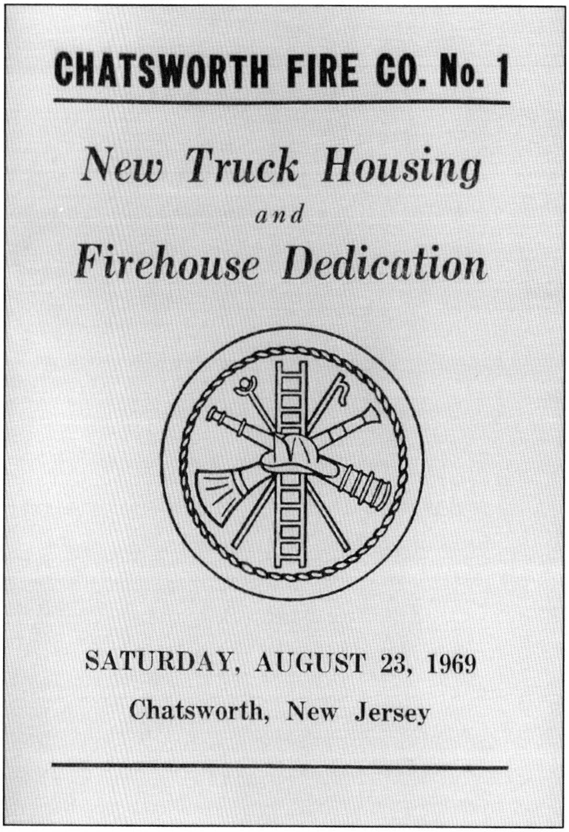

CHATSWORTH FIRE CO. No. 1

New Truck Housing
and
Firehouse Dedication

SATURDAY, AUGUST 23, 1969
Chatsworth, New Jersey

This is a picture of the program for the New Truck Housing and Firehouse Dedication that occurred on August 23, 1969. (Both, Margie Wills Hall.)

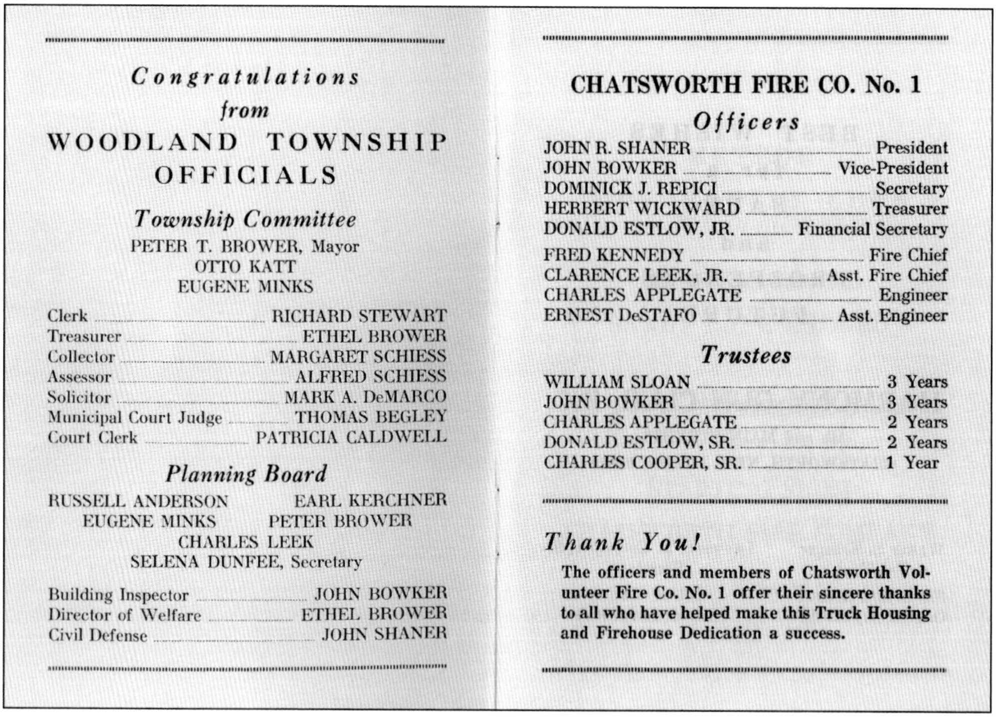

Congratulations
from
WOODLAND TOWNSHIP OFFICIALS

Township Committee
PETER T. BROWER, Mayor
OTTO KATT
EUGENE MINKS

Clerk .... RICHARD STEWART
Treasurer .... ETHEL BROWER
Collector .... MARGARET SCHIESS
Assessor .... ALFRED SCHIESS
Solicitor .... MARK A. DeMARCO
Municipal Court Judge .... THOMAS BEGLEY
Court Clerk .... PATRICIA CALDWELL

Planning Board
RUSSELL ANDERSON EARL KERCHNER
EUGENE MINKS PETER BROWER
CHARLES LEEK
SELENA DUNFEE, Secretary

Building Inspector .... JOHN BOWKER
Director of Welfare .... ETHEL BROWER
Civil Defense .... JOHN SHANER

CHATSWORTH FIRE CO. No. 1
Officers
JOHN R. SHANER .... President
JOHN BOWKER .... Vice-President
DOMINICK J. REPICI .... Secretary
HERBERT WICKWARD .... Treasurer
DONALD ESTLOW, JR. .... Financial Secretary
FRED KENNEDY .... Fire Chief
CLARENCE LEEK, JR. .... Asst. Fire Chief
CHARLES APPLEGATE .... Engineer
ERNEST DeSTAFO .... Asst. Engineer

Trustees
WILLIAM SLOAN .... 3 Years
JOHN BOWKER .... 3 Years
CHARLES APPLEGATE .... 2 Years
DONALD ESTLOW, SR. .... 2 Years
CHARLES COOPER, SR. .... 1 Year

Thank You!
The officers and members of Chatsworth Volunteer Fire Co. No. 1 offer their sincere thanks to all who have helped make this Truck Housing and Firehouse Dedication a success.

The New Jersey State Police were formed in 1921. The people of Chatsworth were afforded police protection by the state police. Trooper Budd Wilson Sr. began his career in the Chatsworth area. He rode a circuit, on horseback, from Troop "A" headquarters in Hammonton. He would ride alone, and when he reached Atsion he would follow the Jersey Central Railroad to Chatsworth. He stayed with a local family named Applegate, where he was provided a stall for his horse, a room, a bath, and access to the outhouse. Communication was difficult; there was a telephone line into Chatsworth, but it was unreliable. The troopers patrolled most of the roads in Woodland, Washington, and Bass River Townships. Below is New Jersey State trooper Bishop, also a mounted police officer, who stayed with the Ritzendollar family when stationed in Chatsworth. (Right, courtesy of New Jersey State Police; below, courtesy of Buzby collection.)

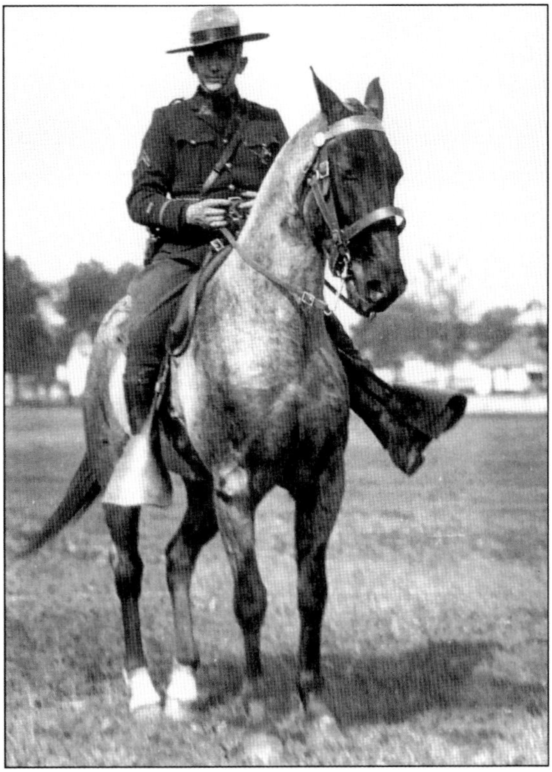

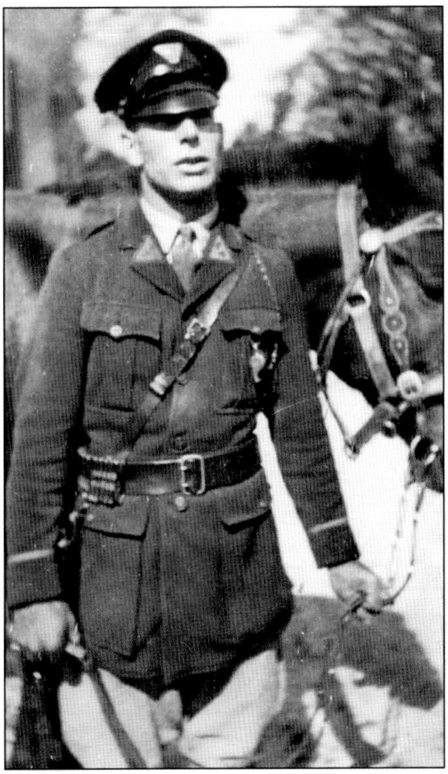

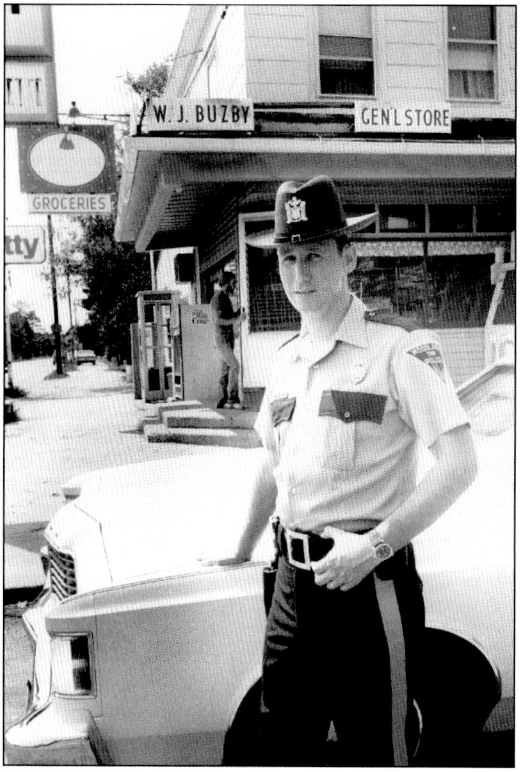

Woodland Township organized its own police department in 1978. It was a part-time police department with officers working shifts during the evening hours and on weekends. Edward Kaufholz served as the police chief, shown here in uniform at Buzby's store. George Wills also served as police chief during the operation of the police department. Other officers employed by the department were George Wills, David Brischler, Ken Gerber, Richard Baum, and Ken Woodworth. The protection afforded to the town by having its own department was greatly appreciated by the townspeople; however, the department was not cost effective. The police department was disbanded in 1982. (Courtesy of Edward Kaufholz.)

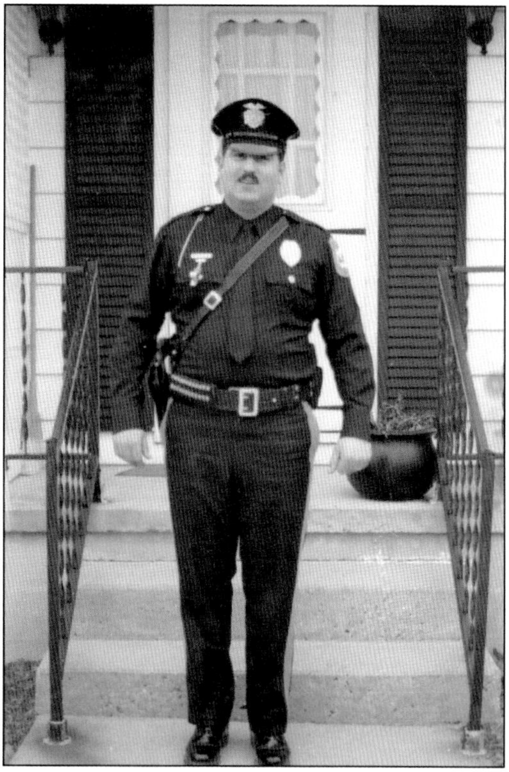

This is a photograph of Ken Gerber who was also employed as a police officer in Woodland Township between 1978 and 1982. (Courtesy of Ken Gerber.)

Seven

RECREATION

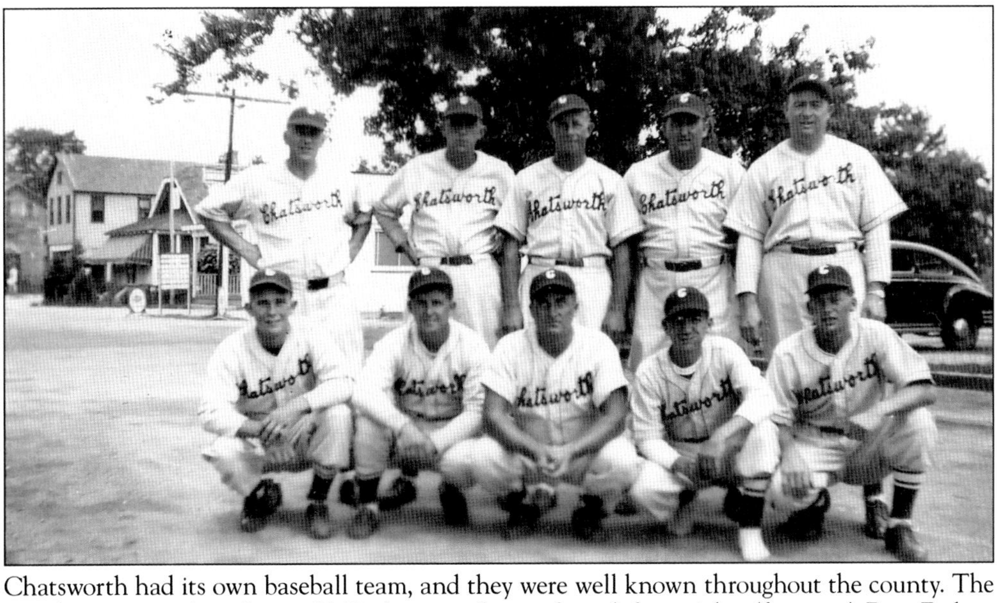

Chatsworth had its own baseball team, and they were well known throughout the county. The members pictured in this *c.* 1940 photograph are, from left to right, (first row) Don Estlow, Norman Adams, Albertus Pepper, Jimmy Doyle, and Harold Stevenson Jr.; (second row) Harold Stevenson, Alfred Stevenson Jr., Richard Green, Ken Dunfee, and Herb Anderson. (Courtesy of Charles Applegate collection.)

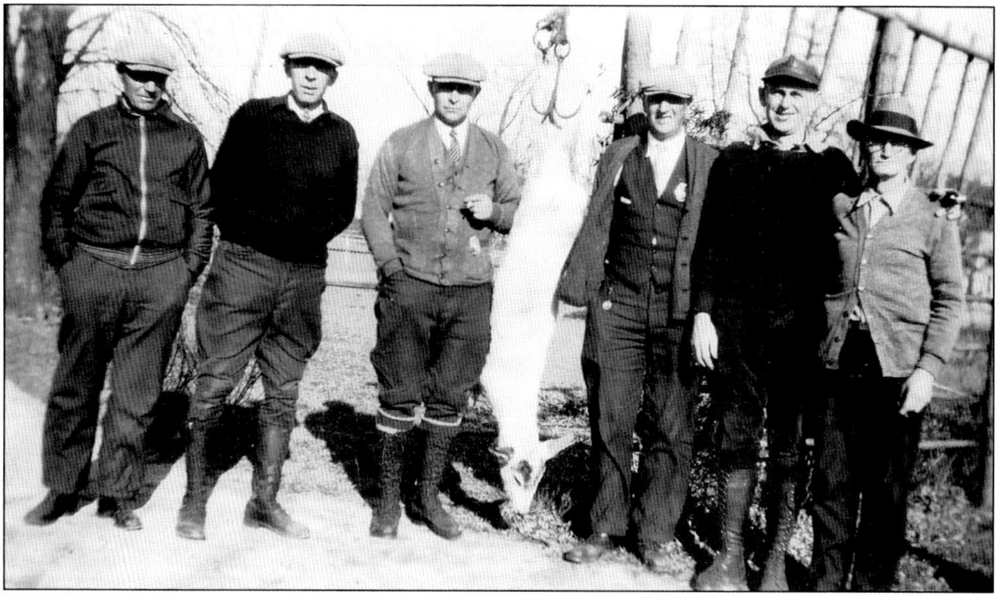

The deer season has always been notable in Chatsworth. In 1935, a rare albino deer was killed during the annual hunt in December. Shown with the deer are, from left to right, Benny Ranalli, game warden Joe Johnson, game warden Corson, Bill Carslake, Roy Applegate, and Jack Ritzendollar. (Courtesy of Buzby collection.)

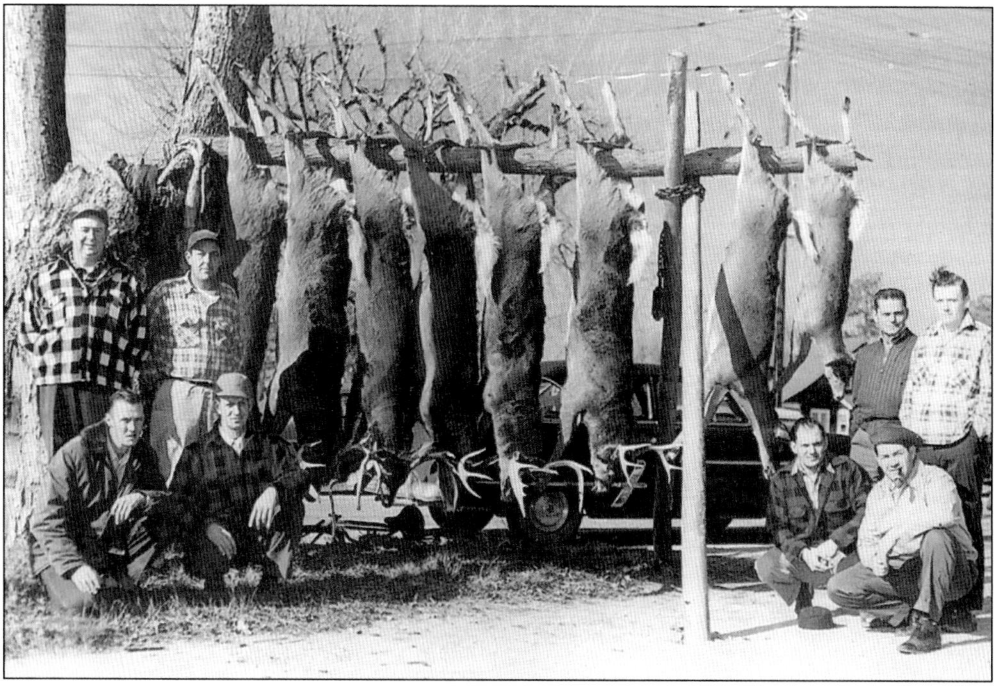

In the 1900s, Chatsworth became a popular deer-hunting region, not only for hunters from varying distances who stayed the entire week in "deer clubs," but especially for the residents. In this 1954 photograph are, from left to right, (first row) Rube Wills, Benny Ranalli, Bill Ranalli, and Jackie Wills; (second row) Herbert Anderson, Alfred "Junior" Stevenson, Freddie Ranalli, and Clarence Poinsett. (Courtesy of Charles Applegate collection.)

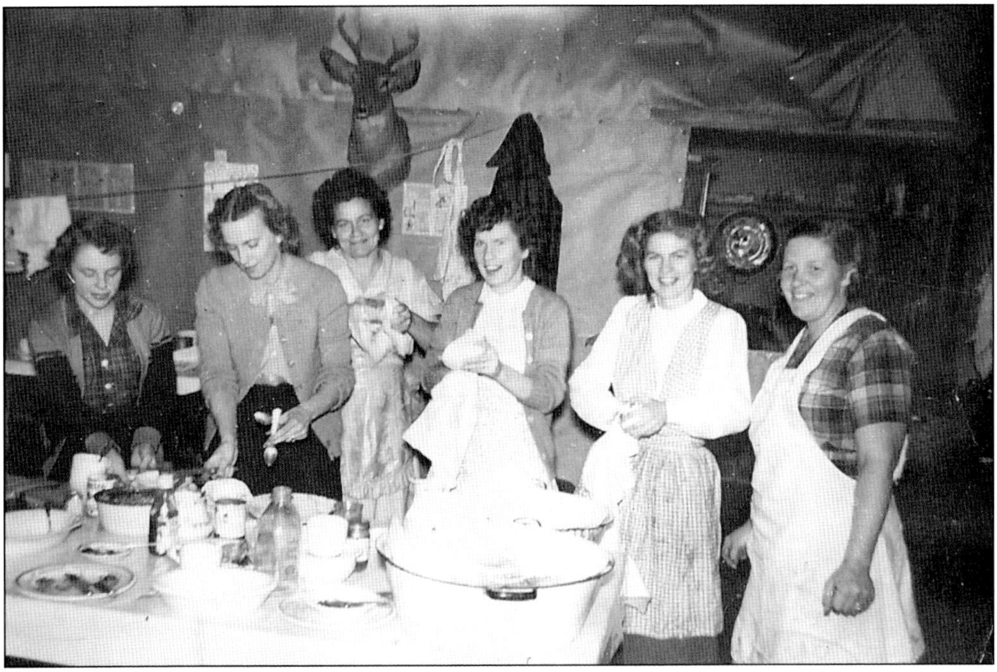

The kitchen crew for the Estlow Gun Club submits to the wish of the photographer after preparing the evening meal for the deer hunters. They are, from left to right, Dorothy Rita Green, Betty Estlow, Kathryn Estlow, Doris Estlow, Virginia Estlow, and Amelia Green. The dinner was always a full-course meal with all the trimmings. (Courtesy of Amelia Green collection.)

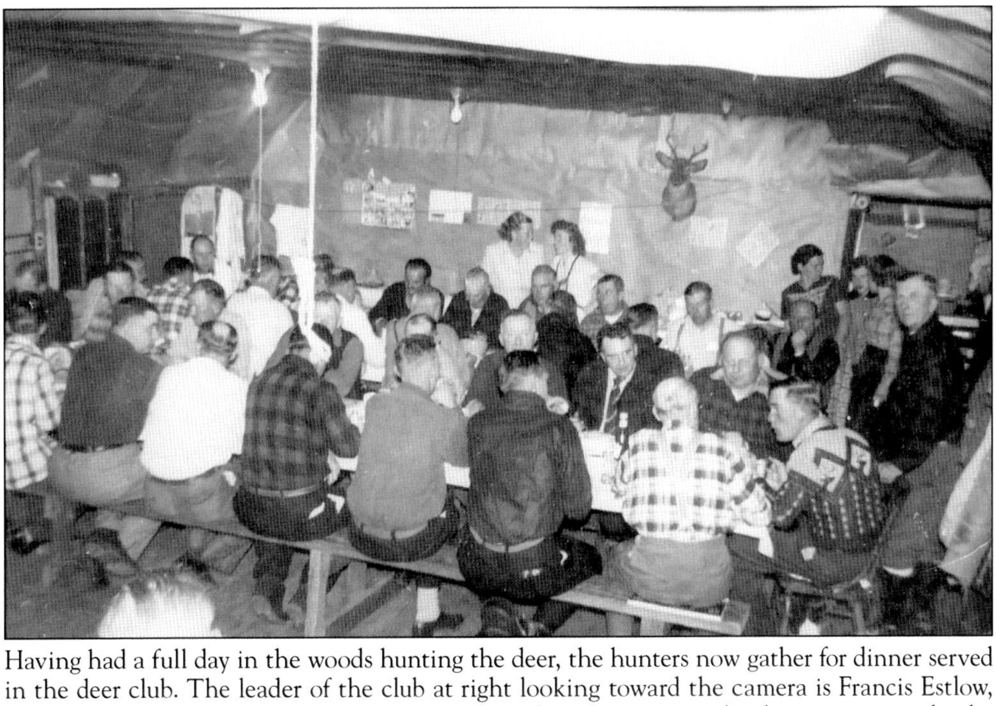

Having had a full day in the woods hunting the deer, the hunters now gather for dinner served in the deer club. The leader of the club at right looking toward the camera is Francis Estlow, who led the club for several years. Flannel shirts and sweaters seem to be the proper attire for the dinner. (Courtesy of Amelia Green collection.)

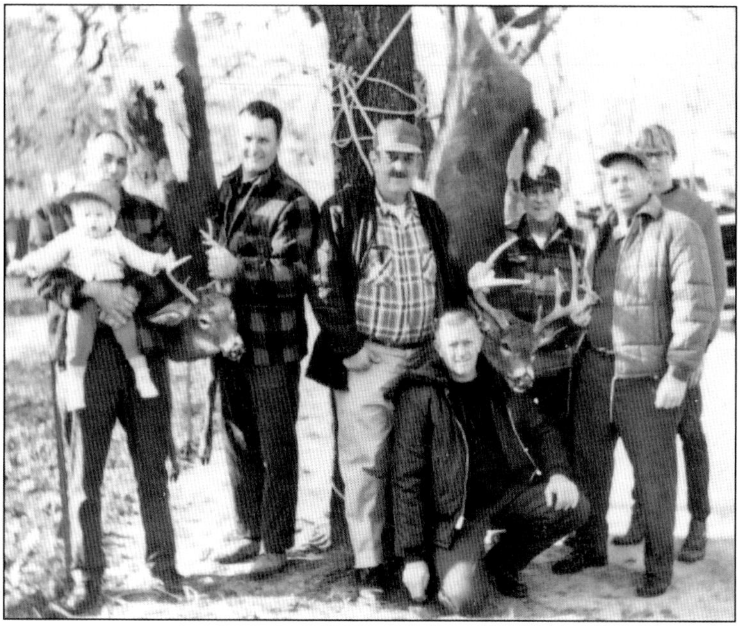

Chatsworth deer hunters pose with a pair of deer brought back by fellow Chatsworth hunters from Maine. They are, from left to right, Buddy Leek, "Wash" Orme, Junior Stevenson, "Frog" Stevenson, Russell Dunfee, Hank Stevenson, and unidentified. (Courtesy of Amelia Green collection.)

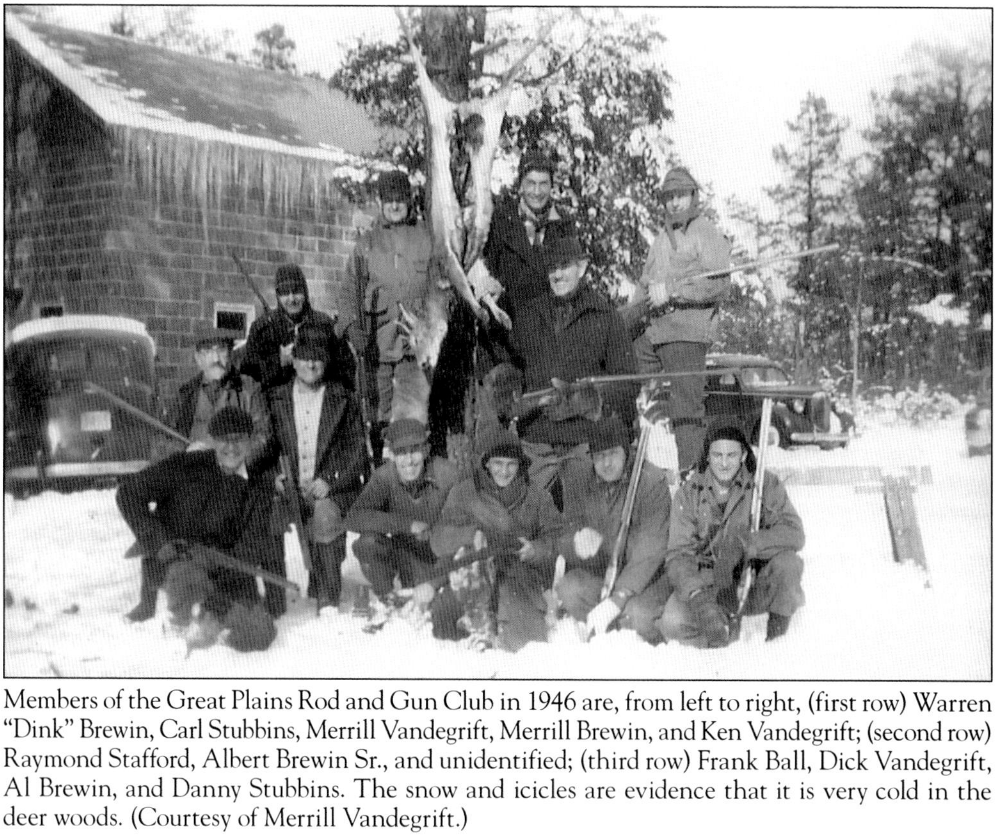

Members of the Great Plains Rod and Gun Club in 1946 are, from left to right, (first row) Warren "Dink" Brewin, Carl Stubbins, Merrill Vandegrift, Merrill Brewin, and Ken Vandegrift; (second row) Raymond Stafford, Albert Brewin Sr., and unidentified; (third row) Frank Ball, Dick Vandegrift, Al Brewin, and Danny Stubbins. The snow and icicles are evidence that it is very cold in the deer woods. (Courtesy of Merrill Vandegrift.)

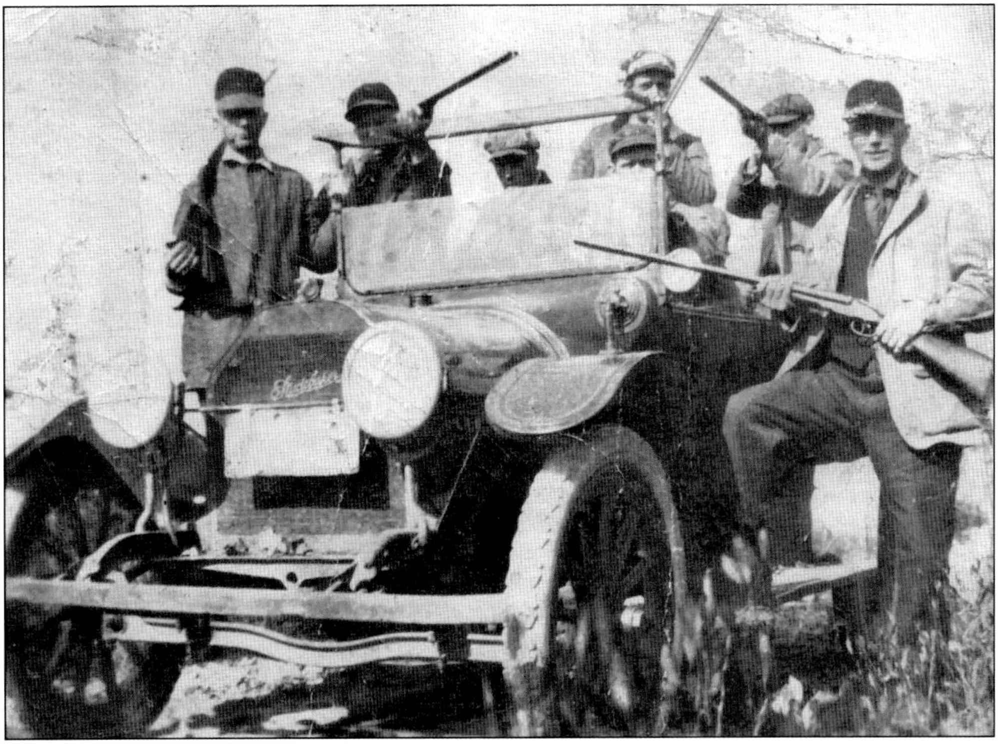

Pat Green (far left) is shown with five other deer hunters. The car is a Studebaker, 1920s vintage. Pat Green was a hunting guide for men not familiar with the dense woods surrounding Chatsworth, and he led fox and rabbit hunters with dogs as well as guiding deer hunters. (Courtesy of Amelia Green collection.)

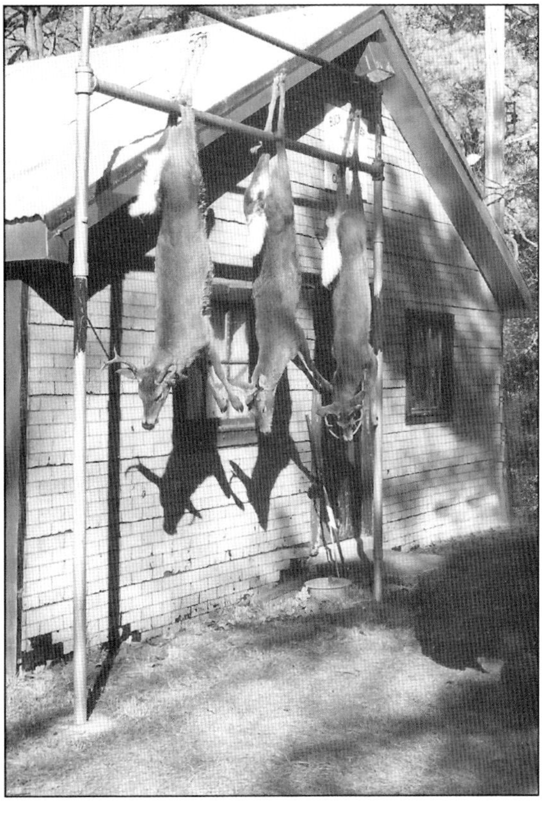

Buck Fever Gun Club was started in 1929. In 1930, they purchased the Clayton Township Municipal Garage (a World War I army barracks) and moved it to Prince Street in Chatsworth. The cabin sleeps 17 men and is heated by a huge potbellied stove. The club hires a cook for the week. Today they have eight members. They love the peace and tranquility of the pinewoods. (Courtesy of Fred Alkons.)

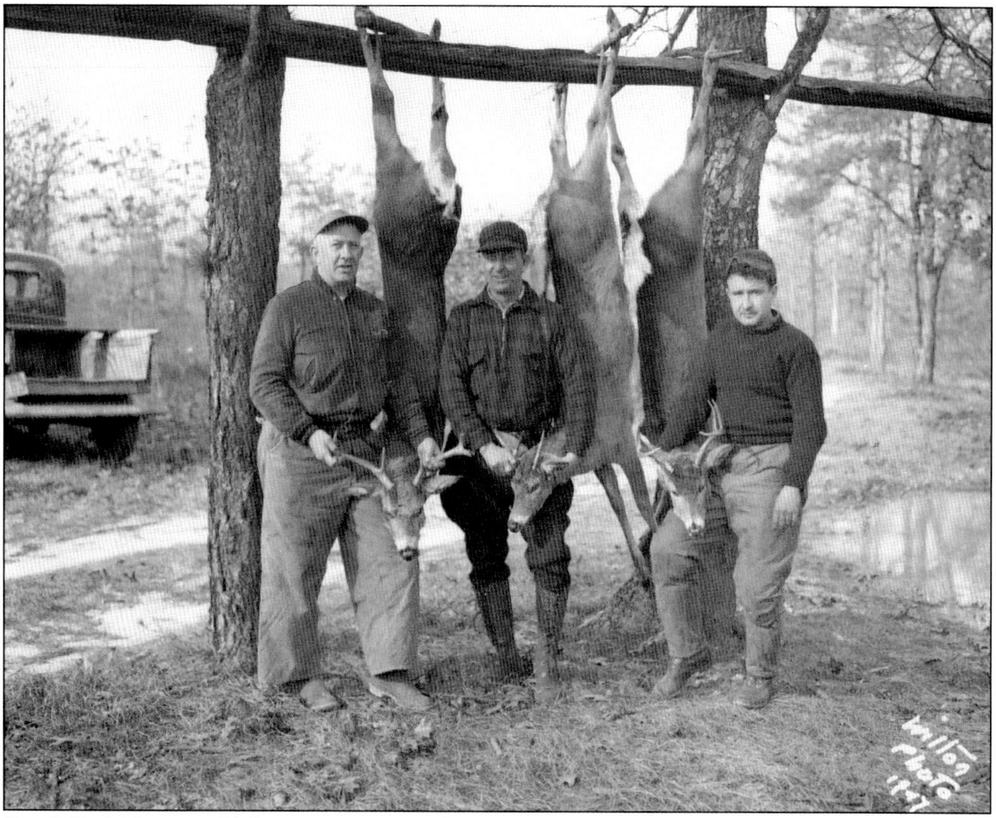

South Park Hunting Club was incorporated in 1922. The club entered into a lease with Constant LeDuc for a house (the old clubhouse) and a lot known as "Lot 68," on a map of the property at Paisley, New Jersey. They also leased approximately 3,500 acres in Woodland and Tabernacle Townships. In 1940, they purchased nine lots in Block 68 from Albert LeDuc and Maude LeDuc for $300. (Albert LeDuc was the nephew of Constant LeDuc.) The lots were 25 feet wide and 100 feet deep. Over the years, they have acquired many acres of woodlands to be used for hunting. They are good land stewards. Three hunters with their trophy bucks are shown in 1947, and the clubhouse is pictured in 1947 also. (Both, courtesy of South Park Hunting Club.)

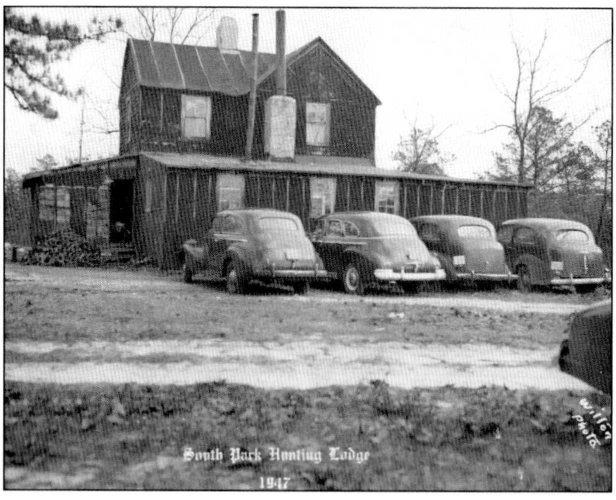

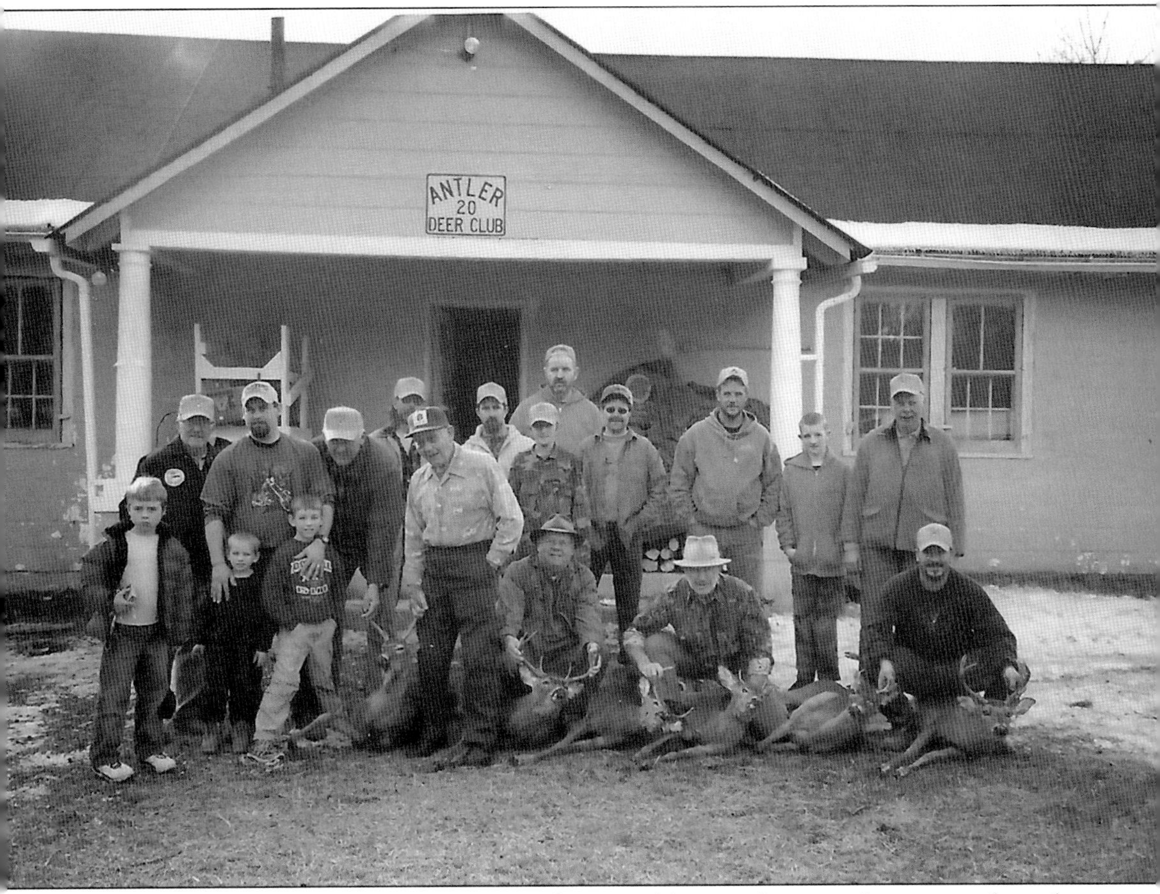

Antler 20 Deer Club has been in existence for over 100 years. A group of sportsmen from the Mullica area of South Jersey and Keyport formed it for deer hunting. Their common bond was not only hunting, but they were all practicing Methodists. The Woodstown Club joined with them in the 1950s, just after they purchased the cabin and property at Sooy Place. They have 20 members, thus the name "Antler 20." Other gun clubs making their home in Chatsworth are Tall Pines Gun Club, Pinewood Antler Club, South River Gun Club, Princeton Rod and Gun Club, Medford Hunting Club, Tri-City Gun Club, Glendora Buck Club, River-Del Gun Club, Harmony Gun Club, Paulsboro Stag Club, Pleasantview Rod and Gun Club, Hamilton Rod and Gun Club, and Blackwood Antler Club. (Courtesy of Stanley Lachiewicz.)

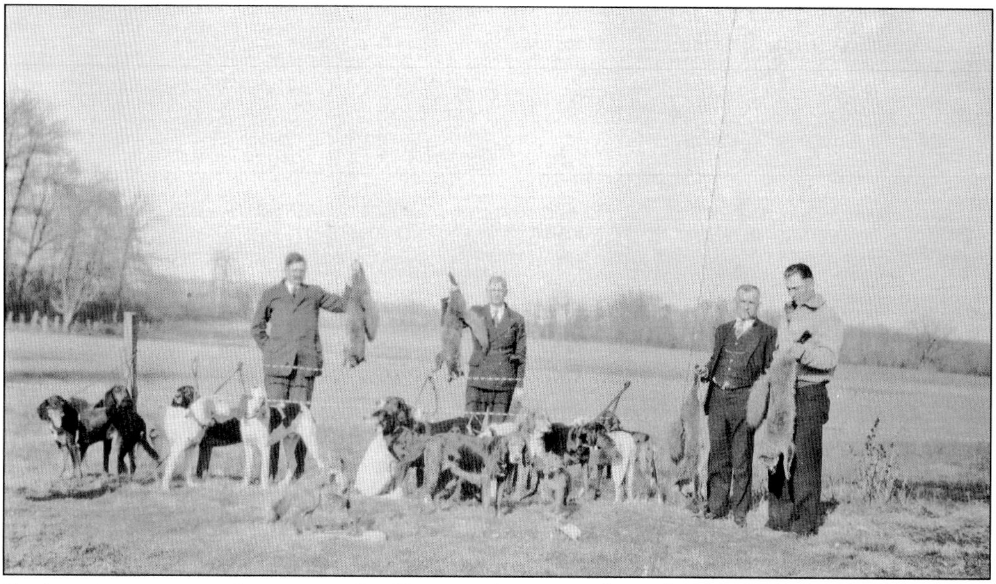

Fox hunting was a popular sport in the Chatsworth areas in the early 1900s. Men in the community led fox-hunting parties throughout the pines for hunters who came to the area from distant locations. Dogs were very much a part of the hunting parties. Four hunters are shown displaying their hunting success of the day. (Courtesy of Sooy family.)

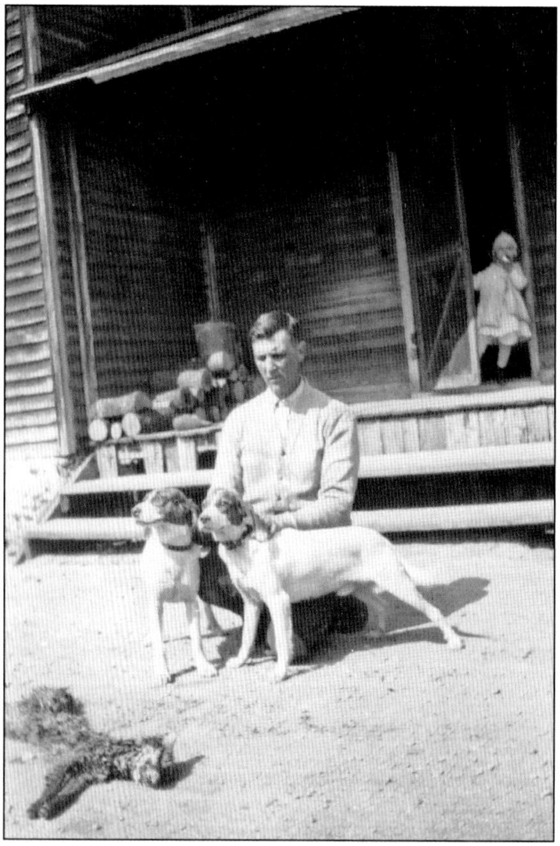

Joseph Holloway poses with his dogs in this c. 1929 photograph at his home in Friendship, a small village near Speedwell. Note the wood on the porch already cut for use in cooking and heating the home. Daughter Jean stands in the doorway of the home observing her dad and the dogs. (Courtesy of Sooy family.)

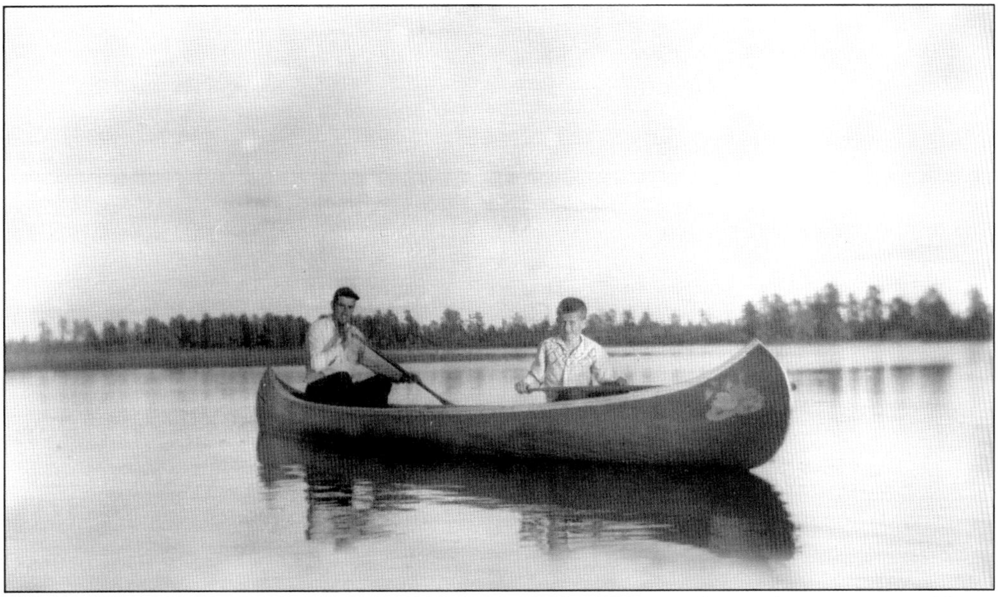

Canoeing has been a popular recreation attraction in the Chatsworth area for many years. Alison "Possum" Sooy and Vinny Henrich are enjoying fishing and canoeing in the nearby Chatsworth Lake in the 1950s. Fishing for pickerel was a popular sport in the spillways surrounding the cranberry bogs, and contests were held locally for the largest catch. (Courtesy of the Sooy family.)

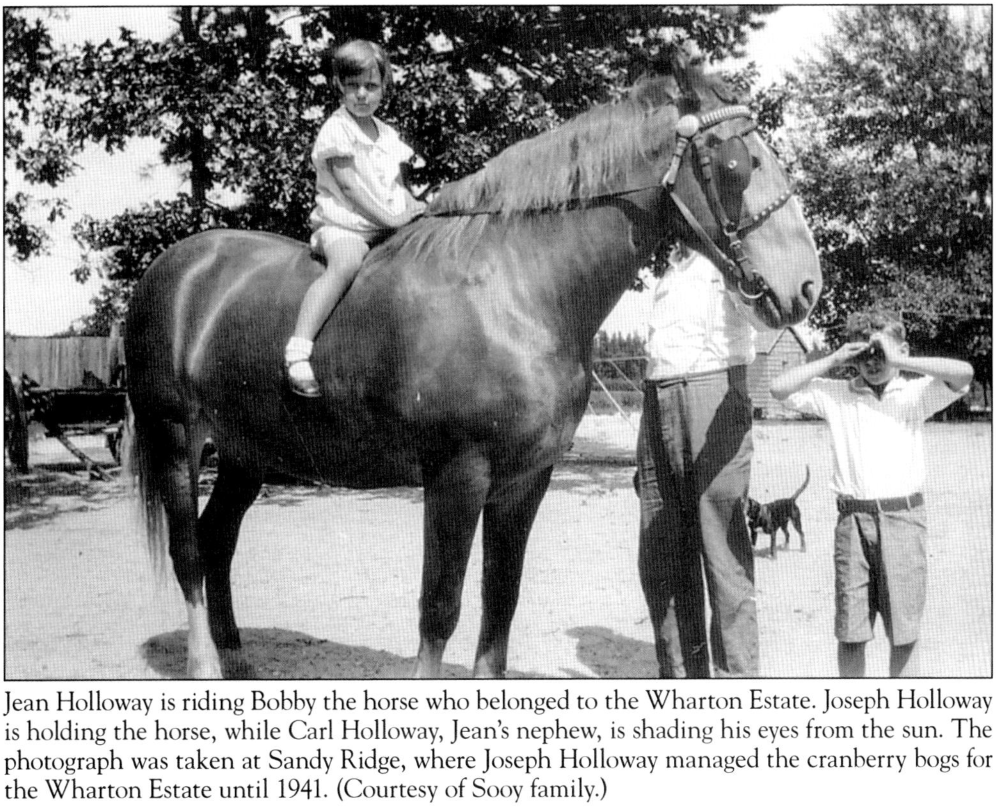

Jean Holloway is riding Bobby the horse who belonged to the Wharton Estate. Joseph Holloway is holding the horse, while Carl Holloway, Jean's nephew, is shading his eyes from the sun. The photograph was taken at Sandy Ridge, where Joseph Holloway managed the cranberry bogs for the Wharton Estate until 1941. (Courtesy of Sooy family.)

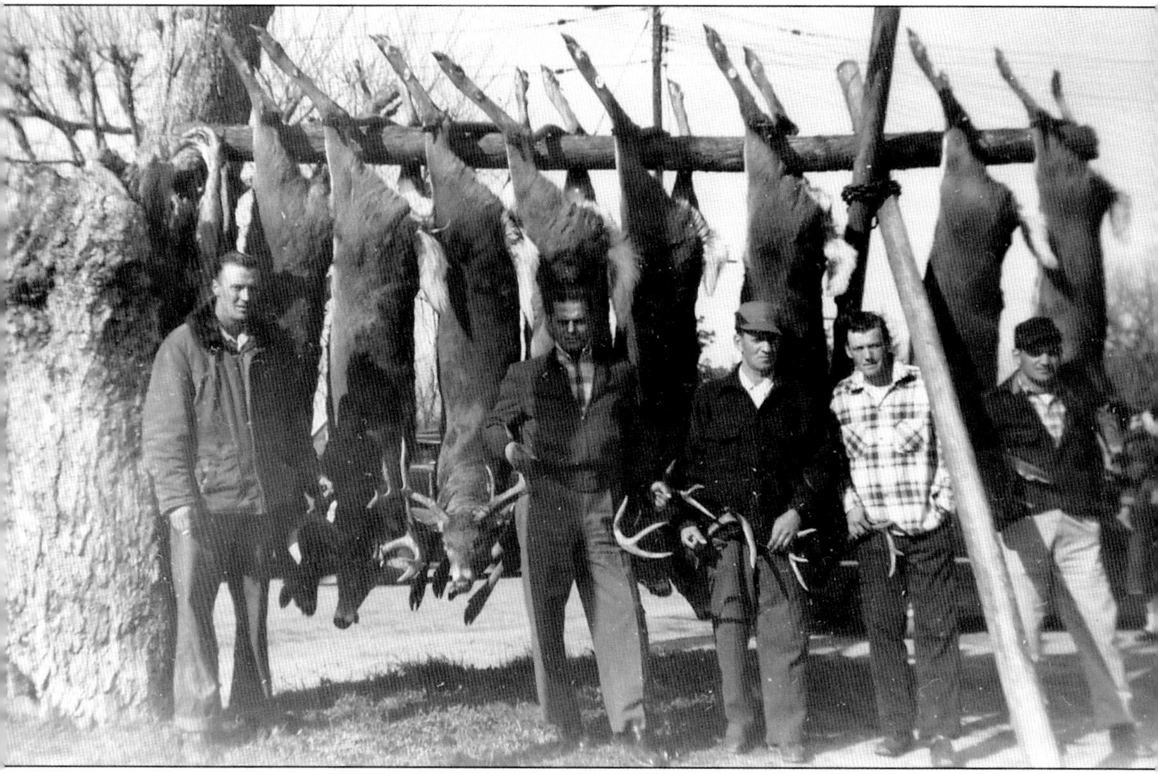

Posing with a fine rack of trophy deer are, from left to right, Alfred Reuben Wills, unidentified, Benny Ranalli, Jackie Wills, and Irving "Diz" Mantell. Many clubs were in competition to see who would "bag" the most deer. The Woodshed, a local bar on Route 72, always had deer hanging out front. Locals drove the roads checking out the deer clubs' trophies. Some clubs built wire enclosures to keep varmints from gnawing at the deer before they could be skinned and butchered. Stories were told around the clubs about the deer being larger in the "old days," and the hunts were always more difficult. (Courtesy of Margie Wills Hall.)

Eight

Potpourri

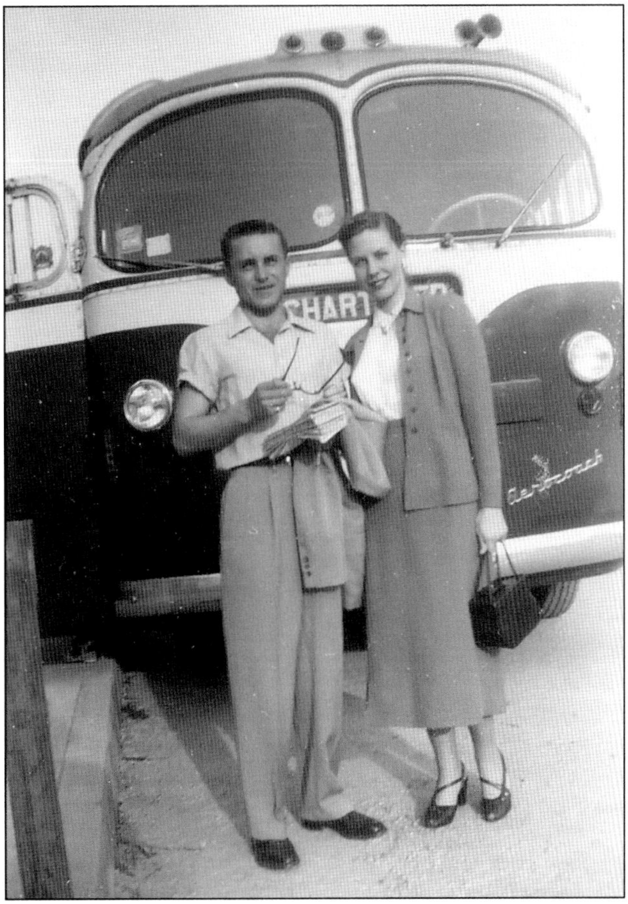

The following presentation is a collection of interesting photographs and information of many persons representing a variety of categories—those who made important contributions to the life of the community. Charles Trutell, left, a teacher of the upper grades in the Chatsworth Elementary School, was a gifted instructor known for his ability to bring out the creative talents of his students. His companion is unidentified. (Courtesy of Margie Wills Hall.)

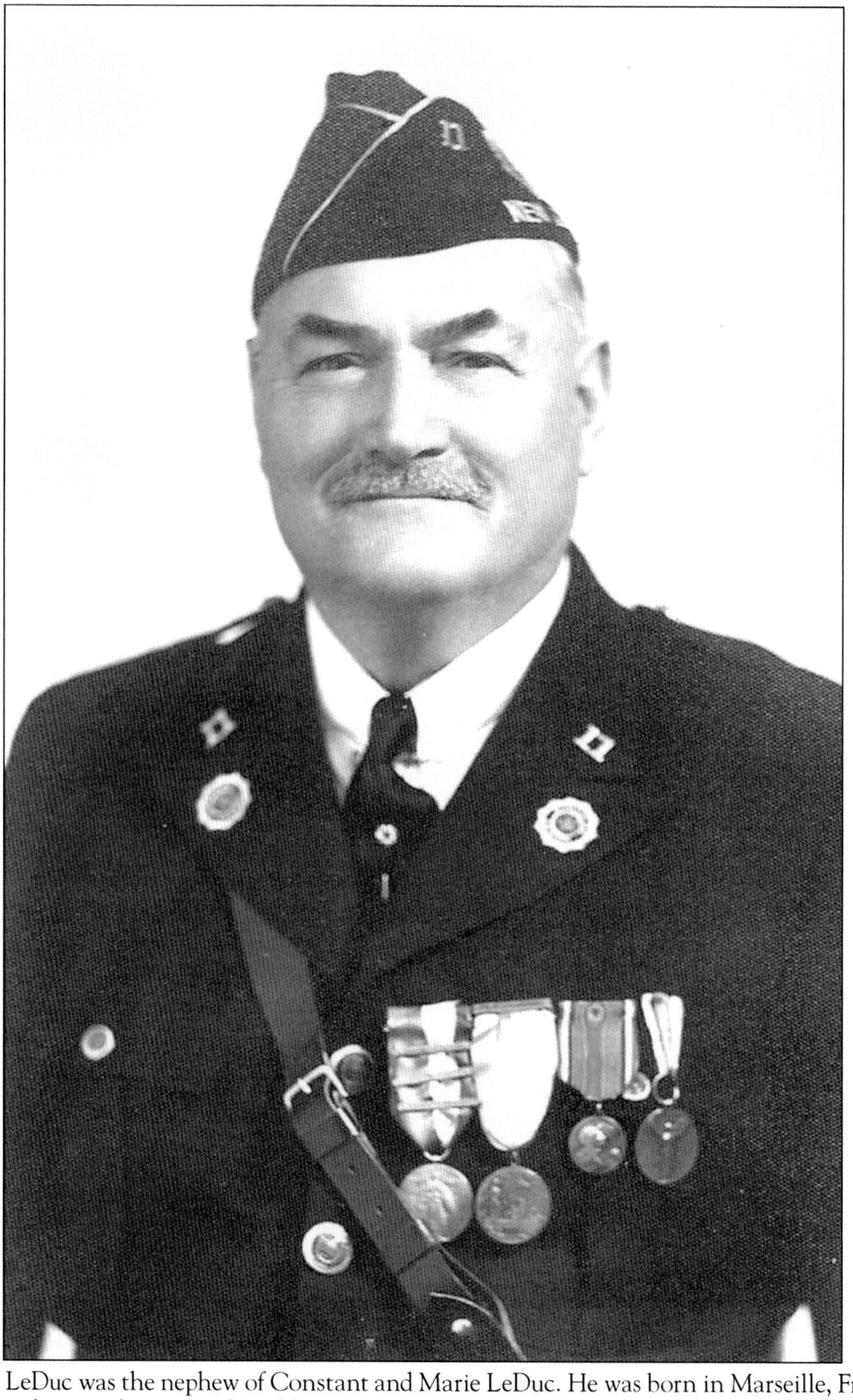

Albert LeDuc was the nephew of Constant and Marie LeDuc. He was born in Marseille, France. He was a decorated veteran of World War I and was fire warden for the Fifth Division, responsible for 80,000 acres. He studied the fire control methods of the Native Americans and advocated controlled burning to prevent the spread of fire and to rejuvenate plant growth on the forest floor. In 1926, he married Maude Baker, the niece of Mary Davis. They resided in Johnson Place, Woodland Township, where Maude Baker held church services. (Courtesy of Lynch family.)

An elaborate marriage certificate memorializing the union of Anna Giberson to John Albert Applegate on October 22, 1899, at Barnegat, New Jersey, is pictured here. John Applegate lived in Chatsworth directly across the street from the Chatsworth Methodist Church. That home looks much the same as it did in the early 1920s. (Courtesy of Margie Wills Hall.)

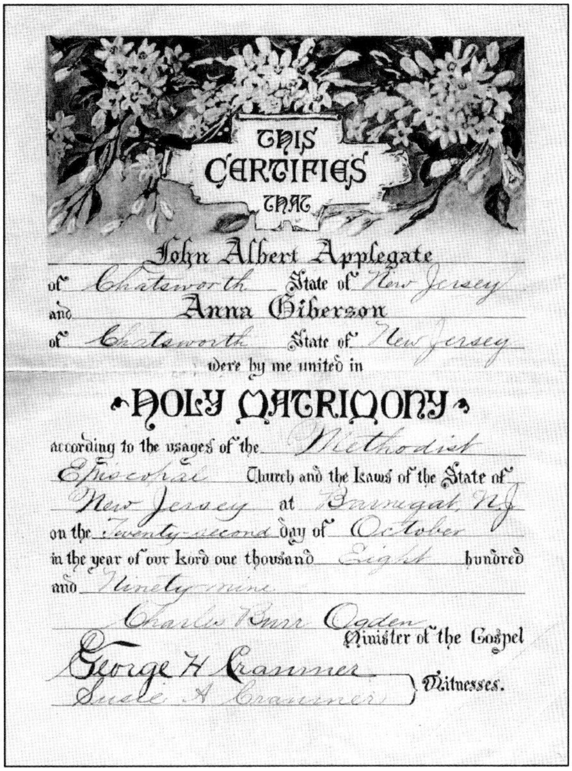

This Certifies that

John Albert Applegate

of Chatsworth State of New Jersey

and Anna Giberson

of Chatsworth State of New Jersey

were by me united in

HOLY MATRIMONY

according to the usages of the Methodist Episcopal Church and the laws of the State of New Jersey at Barnegat, N.J. on the Twenty-second day of October in the year of our Lord one thousand Eight hundred and Ninety-nine

Charles Burr Ogden, Minister of the Gospel

George H. Cranmer
Susie A. Cranmer } Witnesses.

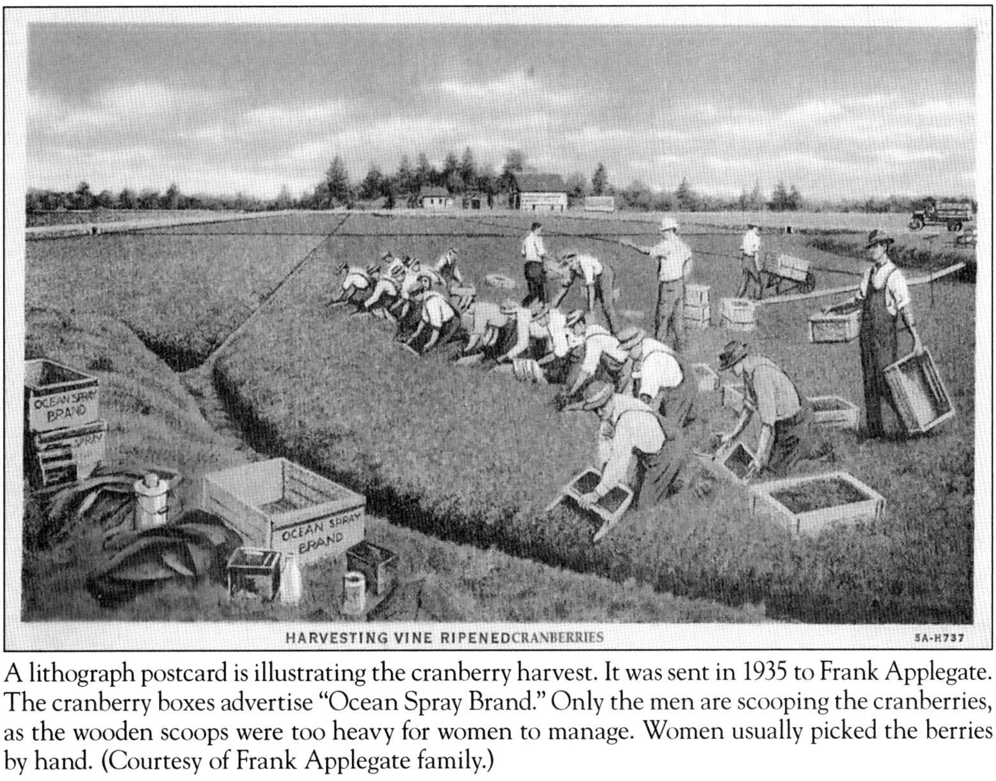

A lithograph postcard is illustrating the cranberry harvest. It was sent in 1935 to Frank Applegate. The cranberry boxes advertise "Ocean Spray Brand." Only the men are scooping the cranberries, as the wooden scoops were too heavy for women to manage. Women usually picked the berries by hand. (Courtesy of Frank Applegate family.)

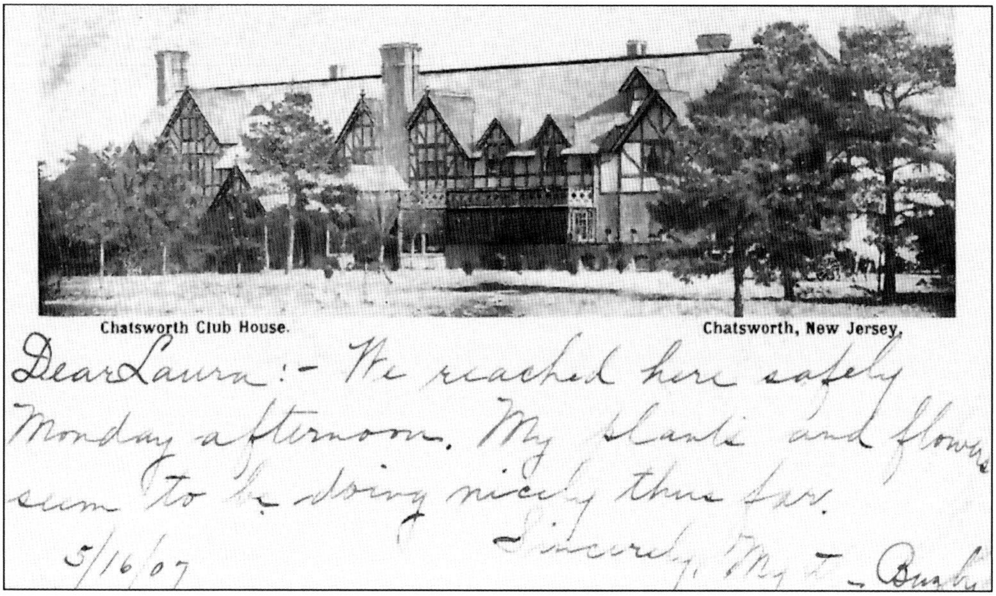

This is a postcard sent by Myrtle O. Buzby, who was the postmistress in Chatsworth, to a friend who lived in Bridgeton, New Jersey. Residents of Chatsworth frequently traveled to Bridgeton by train to shop, and it is possible that Myrtle Buzby had been away for several days, as she tells Laura Broome that "my plants and flowers seem to be doing well thus far." The postcard is dated May 16, 1907. (Courtesy of Deborah Grove.)

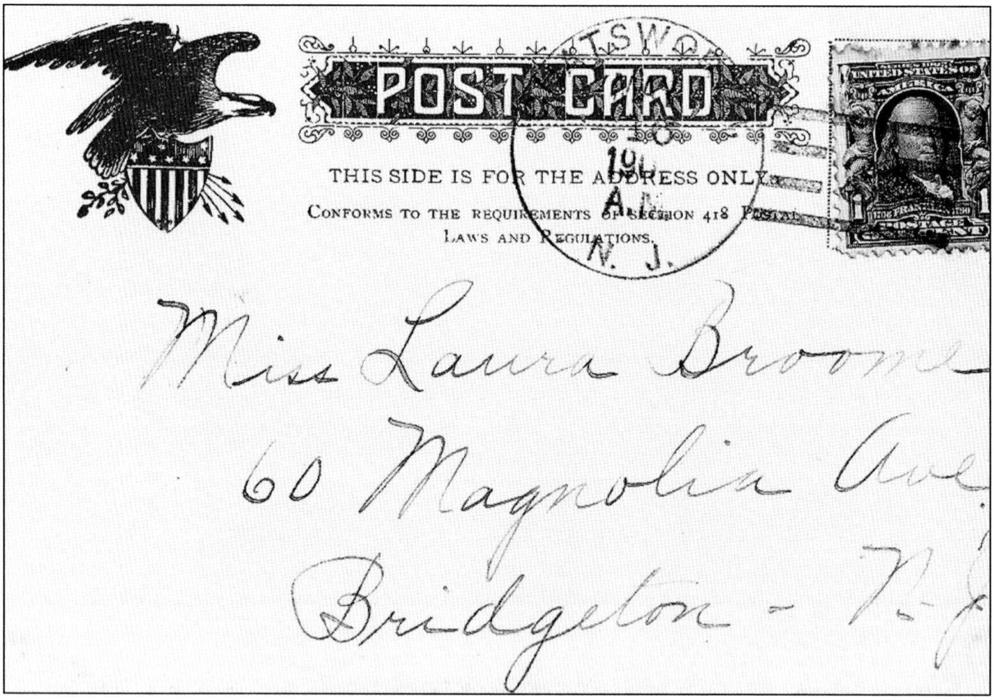

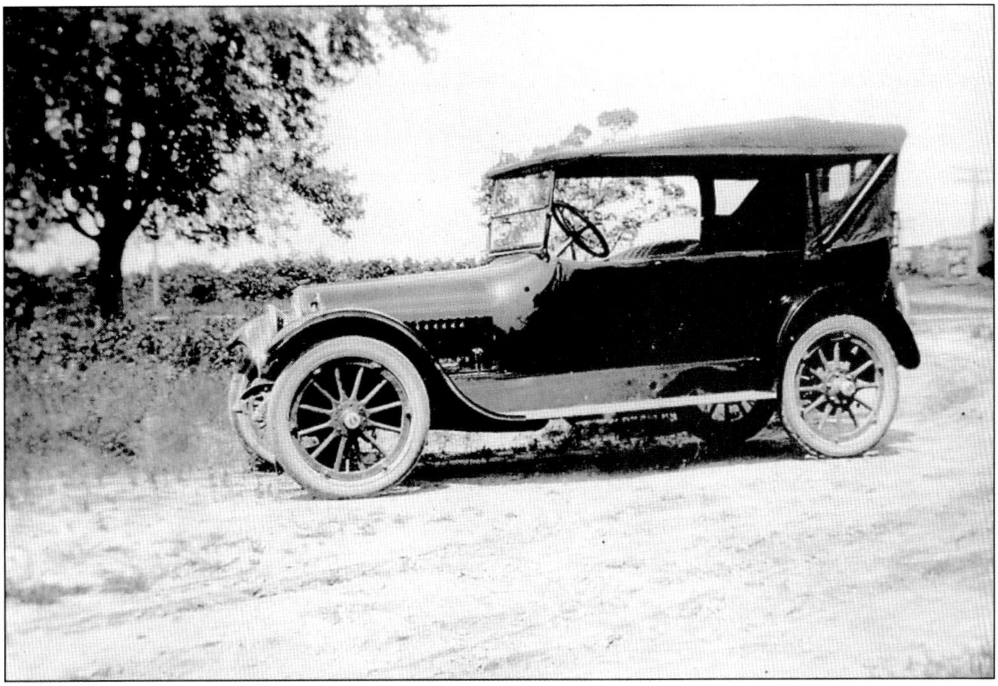

This unique automobile belonged to Katie Buzby. It is a touring car. The picture was taken in 1919. Katie was a proficient driver at a time when there were few automobiles on the road and when very few women were licensed drivers. (Courtesy of Buzby collection.)

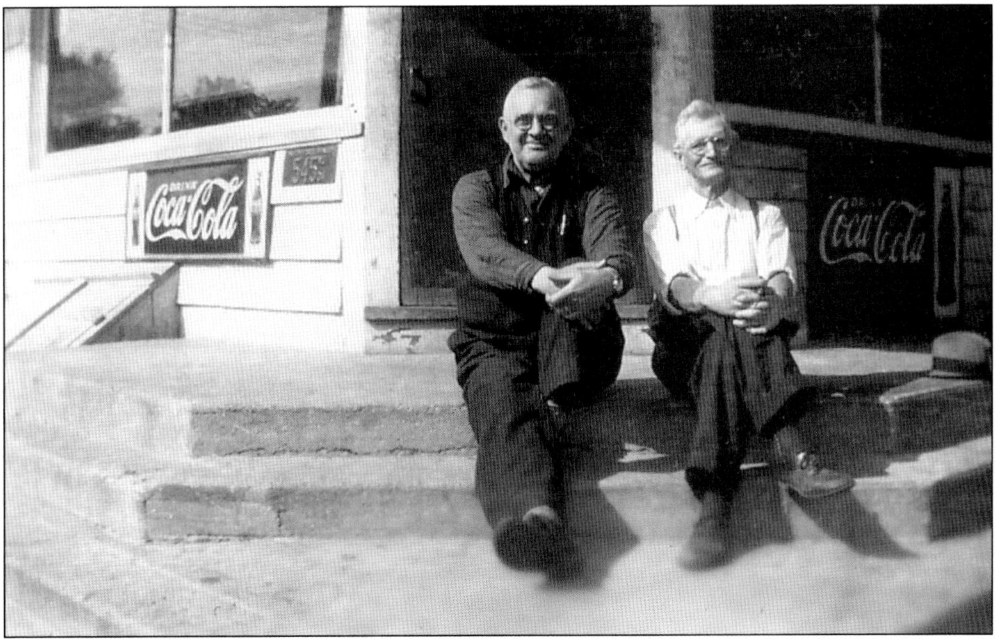

Willis J. Buzby and John H. Ritzendollar enjoy some leisure time on the front steps of Buzby's store in an identical pose. The photograph was taken in the 1920s. It appears that Coca-Cola was the drink of the times. (Courtesy of Buzby collection.)

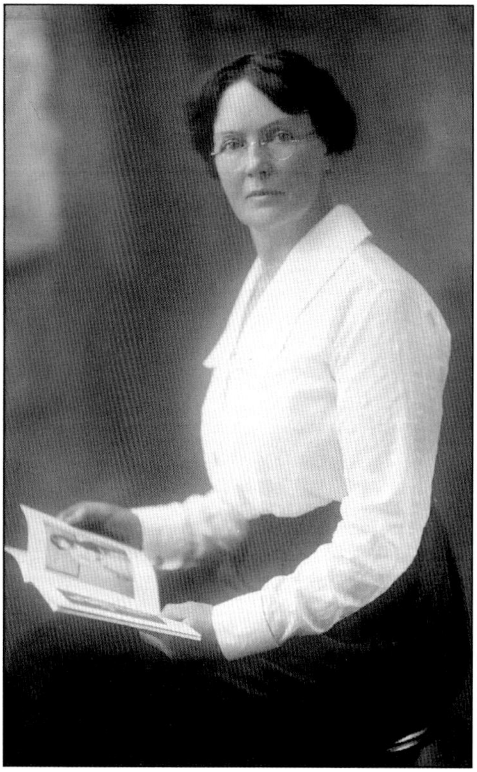

Elise Southworth was the wife of Willis J. Buzby. She was a widow with a child from her previous marriage when Willis married her. She is the mother of Willis Jonathan "Jack" Buzby. Jack was the couple's only child. She occasionally helped Willis in the general store, but was usually a quiet person. (Courtesy of Buzby collection.)

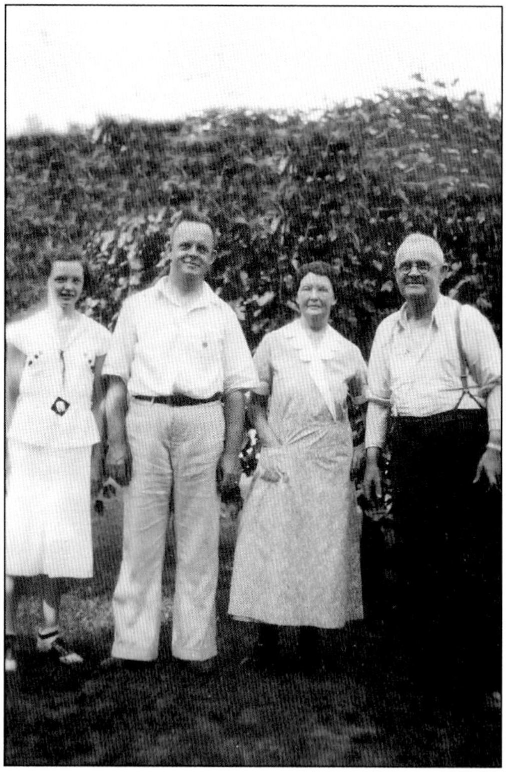

This is a group photograph of three generations of the Buzby family. From left to right are Theresa, approximately 15 years of age; Willis J. "Jack" Buzby; his mother, Elise Buzby; and his father, Willis J. Buzby Sr. Jack and Theresa's mother, Katie, were married on June 1, 1922. (Courtesy of Buzby collection.)

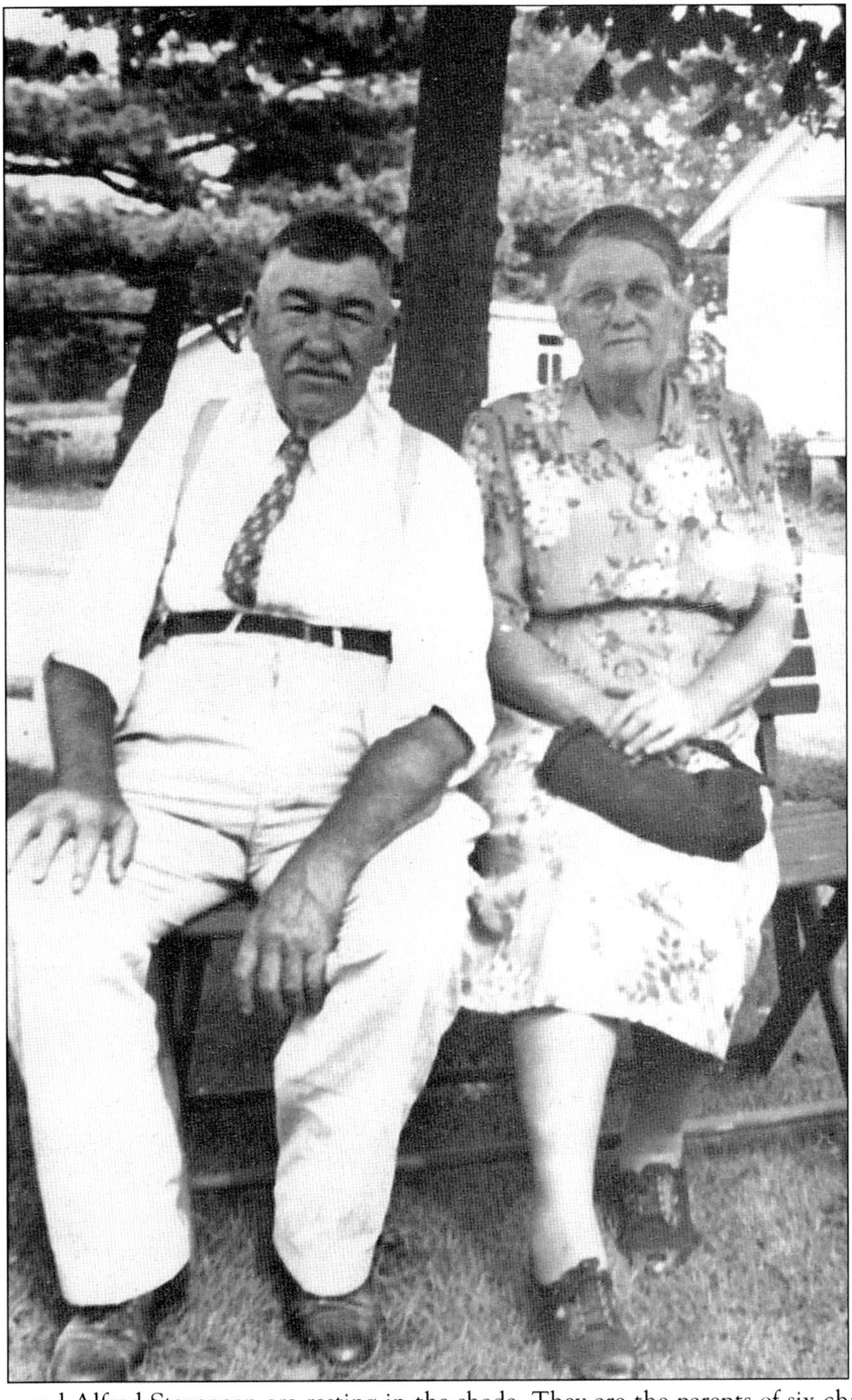

Martha and Alfred Stevenson are resting in the shade. They are the parents of six children, Harold, Paul, Kathryn, Amelia, Alfred Jr., and Jonathan. The Stevenson family came to live in the White Horse Inn in 1911 and later owned the building that was then used as their family home. It has been said that Martha Stevenson always had food to feed anyone who stopped to visit, and she was a good cook. (Courtesy of Amelia Green collection.)

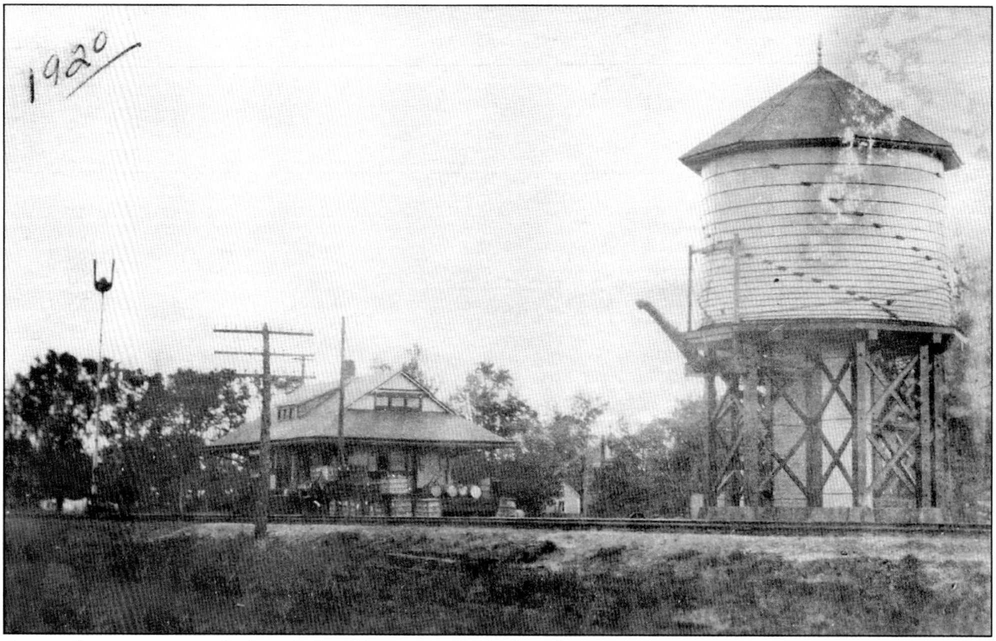

A very large water tank dwarfs the Chatsworth Railroad Station in 1924. It seems that either freight has just been delivered or something is waiting to be shipped by train. The residents of Chatsworth depended on the trains to deliver their daily newspapers and also traveled to New York City, Philadelphia, Bridgeton, and Atlantic City by train. (Courtesy of Frank Applegate family.)

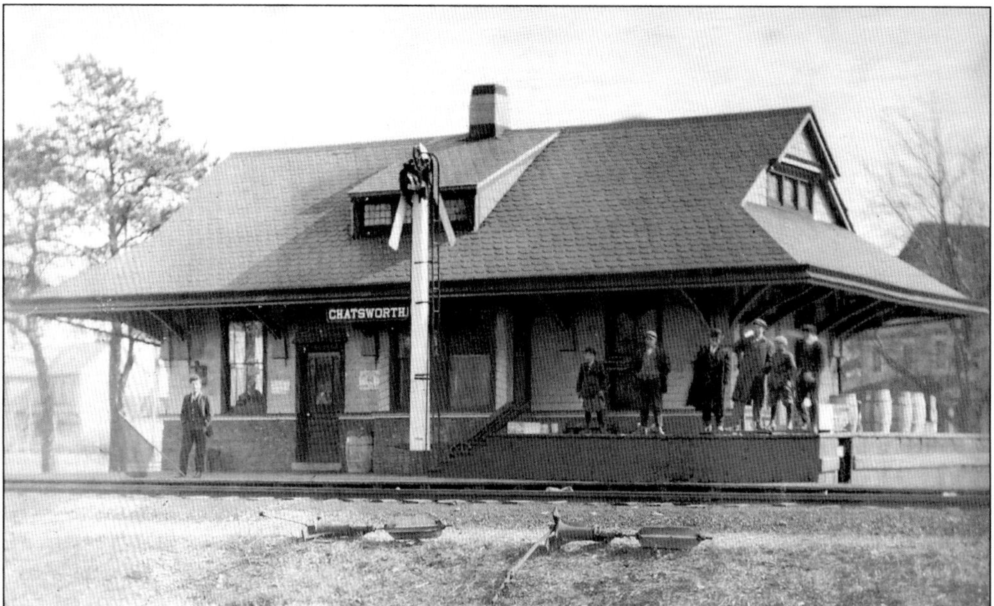

This is another view of the Chatsworth Station taken sometime in the 1930s. The first station was built *c.* 1866, a new station was constructed in 1876, and another station in 1897. The station was sold in 1952, after which it was moved from its original location and turned into a private home. (Courtesy of Margie Wills Hall.)

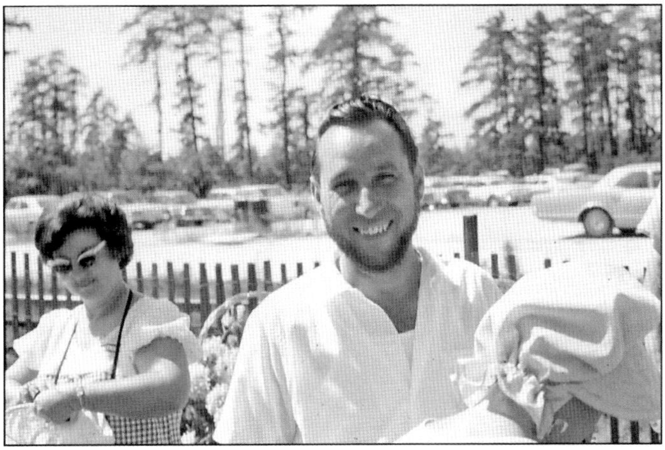

Peg and Earl Kerchner seem to be enjoying themselves at the centennial celebration in Chatsworth in 1966. Earl worked for A. R. DeMarco Enterprises in the cranberry bogs, and his wife, Peg, was a school nurse. Earl is sporting the mandatory beard required for the festivities. (Courtesy of William S. Haines Sr. family.)

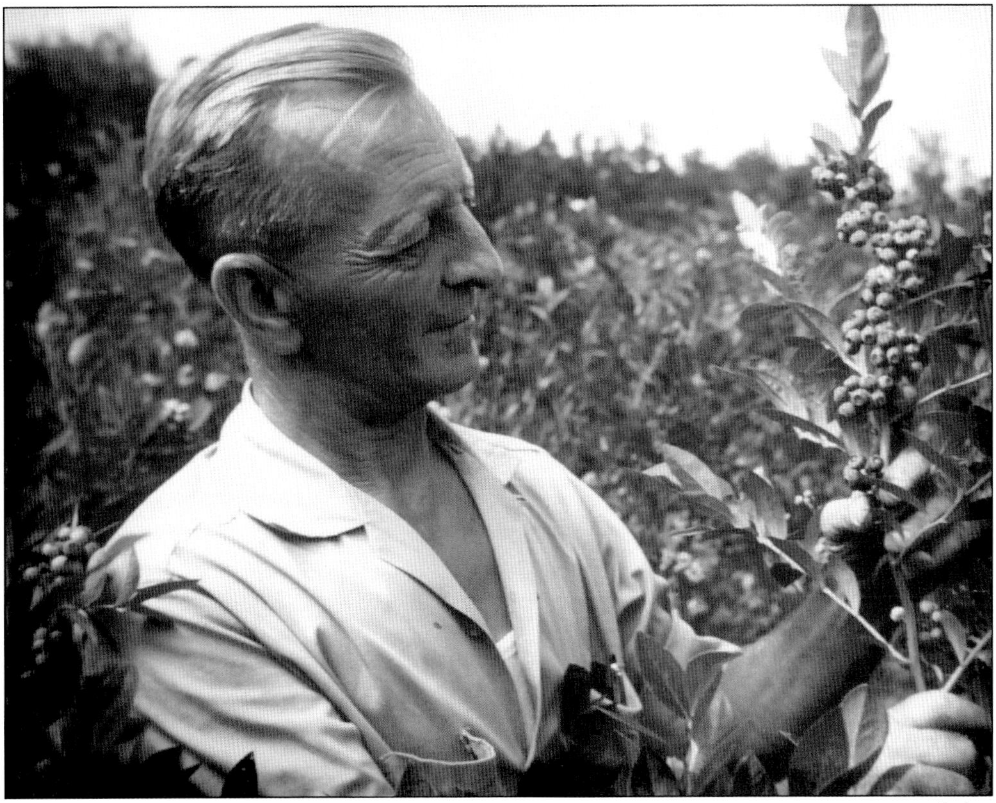

Albert George Ammon is shown here. He moved to Chatsworth from Jersey City, with his newborn son Albert Charles Ammon, to a house on the old farm located on Barnegat Road, now Route 532. He started a freight-hauling business, running three trucks a day between Philadelphia and New York City. In the 1930s, he bought two school buses and got bus routes to pick up the Chatsworth school students. When Route 40 (now Route 72) was under construction in the 1930s, he bought three dump trucks to assist in the paving of the road. During the 1940s, he obtained several tractor trailers to haul airplane parts for the war effort. In 1944, Albert Charles Ammon began driving for Albert G. Ammon, hauling gliders to Pennsylvania to be shipped overseas. In the 1940s, Albert George Ammon began cultivating blueberries, and his grandson continues cultivating blueberry plants today. (Courtesy of Albert Ammon.)